Levinson, Charles, 1920-
Industry's democratic revolution /
edited by Charles Levinson. -- London :
Allen and Unwin, c1974.
3-350 p. ; 23 cm. -- (Ruskin House
series in trade union studies ; 6)

Ruskin House Series in Trade Union Studies

6. Industry's Democratic Revolution

Other titles in the series

Industry's Democratic Revolution

edited by
Charles Levinson
*International Federation of Chemical
and General Workers' Unions*

London   George Allen & Unwin Ltd
Ruskin House   Museum Street

First published in 1974

© George Allen & Unwin Ltd 1974

ISBN 0 04 331062 1

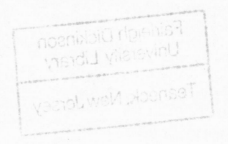
Printed in Great Britain
in 10 point Times Roman type
by Clarke, Doble & Brendon Ltd
Plymouth

Contents

The Contributors and their Organizations

CHARLES LEVINSON
Secretary General of the International Federation of Chemical
and General Workers' Unions (ICF) since 1964. Membership 4
million. Prior to that he was Assistant General Secretary of the
International Metal Workers' Federation (1954–63) and Deputy
Director of the North American Congress of Industrial Organization (CIO) European office (1950–3). The ICF was the first international labour organization to adopt industrial democracy as a
top priority objective. First discussed in 1964, this became official
policy in 1969, following the first international conference on the
subject held by ICF in Frankfurt. A seminar of ICF affiliates held
in Vienna the following year clarified aims and formulated
strategy for extending the principles of industrial democracy
around the world.

Charles Levinson contributed greatly to the development of
study and analysis which became the conceptual background
to the expanding campaign. He has continued to be directly
associated with the numerous action programmes of ICF affiliates,
which in most countries have been innovators and imitators of
industrial democracy approaches in their countries: Sweden,
Denmark, Norway, Austria, United Kingdom, Switzerland, USA,
Canada and elsewhere.

OTTO BRENNER *(Federal Republic of Germany)*
Late President of the Industriegewerkschaft Metall. Membership
2,200,000. IG Metall is the largest industrial union federation in
the world. At the time of his death in April 1972, Otto Brenner
was undoubtedly the single most influential trade union leader
in the country. Unlike the more centrally structured movement
in certain smaller countries, the essential power and strength of
the West German trade union movement is vested in the industry
federations, which undertake collective bargaining, organizing
workers and usually formulate policy within the context of their
industrial branches. The central executive of the organization of
the Deutsche Gewerkschaftsbund (DGB) is composed of the

presidents of the individual unions, and co-ordinates national policies including relations with the Socialist Party of Germany (SPD). This article was probably Otto Brenner's last important article before his death. One of the outstanding leaders of the 'Mitbestimmung' movement in Germany, since its introduction in the steel industry in the 1940s, Otto Brenner's name, like that of IG Metall, has been a synonym for the aims and progress of industrial democracy in the Federal Republic of Germany.

KARL HAUENSCHILD *(Federal Republic of Germany)*
President of the Industriegewerkschaft Chemie, Papier, Keramik. Membership 640,000 (extends over chemical, petroleum, rubber, glass, paper, ceramic and cement industries). IG Chemie is the third largest industrial union in the DGB and together with IG Metall leads the militant wing of the DGB-affiliated unions which together total nearly 7 million members in sixteen individual industrial federations. IG Chemie has been the spearhead of the drive to attain parity, or 50/50 co-determination in place of the 30 per cent representation presently applicable in large corporations over the whole of German industry, as already exists in coal and steel. The union and President Hauenschild are also leading the campaign for expanding still further the rights of co-determination at the level of the workplace.

EUGÈNE DESCAMPS *(France)*
Retired Secretary General of the Confédération Française Démocratique du Travail. Membership 800,000. Eugène Descamps carried out the transition from the earlier Confessional Catholic CFTC. Under the militant guidance of the national executive, this became a new force in the French trade union movement, based upon the principle of workers' self-management. This position has evolved in contrast to the continuing 'democratic centralism' of the communist-identified Confédération Générale du Travail. Closely associated with the Communist Party, the CGT (claimed membership 2,000,000) aggressively opposed openings towards decentralized controls over industry exterior to political authority.

MILAN RUKAVINA *(Yugoslavia)*
President of the Central Board, Industry and Mining Workers' Union of Yugoslavia. Membership 300,000. The largest and most powerful of the industrial unions which comprise the Confederation of Yugoslav Trade unions, the Industry and

Mineworkers' Union occupies a powerful and determining position within the policy-making organs of the country's labour movement. The union is in the vanguard of the current campaign against bureacratic centralism and elitism within the self-management system.

ITZHAK BEN AARON *(Israel)*

Secretary General of the General Federation of Jewish Labour in Eretz-Israel. Membership 1,3000,000. An example of a strong central organization in a small country, its activities and influence extend beyond negotiations of wages and working conditions into the ownership of an important share of Israel's labour economy and administration of the social security system. Mr Ben Aaron has long been among the earliest and staunchest advocates of direct workers' participation in decision making in industry.

LEONARD WOODCOCK *(USA)*

President of the United Automobile Workers – UAW, United States and Canada. Membership 1,500,000. As in other large industrialized countries, the primary force and power of organized labour in the United States rests with the industrial federations. The UAW, the second largest American trade union, and unquestionably among the most effective and influential in the world, has pioneered numerous radical innovations in industrial relations over the years: complementary pension plans; automatic productivity factors and cost of living escalators for wages; guaranteed annual wages, etc. Leonard Woodcock's unequivocal endorsement of the principle of industrial democracy even within the circumscribing framework of current industrial relations practices is a major guarantee that the idea will shortly take off in the United States, despite continued indifference of certain top officials of the AFL–CIO.

TOR ASPENGREN *(Norway)*

President of the Norwegian Trade Union Federation (LO). Membership 700,000. Perhaps the most centralized and centrifugally co-ordinated of the Nordic trade union movement, the Norwegian LO through its organic links with the Norwegian Labour Party and widespread participation in socially owned undertakings plays the key role in formulating and making heard and felt labour's claims upon the economy and social systems. Much of the current campaign and achievements in furthering industrial democracy in Norway has revolved around the LO and the name of Tor Aspengren.

HUGH SCANLON *(United Kingdom)*
President of the Amalgamated Engineering and Foundry Workers' Union (AEWU). Membership 1,300,000. Britain's second largest union, the AEWU together with the TGWU constitutes the locus of power of the progressive militant wing of the Trade Union Congress, the unique national centre which groups some ten million members and which, unlike the national centres in certain of the other countries, such as Israel, Sweden and Norway, carries out a co-ordinating rather than direct function in trade union affairs. Hugh Scanlon, along with Jack Jones, is the foremost fighter for extending workers' control in the UK.

JACK JONES *(United Kingdom)*
General Secretary of the Transport and General Workers' Union. Membership 1,750,000. The TGWU is Britain's largest and most powerful union. It is also its leading advocate and pressure source for advancing workers' control. Militant, and committed to securing these objectives through industrial action, Jack Jones and the 'T & G' are the 'avant-garde' of the new momentum which industrial democracy, under the appelation of Workers' Control, is acquiring in the United Kingdom.

ARNE GEIJER *(Sweden)*
President of the Swedish Trade Union Federation (LO). Membership 1,100,000. Brother Geijer is one of the most representative and influential national trade union officers in the world. The Swedish LO is effective and authoritative as a national centre and its strong, practical centralization of industrial power is reflected in its direct involvement in collective bargaining on wages and working conditions with the national employers' association. This concentrated power is further enhanced by close practical identification of a unified trade union structure with the Socialist Party, which has been in power for over forty years. Central to the Scandinavian labour movement as a whole, the translation of policy into the first legislative application of a special Swedish pattern of industrial democracy provided the impulse to wider progress of industrial democracy elsewhere.

WILHELM HRDLITSCHKA *(Austria)*

President of the Chemical Workers' Federation and Wiener Arbeiter Kammer. Membership 80,000. Including workers in the petroleum, glass, paper and allied industries as well as chemicals, the Federation has been in the foreground of the successful drive for achieving the wide and expanding degree of industrial democracy in the Austrian economy. It has been especially effective in broadening the rights of co-operative decision-making at the plant and workshop level in the industries under its jurisdiction. Wilhelm Hrdlitschka is also the President of Austria's unique Chambers of Labour, a workers' parliament organically related and almost entirely staffed by trade union representatives. The official members and officers are democratically elected by direct voting of all of Austria's workers. Among its many functions in the realm of social and economic affairs is the carrying-out of research and formulation of policy for legislative enactment. In this respect it has given technical and statistical support to the union's 'Mitbestimmungs campaign'.

HENRY LORRAIN *(Canada)*

First Vice-President of the United Paper Workers' International Union. Membership 380,000. Henry Lorrain is also a Vice-President of the Canadian Labour Congress, Canada's major national centre which has an affiliated membership of 1,300,000. A persistent advocate of the need for introducing industrial democracy in the form of trade union participation in management-decision making, both in the pulp and paper industry and the economy of the country as a whole.

EWALD KAESER *(Switzerland)*

National Secretary, Swiss Federation of Textile Chemical and Paper Workers. Membership 20,000. The case of the development of industrial democracy in Switzerland illustrates the axiom that size is not always related to effectiveness. Though small in numbers, the Swiss FTCP has been a pioneer and catalyst in the strengthening campaign in Switzerland. Ewald Kaeser has contributed to the milestone agreements with Firestone and the Basle chemical industry. He is also one of the country's leading trade unionists in the mounting campaign to change that country's constitution to enable the application of joint decision-making throughout Swiss industry. Mr Kaeser is also a member of the

'Mitbestimmung' strategy group of the Swiss Trade Union Confederation (Union Syndicale Suisse) – the socialist-oriented and dominant centre in the country, with some 437,000 members.

EDMOND MAIRE *(France)*

Present Secretary General of the Confédération Française Démocratique du Travail (CFDT). Under the dynamic progressive leadership of Edmond Maire, the CFDT has greatly strengthened its philosophical and strategic commitments to industrial democracy through workers' self-management. The extent of the advance, though not as yet reflected in the practical plant and industry situations, has already created the central ideological and political cleavage between the CFDT and the CGT – one which is certain to become deeper and wider. Under the impulse of Edmond Maire, workers' control and self-management vs. socialist centralism under party and bureaucratic authority promises to be a rising barrier to co-operation and unity between the two organizations on all matters beyond unity of action and collective bargaining in which all major centres are compelled to co-operate.

Chapter 1

An Overview

CHARLES LEVINSON

Secretary General, International Federation of Chemical and General Workers' Unions

Few socio-political phenomena have moved front and centre on the world scene with the speed and impact of industrial democracy. The current impulsion being given this long-standing but largely unrealized aspiration promises to transform the industrial system as no other movement has done since the Russian revolution, whilst its effects will be quite as radical and probably more permanent. In this area, furthermore, practice is far ahead of theory. This is a most uncharacteristic feature of working class history which, since the appearance of the French Utopian Socialists and of Marxism in the nineteenth century until the present, has been as prolific in rhetoric and rich in concept as it has been lacking in achievement and limited in practice. The reverse has been true of the history of the privileged groups, and the ensconced hierarchs of power. For them theory and slogan has always lagged, beneficially, far in the wake of practice. This has never been so acutely evident as it is today in the irrelevance to reality of much of the campus economists' wisdom and the social and economic policies of governmental gurus.

A principal explanation for the new inversion of this traditional relationship between the slogans and dreams of workers' emancipation and the hard realities of their work and social environment, is that the initiative has been taken by the workers themselves. The thrust for industrial democracy, especially in the West, is coming from the trade unions. Because of this, the approach has been pragmatic and direct, rooted in the practical necessity to find new effective systems for advancing workers' rights and interests in a rapidly changing, technological-industrial society beyond mere rhetoric and party ideologies. A corollary of this trade union pragmatism is that the idea has acquired momentum precisely because of the differing national options and approaches, which have probed for opportunities of advance on the broadest front. The German co-determination system was, for some time, held by many national trade union movements to be a negation of the universal ideology that trade unions could not participate in management without intrinsically qualifying their independence and their right to contest the power of employers. The now conclusive proof that co-determination has not integrated the German unions into the system of the capitalist ruling classes nor conditioned their independence of action in defence of the interests of their membership has modified these earlier reservations. Support for the co-determination principle has become extensive among the major national trade union movements in the West, although there is still ideological opposition from party bureaucracies which continue to proclaim economic policy to be the primary responsibility of political action, whilst social policy alone is seen as the domain of unions. This philosophy extends from moderate reformist social democracy through the Marxist-Socialist, Marxist-Stalinist, Marxist-Leninist and new anarcho-revolutionary leftists, to the unyielding anachronism of certain AFL–CIO leadership. The strictures of classical socialism have had to give way before the hard, positive experience of six million organized German workers. Similarly the recent advances in Norway and Sweden, in Austria, in Peru and Tanzania have taken place with only incidental correlation to a broad ideological wave. This would not have occurred had the issue been handled as a political responsibility and left to politicians or academics to formulate or introduce. As a result the inherent, congenital need of each man as a social being to become directly and personally involved in the decision-making processes determining his life, once his basic biological and rudimentary social needs are requited, is certain to be the dominating force behind future social and economic demands.

PARTICIPATION AND SELF-DETERMINATION IN HISTORY

The claim that pragmatic trade union action is the decisive force behind the emerging revolution of involvement, does not deny the historic importance of the numerous philosophers and social critics who have proclaimed the principle in different forms and guises. The idealists of nineteenth century England clarioned 'workers' democracy' in industry as their theoretical response to the oppression and squalor of the industrial revolution. Out of this grew the concept of Syndicalism, advocating seizure of industrial power by strong trade unions. Too contradictory of the triumphant principles of the industrializing society (authoritarian efficiency, economy of labour in relation to the other factors of production for greater productivity, the dominance of mechanical processes, the synergy of vast accumulations of capital) to withstand the pressure, these ideas were crushed in the Victorian rise of capitalism with the new capitalist bourgeoisie at its head. Power and capital had now joined hands and the ascendant owners or managers of capital and machine tools had little difficulty in subjugating man as worker. It was not until the early 1920s that, under the inspiration of G. D. H. Cole, the idea of Guild Syndicalism emerged linking the syndicalism of a single industrial union in each industry with the concept of the Guilds. G. D. H. Cole saw in a pluralistic system in which the state represented consumers and unions represented workers as organized producers, the way towards industrial democracy and workers' control. But the inexorable crunch of recurring depressions, mass unemployment and subsistence-level existence brought about by the capitalist system on free rein and the Second World War again proved too strong for the concept to conquer and it returned to the impotence of a slogan.

The notion of workers' self-management or producer societies lay at the heart of European nineteenth century socialist doctrine from the French Utopians through the anarchists, syndicalists, left-wing social-democrats, non-communist party Marxists as well as many others. It is profoundly rooted in the history of radical and socialist theory. It is not surprising, therefore, that the call for workers' control over production and the establishment of workers' self-governing councils accompanied the numerous uprisings of workers against industrial tyranny: the Paris Commune of 1871, the revolutions in Russia of both 1905 and 1917, Spain in the 1930s, Hungary and Poland in 1956, the Prague Spring of 1968 and Gdynia of 1970.

Concurrent with such spontaneous political explosions and more tenacious have been the extensive creation of varied types of plant committees, works' councils and workers' assemblies at the place of work, which shared at least some limited claims to participation in decision making. Among the more salient were the joint councils created in British nationalized industries in 1918, the factory councils in Austria in 1919, and the plant committees introduced in Czechoslovakia and Germany in 1920. From the shattered industries of the Second World War evolved a renewed general movement towards establishing plant committees in the factories in a number of European countries, all formally purporting to extend the participation of workers in industry and 'granting' rights to be informed on production and financial affairs of the enterprise, on important changes in technology, investments, dismissals, etc. The Comités d'Entreprise in France, the Conseils d'Enterprise in Belgium, the Commissione Interne in Italy, Works Councils in Switzerland and Holland, labour-management consultation committees in the UK and the Betriebsräte in Austria and Western Germany, were all initiated with ardent hopes that they would constitute a solid institutional base for further advances towards industrial democracy at the workshop level. In their wake similar systems were established in many countries of the developing regions, notably in Latin America.

THE GERMAN FORMULA

But by the middle of the 1960s these aspirations had proved illusory, again emasculated and contained by the dominant power of the political-industrial complex. Perhaps with the single exception of the German and Austrian Betriebsrät, most of the national forms of plant councils had been adroitly transformed by management power into token organizations with only formal rights of participation. Even the usual 'letter of the law' explicitly calling for management to 'open the books' and 'inform the personnel' on important future plans common to all systems was seldom respected or enforced upon employers. The fact that the majority of such councils had been legislated into existence and consequently were held to be legal entities distinct from the unions, facilitated the domestication strategy of the employers and politicians (socialists included), which sought to tie them to the company rather than the union. In the Federal Republic of Germany, a different tradition and a more extensive unity than prevails in the trade union movement elsewhere in Europe (with the exception of the Nordic group) resulted in an absence of union rivalry at the factory and company levels, allowing unions to integrate the shop councils more effectively into the union structure. The distinction between union- and 'company'-based councils remains in law, however, and is utilized by employers to keep the national union out of the plant. This, in large measure, helps explain the much more positive assessment of the functions and utility of such councils in Germany. Unquestionably, they have been accepted by German unions as the principal channels for the democratization of the work environment. This strategy is supported by the continuing effort to defeat managements' attempts to domesticate the councils.

The total commitment of the German trade union movement to the achievement of co-determination at the level of the boards of supervision (Aufsichträte), which corresponds roughly to the senior American-style board of directors, contributed to the comparatively better functioning of the Betriebsrät. This opened up a second front in the German trade unions' struggle to achieve industrial democracy and added a new dimension to the definition. Concurrently with demands at plant level and work-site, the issue was extended to the levels of the boards of supervision and executive boards (Vorstände), where most strategic and financial power of the modern corporation lies. This was the first articulated recognition that the conquest of power by the workers in the decision-making process of industry was a practical reality. The terms 'workers' control' or 'workers' participation', though often used interchangeably by partisans of industrial democracy, usually reflect differences in perspective of the role and power of the unions vis à vis political parties. 'Workers' control', at the shop level considered as a check upon political and managerial authority, is widely preferred by politically motivated and oriented groups, while 'direct participation in the decision-making process' by workers usually denotes a trade union point of view. But an effective campaign for the shifting of power requires complementary and parallel offensives against the concentration and authority of management both at the level of policy (supervising and executive boards) and the application of such policy to the factory floor (works' committees).

EVOLUTIONARY IMPERATIVES

Scientists claim that Man is only 35,000 years old, a brief span on the evolutionary calendar. Societal man is a much more recent phenomenon, and industrial urban man a mere foetus still awaiting his humanity. Man's supremacy has expressed itself to date largely in his ability to change his physical environment by developing effective tools and instruments in an effort to turn nature to his advantage. Such inventiveness in the modern phase has built the supertechnology that underpins the economic systems within which he labours. On the biological front also, his evolution is on the threshhold of a fantastic quantum jump which has been called 'the great biological synthesis'.

Through recent mind-boggling discoveries which have unlocked the most fundamental life processes, man may soon be able to control and alter his own vital biological forces. The understanding of how life's master molecule DNA transfers through RNA hereditary information from one generation to the next and directs and orders the making of proteins, life's critical building blocks, has entered the area of miracle science. As new power to control cancer-creating viruses and engineer genetic structures comes within his grasp, man will shortly be in a position to modify and develop his own physical and mental future.

It is doubly ironic, therefore, that the effects of man's achievements in the realm of science has been to subordinate his primary social needs in an almost philosophical pursuit of the economic ends proposed by his genius for gadgetry. Because of the economic environment which he has created through technology, he is, as a social species, condemned to greater and greater social pressure, intimacies and interdependencies. It is not sufficient merely to 'revolutionize' himself biologically. It is equally necessary to revolutionize his social and economic environment. Failure to do so will call forth inexorable pressures, tensions and conflicts and induce new ailments and maladies in forms untouched by new medical techniques. From the moral agonies and nervous tensions produced by contradictions between vastly better physiological, psychological and biological qualities and a deteriorated, oppressive and malignantly obsolete social environment will come new and perhaps deadlier, more devastating diseases. Coronaries produced by alienated life-styles, for example, will replace cancer and genetic deficiencies as the chief scourge. A recent US study made by Sidney Cobb and Stanislav V. Kasl, both of the Institute for Social Research at the University of Michigan, shows the severe psychological and physiological ill effects experienced by factory workers who are redundancy victims. The research centred on shop floor workers (not on the much-pitied executive grade, for once) aged between 40 and 59 who had lost their jobs after closure of two plants in the United States. One plant was in a major city and the other in a small rural town with a population of just over 2,000.

The researchers studied the men through three phases – the period immediately prior to redundancy, the out-of-work period and the resettlement phase when most of the men started new jobs. The study revealed a significant rise in the incidence of ulcers, arthritis and high blood pressure. The prevalence of ulcers was also evidence of the psychological toll redundancy takes on a man. Even more significantly, several of the men's wives developed peptic ulcers, which are rare in women. The study also detected a high level of symptoms which can ultimately lead to coronary diseases and gout. There were two suicides, which is about 30 times more than the normal rate for shop floor workers of this particular age group. There was also at least one unsuccessful suicide attempt.

The study shows that the men had a very low opinion of their future career prospects, which did not improve even after they had settled in new jobs. 'It is as if their experience had permanently uprooted optimistic evaluations of their life and of their future', states the report.

The report suggests, after these findings, that 'portable' pensions should be introduced to protect older workers who have invested years in a company and lost their rightful benefits. It also recommends that health insurance should be an automatic part of unemployment compensation, since redundant workers are usually reluctant to pay the increased rates for individual subscribers. Another suggestion is that firms should introduce flexible termination periods of between 30 and 90 days. This would allow the employee to leave the plant when his next employer was ready for him. The employees in the study had to work the full termination period or lose severance pay.

In the face of this and increasing similar evidence, what good will curing illness at the level of the cell be if the incidence of nervous stress and destruction continues, or even increases, at the level of vital organs? Failure in this domain could condemn man to follow along the evolutionary path towards extinction, such as happened to 98 per cent of the hundred million species of animals and plants which have vanished from the Earth throughout its history. Perhaps 'homo sapiens' will be the first species simply to worry himself to extinction.

Spanning the gap between the dynamics of his new discoveries and the stagnant dereliction of his economic and social condition will be a task worthy of man's highest genius. Despite the possession of will which has elevated him thus far beyond all other living species, and despite his proven scientific and creative faculties, the skill of building just, peaceful and co-operative social orders seems to have eluded him throughout social history.

THE ECONOMIC RELATIONSHIP

Few today contest the primacy of economic and industrial structures in the determination of social man. It is the foundation upon which all the interrelated cultural and institutional edifices rest, including man's patterned social relationship to his fellow men. Throughout modern social history, the economic order has been inspired by a code dating back almost 3,000 years to the ancient Roman Empire. Roman laws of property consecrated slavery as the principal factor of production. The slave was viewed as a means of production, belonging to the master in identical fashion to all other instruments of production: animals, tools, materials, etc. This origin of the worker–boss relationship has continued the oppression of man as worker throughout the ages.

The industrial revolution saw vast new industries emerge (steel, railroads, electricity, petroleum, public transport, agricultural machinery) and tremendous changes in the structure and scope of older ones (meat-packing, textiles and clothing, coal). The chief technological cause of this development was the availability of mechanical and electrical energy to complement human brawn and animal power, which enormously increased the worker's productivity and profitability for the owners of property and of the instruments of production. The 'mass production' thus made possible, which turned slave-owners and serf-barons into capitalists, demanded a mass market. Slaves, owning nothing, do not make good customers, so workers were progressively 'liberated' from the tutelage of the owners of capital in their non-work functions. Outside the mine, factory, office and plantation, the worker acquired rights of citizenship and in capitalist countries democratic rights of individual liberties, though the pressure necessary to effect this social change was usually brought to bear at the workplace as the new productivity of labour enhanced its value to the point where its withdrawal by strike became an effective weapon. This uneasy equilibrium has since defined the employer–worker relationship and changed the system from slavery and serfdom to a contractual or economic obligation or compulsion. Because of the nature of the ownership/power equation, it has remained an authoritarian–subservient relationship – master–servant or boss–employee. In other words, the capitalist had the 'right', granted by possession, to command and dictate terms and conditions of labour under threat of dismissal or refusal of gainful employment to workers who remained a factor of production – an input along with other factors such as capital and raw materials, etc. Not having capital of his own to fall back on, his critical dependency on his labour for subsistence compelled subservience in the worker.

In the evolution of Western societies, especially industrialized ones, this crucial master–servant relationship of the worker to the owners or controllers of capital assets has continued essentially unaltered. True the growth in strength and influence of trade unions imposed significant limitations upon the degree of arbitrary power which capital ownership and management could exercise over workers, particularly over wages and working conditions. This area of exploitation was further reduced by legislative restrictions upon the social authority of capital over citizens, imposed as a result of the acquisition of effective political power by labour and socialist parties. But though such forces curtailed and mitigated some of the extreme forms of material and physiological abuses, they did not alter the essence of the economic relationship. The worker was still under the dominant power of those who controlled and managed capital assets, even though his collective strength in trade unions qualified its application in certain specific areas.

Recent evolution, especially of the last few decades, has seen the movement of capitalism towards a system without capitalists or owners under the control of professional managers and a few minority stock-holding fiduciary institutions such as banks, insurance companies, mutual funds, etc., but has seen no modification in the autoritarian structure of economic and administrative enterprises. The entire thrust of the technological revolution of the 50s and the 60s, intensifying and accelerating the substitution of capital for labour, has been to concentrate power of economic decision-making into fewer and fewer hands, and to sharpen the elitist control of power by vested interests. Concurrently it fostered the absolutist and technocratic philosophy that the powerful and superior few were obliged to govern the inferior masses in an ill-defined and insubstantial pursuit of efficiency, success and progress.

A CRISIS IN CONFIDENCE

Either because of the immutable dialectic of history or the structural demise of the market economy, the world's economic systems have become anachronisms and increasingly dysfunctional. This applies with but very few exceptions to all types of economy: to the socialist East and the capitalist West, to the underdeveloped South and the industrialized North. Human society as a whole seems to have reached a cultural turning point. Traditional structures, both administrative and ideological, can no longer assimilate or neutralize the criticism and challenges levelled at them. Popular confidence declines as the system fails to meet the illusions it nurtures. As the system depends on confidence for its continuation, economic theory is seen for an elaborate sham of self-promotion on the part of the system's operators and apologists.

The factory, office and other places of work have become critically obsolete and their programmes for greater efficiency and productivity, with their underlying values and assumptions, are increasingly confronted with repugnance, rejection and outright hostility from workers. The enterprise is delapidated and malevolent, a physiologically and psychologically harmful and debilitating environment for working men and women. In certain branches it has already reached a peak of self-destructive contradiction: the more successful it is economically and the proportionately greater the earned incomes negotiated, the more intense the desire is to leave the enterprise entirely or luxuriate in absenteeism. The automobile industry has become the modern symbol of the surging revolt against the factory, especially among blue collar workers, whose absenteeism is pushing towards 10 and 15 per cent. In the USA, this has been labelled the 'blue collar blues'; in France, 'la revolte des os chez Renault' has become a national trauma; in Italy the slogan 'Potere Obrero' (workers' power) is keeping FIAT in a state of policed tension; in Great Britain occupation of factories has become a commonplace occurrence. Attacks against the economic order are centering upon the enterprise and workplace, the site where most people pass the greater part of their productive lives and lose most of their hopes and health. The revolt is a populist, grassroots protest, which does not fit readily and symetrically into either radical, liberal or conservative concepts. Socialists and rock-ribbed capitalists alike, while advancing contrasting solutions, are remarkably close in their diagnosis of the problem. But neither has yet awakened to the fact that if any solution, socialist or liberal, is to be effective, it must concern itself as a fundamental matter of priority with the reform of the factory, office and enterprise. The mounting criticisms, coming from all points of the culture compass – economic, technological, sociological and psychological – focus on the workplace and highlight the outdated structures and methods still in force which seem incapable of accommodating to the new values and demands of our time. In the extant economic and social environment, the relation of the worker to his job, the system through which he communicates and interrelates with the rest of the enterprise, the status accorded him as a person and as a human being in the production process, the equilibrium between his intelligence and creative faculties and his work functions and responsibilities are mostly negative and destructive of total human personality.

SOCIALIZE THE ENTERPRISE

The total failure of the market place to optimize the aggregate social results of the independent decisions of private enterprises is today as evident and acknowledged as the failure of the national coercive economic plans of the so-called socialist economies to achieve social equality and justice. What has been good for General Motors, or what has been good for the Steel and Engineering Trust of the Soviet Union, has manifestly not been good for the country. In fact in both cases it would be easy to show that on balance it has been bad. The free or enforced controls of economic systems or 'isms' have therefore turned out to be, as far as the ordinary 95 per cent of the people are concerned, bankrupt. As a result, attention must be redirected to the enterprise itself as the place where real reform must start. Socialism without a socialist enterprise, without factories and administrations which are inherently socialist in their structure and operations, cannot solve any basic problems, let alone produce true socialism. Bureaucratic centralism and state capitalism have been the inevitable results of the authoritarian military-structured enterprises on which production-consumption society has been built. As long as reforms undertaken are external to the factory, its damaging, anti-social effects will remain. Western enterprise has been proved incapable of serving the social needs of the commonweal by pursuing its own narrow economic self-interest. The proof is both statistically and empirically beyond responsible doubt. The overwhelming necessity is for social aims to take precedence over the economic objectives of the enterprise, whether those objectives are currently measured in socialist production or capitalist profits. Every large enterprise must be considered as a social undertaking, an entity whose strategies and existence are legitimized exclusively in their social and public utility.

DESTRUCTION OF THE PYRAMIDS

No aspect of modern society is more thickly shrouded in mythology and moribund dogma than the area of industry and management. Large corporations today have virtually no resemblance whatsoever to the prevalent public ideology. If these entities are to be subjected to social control and accountability, the verities of their present functioning must be revealed and new systems for their operation innovated. There is no other route to meaningful change and progress, whether it is labelled 'reform' or 'revolution'. Political revolutions and vast legislative governmental reforms alike have failed to modify the fundamental shortcomings and defects of industrial society, dealing only with the happenings of change. Working from the top down has reached an impasse – any hope for real change depends upon action that moves from the bottom up.

The age of the hierarchical pyramids of organizational structure is dead. The rulers of these moribund pyramids of power must be buried within them, to be consigned to the corporate Valley of the Kings where they can be analysed by historians as vestigial totems of an unjust and undemocratic culture. In place of these monuments to misery raised and maintained by the physical toil and mental tension of the slave race at the base for the self-glory and affluence of the few at the peak, new geometric forms of corporate and factory organization are needed: equi-centred shapes with no triangular inequality between the top and the bottom. Boss-men, father-figures and demi-heroes endowed with supernatural leadership qualities have no place in the new geometry either at the top or the centre. Few today are unaware that it is much easier for anyone to do the job of a top politician than for a politician to do the job of anyone else. If an electrician, plumber, doctor or lathe-turner became a President in most countries, they would do a pretty good job in listening to the technocrats and the state would function reasonably well. But if Presidents, senators and their like were sent to man the generating plants, repair the plumbing and diagnose ailments, our organized civilization would most likely come to a crashing halt. Society today is composed of working specialists ruled over by managing generalists. The critical need today is to get the practical social wisdom of the specialists into the seats of power at present occupied by generalists who are propped, aided and abetted by cabalistic technocrats.

The myth of the enterprise and the myth of industrial management are twin supports of society's present totems. Supposedly super-skilled, for leadership born, and possessed of the science and technology for running large organizations well and efficiently, the top management of the major corporations have become the warrior-princes or the nobles who maintain and make prosper the realm. But this promoted image of the corporate manager-king, like that of his corporate empire, is mostly vested interest public relations, with very little substance. Far from being skilled technocrats, trained in quantitative science-based disciplines, most successful managers, like their successful political counterparts, are egocentric, ambitious aspirants to power. Their skills are wholly developed in amassing power either aggressively or stealthily, and using it to manipulate relationships. Management consists to a rather large extent of pressuring people to make them compliant to the needs of things. The predominant skill in management is therefore one of politics, or the ability to achieve results through the activities of other people. This largely amorphous, indefinable function defies a more precise description and its techniques vary almost infinitely with different types of corporation, industry and economic system. For this very reason its effects are the more corruptive. About the only discernible commonality is the obligation to impose a discipline upon the human factor, to minimize costs and impediments to the best utilization of things. For this reason the fundamental trait of all management systems organized along militaristic hierarchical lines is the suppression of natural human emotions and personality and the basic needs of workers to express individuality. As Alistair Mant, author of the British Institute of Management Report on 'Management Education in the 70s', has said: 'In my view, there is no managerial job in British industry at any level which an intelligent person couldn't master in six weeks. Where the interest and skill comes in is in the practice of politics.'

Nevertheless, a vast industry has grown up around the training of managers. Universities and business schools are proliferating around the world, according doctoral and master degrees to authenticate the ephemeral science. Management consulting has become the principal source of affluence for many practitioners, and especially for academics, who use their campus and theoretical status to sell their reputations to big business. As these services are accountable as costs, and therefore figure as tax write-offs, the corporate managers are always ready to take a chance on a long shot to see whether some of the proposed wisdom will not help their task of containing the innate opposition of labour to their profit-maximizing schemes. Management is basically the art of power politics, or the manipulation and direction of people, and the industrial subjects of this effort are the manual and intellectual workers who are used to drive the profit/production machine.

The failure of economic systems to provide security and equality, to eliminate poverty and above all to promote human progress and personality, has therefore led to rejection of the systems. Bitter experience of the failure of politicians and bureaucrats to make these systems work for the common good has demonstrated that, being an integral and motivating part of the system itself, such men have no stomach for the imposition of effective external controls on the enterprise. This leads to the obvious realization that abuses of the social corpus, being due to the structure of the corporation and especially of its management, are not likely to be ended by the entrenched administrators and manipulators of that system itself. Clearly a profound restructuring of managerial power within the corporation would be necessary to achieve a substitution of values and objectives and a replacement of economic goals by social goals.

OWNERSHIP AND CONTROL

It is evident that the ailing world economic systems have entered a period of upheaval and tension, if not revolt. The symptoms of this upheaval are everywhere. In the debacle of the 'development decades' for improving the societies of the developing regions; in the difficulties besetting Soviet, Czech and Polish leadership to contain their 'revolted' working classes; in the rising criticism of morally sick capitalist society and the failure of that system to eliminate poverty, job insecurity, elitist and ill-adapted education, inadequate social security and public health. These crises are the reflected failures of enterprise to carry out either its external responsibilities to the collectivity and its internal responsibilities to its employees. The rise in the private affluence of the managerial-based elite has been accompanied by public decay of cities, environmental pollution, breakdown of mass transit systems, and social neglect of health, education and leisure needs. Classical definitions of the causes and symptoms of this public degradation are of little relevance. It is not capitalists as owners of the means of production who are the cause – the identification of such personifications has become virtually impossible, for most shareholders have been removed from any operating power in the corporation.

It is the control of economic power which counts today, not ownership. The average stockholder in the United States is as much an owner or capitalist as the Soviet worker is the socialist possessor of the means of production. In both cases the ownership is of an absentee, formal nature distributed theoretically among the stockholders, fiduciary companies and banks in the former case, and the peasants, intellectual and manual workers in the latter. Effective power, however, rests with those who control and manage the consolidated capital assets, not with those who 'own' a part of them. In both cases the top managers and their technocrat subordinates are the effective controllers. The relationship between these controllers and the stock-owning minorities (5 per cent of the stock of a major US corporation usually ensures sufficient representational strength to 'elect' the top management) is less binding than is often imagined. As long as the managers 'make money' in sufficient quantity they are left alone to do as they please, usually encouraged by important gifts of stock options and bonuses in addition to lavish salaries. The stock option and stock bonus serves a double purpose of providing tax-free or tax-privileged capital gains to managers for whom increases in salaries would merely be given to the tax collector, whilst at the same time tying them by such capital gains riches ever more firmly to the company and the system.

For the Soviet analogue, what identifies the manager in control with an attitude of ownership is a comparably tenuous and self-interested set of ties. The direct ties are not with the state, which owns the means of production, but with the party and with personal bonuses and other rewards for exceeding the norms of the plan. Both castes of managers have moved beyond restrictions by the vital exercise of unbridled power to fructify the investment and achieve a high rate of expansion.

One of the crucial elements in this transfer of control is that the far-reaching changes and disruptions caused by the incipient social-economic revolution makes it difficult, if not impossible, for those who see themselves in traditional terms as leaders to keep abreast of switches in the current of demand, much less to give direction. The result is that contemporary 'leader' figures of the left as well as the right, talk about new problems in nineteenth century terms, or about the industrial problems of yesterday instead of those which will cry out for solution in the latter 70s and the 80s.

Already the process has altered the nature and distribution of property, the system and values of economic life, the potency and comportment of government and, above all, the relative loci of power. The heart of the new revolution is the modern corporation and the chief victim is the nation-state. No longer is a national economy the simple aggregate of its home-based individual corporations. A nation's gross national product, national revenue, per capita consumption, investment, foreign trade, balance of payments and the condition of its currency no longer balance the production, sales, taxes and employment of its corporations. The power of any government to control and guide a national economy has been decisively reduced. It can no longer prevent unemployment from growing, inflation from galloping, the value of its money from eroding, the environment from being polluted, or the social fabric of its cities and communities from decaying. Even its control over the direction of politics has been drastically curtailed, for the strength and power of corporations can no longer be contained within the traditional boundaries of a national political democracy.

Governments are being forced into open alliances and coalitions with large corporations which makes the concept even of the mixed economy obsolete. Nationalized industries and firms, even to survive have to adhere to the rules of the prevailing system, and usually merge or engage in joint ventures with private giants to maintain momentum and prosper.

Two complementary and interrelated factors have been largely responsible for the structural transformation of the economic system: the complete domination of national economies by large corporations and their global extension into multinational companies whose dynamics are dependent only upon a global or world market. Both factors derive from the rapid scientific and technological advances in recent decades, propelled by the new global dimensions of modern communication and information networks.

BIGNESS AND MONOPOLY

The modern corporation to be efficient must be big. For reasons of efficiency in a special field many sub-units, factories, research facilities and other ramifications, may appear small-scale, but are in fact increasingly co-ordinated, directed by and made accountable to a consolidated corporate plan. In this way, the advantages of small-scale flexibility are combined with the power of grouped resources to prevent a destructive dinosaurism and inadaptability to specific situations. Similarly, certain unmonopolized functions are best performed by unorganized, imaginative, free talents, such as in basic scientific discovery and in some cases day-to-day operation may remain small scale and independent. But, although most important discoveries in medicine, electronics, biology, chemistry, etc., were the work of individuals and not of large corporation research laboratories, most if not all such discoveries were ultimately exploited and commercialized by the large companies. Even if the discovery is held by the inventor and commercialized by him alone, he 'succeeds' by growing into a giant himself. Nevertheless, in technology, product improvements, new types of industrial substances, electronic devices or space technology which requires important capital, the giant corporations are the prime producers.

The point of no return has already been reached and the big enterprise will increasingly dominate the economy. By 1985 some 300 corporations will control between 75 and 80 per cent of the West's capital assets. Under 200 corporations possess over 60 per cent of US capital. Seven oil companies, for instance, control 75 per cent of all oil refining and distribution. The West's automobile industry likewise consists of nine main companies which assemble around 90 per cent of all the vehicles. Computer manufacturing is done by a dozen companies, of which four do over three-quarters. And in Europe, over 75 per cent of production is in the hands of twenty firms. The important tyre producers in the West are less than twelve and will, in a few years, be less than seven or eight. In pulp and paper, glass, ceramics, production is largely in the hands of a few firms. Likewise, on a product basis in most countries the leading three or four firms usually account for over 80 per cent of total shipments.

The *Fortune* magazine's famous annual listing of the 500 largest US industrial companies put their share of total industrial sales in 1971 at 66 per cent, which is up from 50 per cent a decade earlier. Their profits accounted for 75 per cent of all industrial profits on sales of nearly $503 billion. Though this figure represented an increase of just under 9 per cent, it was achieved with a reduction of their employment (14·3 million) by 2 per cent highlighting the general characteristic of large enterprises of cutting their workforce while increasing sales.

The leading 120 British firms account for over half the country's exports. 15 to 20 per cent of these account for more than a quarter. Dutch industry, like its foreign trade, is largely dependent upon the health and prosperity of a dozen leading firms, but especially its top four: Royal Dutch/Shell, Unilever, Philips and AKZO.

The future of industry lies in the science-based, capital-intensive sectors which by 1985 will receive about 60 per cent of total investment: petroleum, chemicals, plastics, electronics. Only large 'monopoly-sized' firms will survive for only the giants will be capable of raising the necessary growth capital of $1·3 trillion, 95 per cent of which will need to come from retained earnings or cash flow. The others will shrivel from lack of capital or will be merged into the giants. In non-manufacturing sectors the growth will be in service trades. Nearly 75 per cent of all workers will be in some service profession by the year 2000. Many will be employed in education and training, health service institutions, police and civic services, which hopefully will remain largely under public control. In the commercial service sector, hotels, leisure activities, travel, catering, etc., the trend to large organizations is already under way and will grow.

Despite much nostalgia, and demonstrations to the contrary, the large corporation is expanding because it is more efficient. It can afford to invest for higher productivity and it also has the capital necessary to be innovative and aggressive. The amassing of vast amounts of capital implies market protection, and sheltered, monopolistic conditions in which to operate. Enormous capital is required even to enter modern industry. In petroleum, for example, the amount of capital employed per worker has reached about $400,000. To exist even on a modest scale in the automobile industry would demand an initial investment of around $50 to $60 million. Chemical process plants of a size necessary to benefit from modern economies of scale (a precondition to success) above all demand hundred million dollar strategies. Capital is the key to modern business enterprise and the chief concern of modern management. Technology can usually be purchased, frequently from competitors. In chemicals, tyres, pharmaceuticals, electronics, glass, steel, automobiles and most other industries, many large firms operate under licenses and patents held by competitors. The key to success is in the distribution, sales and packaging, where the sole possibility for competition remains between the giants in many areas.

There is no stopping this trend. It has been suggested[1] that the emergence in the UK of just twenty or so national companies is plausible by the end of the 1970s. In France, Germany, Italy, Belgium, Holland, Japan, Australia and the Nordic countries, also, a similar pattern of a handful of 'national' multi-product, multi-industry combines is beginning to become apparent. As at present, these giant concentrations will all be inter-linked, and inter-connected within a vast systems matrix through joint ventures and common participation in production, distribution and financial operations.

This giant fact of economic life has forever made traditional notions of competition, anti-trust controls, public regulation of productions, of health and safety, of prices and incomes policies, controlling modern inflation produced by cash flow maximization and most recently a new rising strain of technological and structural unemployment caused not by a lack of but by a rise in industrial investment.

The effects on workers involved in these huge combines, or

[1] A. Jackson and G. Newbound, *The Receding Ideal*, London, 1972.

B

thrown out of employment by massive shifts of capital, or simply living as consumers in a marketplace dominated by monopolistic practice, are obvious. If the worker does not take a hand in the primary control of these enterprises directly there is no other agency who can stand in the social interest against their profit-motivated managements.

THE MULTINATIONAL ENTERPRISE SOCIETY

If the demand for industrial democracy is to become more than a mere slogan, it must embrace an appreciation of the macro- and micro-economic aspects of the new enterprise system into which it seeks to extend its catalytic influence for change. It is not enough simply to describe effects. Causes and wider tendencies must be identified and discussed if workers are to understand the implications of their involvement and be at no disadvantage in their confrontation with the corporate strategists. Therefore, it will be necessary to study the new dimension added to these enterprises by their involvement in a global marketplace from which perspective the world looks, indeed, like Marshall McLuhan's 'global village'. It is at this level that today's, let alone tomorrow's, firms will need to operate to survive and grow.

Advancing at a rate well beyond the capabilities of other institutions to match, the new monopolistic, multi-product, multi-industry enterprise has expanded beyond the reach of the nation-state and the national economy. The extent of its growth has already permanently transformed the co-ordinates of the important socio-economic problems. By the end of the decade it will have altered social and economic systems beyond all recognition. But the phenomenon is not new in itself; leading enterprises of the petroleum industry, the automobile industry, the chemical industry, the tyre industry, etc., have long been multi-national. What is new is the magnitude of the phenomenon's exponential growth rate and the extent of its spread. Already the foreign production of subsidiary firms in the West exceeds $500,000 million, and American subsidiaries abroad have assets of nearly $100,000 million in book value. The real or market value of these assets is more than double this amount. Sales of these direct investments (around $400,000 million) were nine times US manufacture exports in 1971. Furthermore, over half of the recorded manufacturing exports are shipments from the parent company to its foreign subsidiary in the form of equipment, raw materials or semi-processed products. This little-appreciated fact represents a traumatic transition of US foreign trade from home-based exports to overseas direct production, with a growing share of the locally produced exports dependent upon overseas investments.

American multinational firms are to a large extent self-financing for growth requirements. The magnitude of their capital needs is rising vertiginously, tripling and quadrupling their levels of the 50s and 60s. As 95 per cent of this investment capital derives from cash flow (depreciation + retained earnings + special investment tax allowance and reserves), a cash plan must be optimized on a global basis to profit from low wages in Taiwan, Hong Kong and Indonesia from where goods are then imported back to the home market (textiles, clothing, electronics, sewing machines, etc.), to benefit from reduced transportation costs (automobile, agricultural implements, petroleum) and, above all, to achieve minimal taxes on earnings by judicious chanelling of income in and out of the proliferating tax havens (Switzerland, Lichtenstein, Luxembourg, Panama, Liberia, Nassau Bahamas, Curaçao, Singapore, Hong Kong, etc.).

It has been estimated that the net earnings of US multinationals on overseas operations are at least 30 per cent higher than their home-based export earnings. Little wonder that sales of the leading US corporations are increasing three or four times faster than their sales inside the US, or that the number of US production facilities abroad will soon exceed 10,000. As a result, one may estimate that by 1980, US and US-associated production abroad will comprise nearly a third of the West's output outside the USA. The US-associated portion of production reflects the heightening involvement of middle- and even small-size enterprise through licensing and joint ventures. The large multinationals are, of course, extensively inter-linked through numerous joint ventures with each other, both American and foreign. Through such devices the smaller firms, who are better able to specialize in management and products, may also tap the capital strength which only the giant firm can muster. Canada has learned this through bitter experience. Territorially large but capital-scarce, her thirst for capital has culminated in around 60 per cent of her industry being foreign-owned. Small-sized Canadian firms are forced to associate with foreign giants or give way entirely through mergers in order to secure the capital necessary for survival.

If the US multinational firm has been the prime mover of the 50s and 60s, European and Japanese firms have already started making their counter-moves on a broad front. European annual direct investment in the US is expected to triple in volume by 1975 and quadruple thereafter. Japanese direct investment in US rose to nearly $1·5 billion in 1973. It was 12 times greater in 1973 than in 1972. By 1975 or 1976, European and Japanese associated investment will account for nearly a quarter of US Gross National Product. By that time, direct sales of US subsidiaries overseas will account for the largest share of total foreign sales with exports amounting to only 10 per cent. Historically, large multinationals have dominated European economics, especially in the smaller countries whose limited domestic markets alone could not sustain enterprises of the new dimensions needed to prosper. Switzerland is perhaps the outstanding example. Virtually all of its important firms are multinationals, with more of their production, sales and employees abroad than at home. Nestlé, the food giant, has only 0·05 per cent of its personnel in Switzerland; CIBA-Geigy, the world's thirteenth largest chemical firm, has 20 per cent; Hoffman la Roche, the largest Western pharmaceutical producer, does only 2 to 3 per cent of its business at home. Holland's four largest giants are members of the billion dollar sales club. Its firms – such as Unilever and Royal Dutch/Shell – besides being half English, have hundreds of plants scattered around the world. Philips in electrical production, and AKZO in chemicals have less workers in Holland than abroad. World famous names such as Purfina and Solvay in Belgium; Hoechst, Bayer and Siemens in Germany; Pirelli, FIAT, Montedison and Olivetti in Italy; Rhone Poulenc, Renault and Michelin in France; ICI, Dunlop and BP in Britain and Billeruds, Eriksson and RKZ in Sweden, as well as the leading pulp and paper firms of Norway and Finland, symbolize the real extent of the multinationalization of European industry. Most of these are investing more abroad than at home and all are bidding up their stakes in the US market.

Significant also is the amount of European portfolio investment in the USA. Nearly 70 per cent of total European investment in the USA is portfolio and only 30 per cent direct.

The degree of bank control over productive enterprise in Europe is very high, exceeding that in the USA, where a 1969 report of the Banking and Finance Committee of the House of Representatives even so charged that 49 important banks possessed effective ownership in 147 of the 500 largest American companies. When both direct and portfolio investment are added, West European investment in America is just slightly under combined American investment in Europe. England, Switzerland, Holland and Germany have a bigger stake in the USA than vice versa. Switzerland, for example, has over $60 billion worth of financial assets under its administration in the USA, and Germany's foreign portfolio investments (73 per cent of total) is largely 'invested' in stocks listed on the New York Stock Exchange; Holland, even on its direct account, has a stronger position in the USA than the USA has in Holland. When its considerable portfolio and real estate investment is included, Dutch imperialism in the USA considerably exceeds Yankee imperialism in Holland. France's situation is about in equilibrium. But with French direct investment programmed to expand tremendously, Marianne will shortly have a larger claim on Uncle Sam than Sam will have on her.

THE JOINT VENTURE

A concomitant to this European invasion of the USA is, of course, the extensive integration of European into American business through joint ventures ranging from large majority holdings (90–75 per cent), through partnerships (60–40 per cent), to minority participations (less than 40 per cent). Although the percentage is less now than in the 50s when nearly 70 per cent of US foreign holdings were joint ventures with non-US enterprises, the figure is still over 50 per cent and a new surge has begun. In many cases this linkage provides the European enterprise with a participation in the Stateside results of the joint venture operation. A measure of the scope of the joint venture system (some firms maintain up to twenty with other independents, notably in petroleum, chemicals, paper, rubber, etc.) is that there are nearly triple the number of such links between Common Market headquartered firms and non-Market firms, than between two firms headquartered in the Market itself. Just as US firms seek to purchase locally knowledgeable management and already established commercial, financial and politically integrated operations in order to reduce significantly the initial costs and risks by buying into European, Japanese, and other firms, so European and, incipiently, Japanese firms are buying into well-managed medium- and small-sized American companies to start or to expand their American penetration.

The phenomenal success of Japan's rising economic sun and the flood of occidental moneys has created an embarrassing surplus in that country. To alleviate the new foreign pressure for upward revaluation of the yen and to move into the economic orbit of the late 70s and 80s, Japan is switching its emphasis from exporting goods over to exporting factories and money. At first the area of concentration was South Asia, in neighbouring Taiwan, South Korea, Indonesia, etc. With much lower wages, abundant labour and only infant labour unions, these regions offered quick relative benefits for the managements of labour-intensive industries such as electronics assembly, textiles and garment manufacture. Recently the thrust has extended world-wide, even into the highest wage zones like the USA itself. TV plants, home building firms, food factories and even textile mills have been started there. Japanese chemical, electronic, camera and other firms are setting up in the Common Market, Ireland, UK and Switzerland. There are over fifty Japanese firms already established in Holland alone.

The Japanese Ministry of International Trade reports that the US–European invasion of Japan will soon be paralleled by direct foreign investment, which may reach close to $30 billion by 1980, representing nearly a tenfold increase over the $3·6 billion direct foreign investment in 1972. To this sum will be added the release of Japanese portfolio and loan funds to Western enterprises in conjunction with major American and European banking consortia. It is expected by the end of the present decade that the volume of such financial exports will approach that currently being pumped into direct investment to a heady total of nearly $50 billion.

Unsurprisingly, such a vast structural upheaval is triggering a chain reaction in banking and finance. To service their prime clients, large banks have gone multinational in search of scale: US banks such as the Bank of America, First National City, Chase Manhatten, etc., have hundreds of branches in dozens of countries. Barclays, Lloyds, Westminster and the sister British giants of the City have thousands of branches abroad. The major European banks, such as Société Générale (Belgium), Union de Banques Suisses (Switzerland), Banca Nazionale del Lavoro (Italy), Deutsche Bank and Dresdner (Germany), Banque

Nationale de Paris and Credit Lyonnais (France), and their half
a dozen largest co-nationals, have all become multinationals and
are expanding four to five times faster abroad than at home.
They are also exploding into joint-venture banking between themselves to form networks capable of accumulating, distributing
and managing the tremendous volumes of capital required across
the continents to support their industrial, commercial and
speculative clients. Already some 1,000 people in the leading
merchant or trading banks dominate the world underwriting
business, which raises around $50 billion of new 'entrepreneurial'
risk or debenture capital annually. By the end of the decade
about ten multinational global banks will sit securely upon the
money markets of the world.

This complete restructuring of finance at the global level has
already drastically impacted key areas of international economics
and propelled them at least a quarter of a century in advance of
pragmatic politicians and as much again in advance of conventional academic wisdom whose institutionally accepted
assumptions and hypotheses are, as a result, so outdated as to
be irrelevant to the functioning of real events.

Some of the new problems arising out of the dynamic changes
of concentration, multinationalization and the cash flow
maximizing of industry include:

1. Reduction of any meaningful relation between national
   exports, balance of trade and payment measurements as
   direct investments replace exports in foreign trade.
2. Emergence of permanent and rising levels of inflation well
   beyond the 3 to 4 per cent levels previously considered
   compatible with Keynesian-based full employment policies.
3. Appearance of 'stagflation' with rising structural employment
   and recurrent monetary crises, which are symptoms of the
   changing patterns and magnitudes of industrial investment
   provided essentially by consolidated cash flows and retained
   earnings.
4. Decrease in influence and control by the nation-state over
   important sectors of its economy and the transfer of effective
   centres of decision making from the territorially circumscribed
   national economy to the global corporation.
5. Introduction of a new stubborn strain of structural and
   investment-induced unemployment, laying the foundation of
   a 'jobless prosperity' in the corporate economy.

THE OBSOLETE ENTERPRISE

These global considerations have direct and obvious consequences for the individual enterprise in which the worker at present functions. As the enterprise is both the product and the accelerator of the system, change will be felt here in its crudest and earliest configuration. If the movement towards industrial democracy is to seize the advantage of the time, it must be prepared to use change as a positive medium for its advancement.

The combination of great corporate scale, greater market control and the explosive transformation of the enterprise into a multinational institution has produced an irreversible and inevitable trend towards the corporate economy. As we have discussed, dynamic and radical investment strategies, fed by growing cash flows, are making the corporation or enterprise the locus of economic power in society. Largely immune from public controls and regulations such as tax laws, anti-trust legislation, or from social obligations to their employees and customers, the new power centres have created new insecurities and dangers for most of the world's workers who are employed by them. Thus sheltered from the theoretical constraints imposed by governments upon their comportment, corporations are becoming introspective and directing more attention to the trade union and social challenges to its internal power. Workers and consumers have grown increasingly aware that public efforts to control the corporation meet with only limited success. Hard experience has demonstrated that hopes for self-policing or a social sense of corporate responsibility are in vain. This new consciousness of the political realities of the modern economic system is the source of much of the violent attacks against managerial prerogatives and against the entire corporate structure. It reflects the reality that effective control can be achieved only from within the enterprise not from the outside.

The conventional structures and decision-making processes of the enterprise have become obsolete. The culture of factory and office has not evolved in compatability with the widening cultural expectations of society. The personality, intelligence and life style of people who in the past were referred to as 'the masses' are no longer in tune with work systems which were developed from that perspective. Increased social awareness, wider communication and greater social mobility have come hand in hand with the expansion of the production systems to their natural boundaries at the global frontier. But the central dynamic of the system within which the worker/consumer is bound has increased rather than relented its compulsive vigour. The same 'freedoms' which have broadened man's potential as a user of things from the system, also now reduce his tolerance of the physical and social limitations imposed by the system's logic of operation in the work area. The recognition of his restrained and exploited condition makes the factory a repressive, demoralizing place for the contemporary worker, especially for the younger people, who have no history of deference. Repetitious, boring work carried out under adverse physical conditions usually inimical to physical and mental health and organized primarily for the benefit of machine utilization and productivity is in conflict with their living habits, values and expectations.

MAN AS MACHINE

Conventional management is geared to financial engineering and technological priorities. Its skill is expressed in terms of productivity, mechanical efficiency and lower costs through the application of complex equipment, rapid changes in technology, product diversification and sales requiring the subordination of human needs to machine and capital requirements. Authority in this system is necessarily autocratic, centralized and linear, flowing from the top down only. Decisions are taken far away from the workplace and in total disregard of the inherent needs of the human personality for equality, freedom and involvement. The need for creative and challenging work is deliberately engineered out of the system to avoid deviations and the job is evaluated and classified to keep it infantile or subordinate. The worker leaves his adulthood outside the factory and assumes the posture of an infant; the adults in the factory are only allowed in the upper executive echelons, foremen are a sort of supervisory adolescent or 'prefect' and those executing the orders are mere children. It is recognized that the really intelligent child rebels at a very early age, protests and defends his turf, even within the family in response to his budding self-consciousness and realization of personality. At maturity, at least before economic intimidation has rendered him thoroughly craintif and passive, a person desires to participate actively in his milieu.

Historically, the art of supervision and plant management has been, to quote Frederick Taylor, the founder of the school of so-called scientific management, that of 'knowing exactly of what you want men to do and then seeing that they do it in the best and cheapest way'. Its application through the years has turned the place of work into a pathologically destructive place for mature, independent and intelligently creative people. The underlying concept of scientific management is that the workers, because of their limited material means are primarily economic beings motivated by money. Taylor counselled management to pay workers well but to remove all but mechanical involvement from work. This philosophy fitted the factory system very well for it was entirely consistent with the culture of bureaucracy which demands centralized, authoritarian control and routinization of an essentially passive work force. The moral justification was, of course, that this was the most efficient system for providing everybody with material bounty to be enjoyed outside the working periods.

This in-plant bureaucratic culture has continued fundamentally intact up to the present time. But as workers succeeded in organizing stronger, more powerful unions on an industry-wide basis, the wage-fixing power of management was progressively transferred from the board room to the negotiating table and bargained rather than dictated. With base rates written into collective agreements, management switched the emphasis to incentive pay systems and production bonus systems over these negotiated base rates for purposes of retaining some production-related control over economic man. Though applied throughout the industrial world, scientific management and wage incentive schemes had only limited success relative to their philosophical aims. Over time, the trade unions successfully imposed a negotiating framework around the systems and standardized their applications within the enterprises. The concept thus lost most of its potency for promoting conformity and slavish fidelity to corporate goals.

MAN AS A DELICATE, BUT SUSCEPTIBLE MECHANISM

The continuing challenges of workers and the consequent frustrations of optimum efficiencies as calculated nicely by linear programming techniques, input–output matrices, and other more recent mechanistic planning devices, have encouraged managements to look towards the 'humanities' of academe to earn their keep by reducing antagonism.

It was natural therefore that the ideology factories of capitalism, the universities, and the academic business schools, should turn from the economic to the social motivations as a means for securing the passivity of workers to bureaucracy's games plan. A preliminary strategy was devised in the famous, but now moribund doctrine of human relations in industry, elaborated by Elton Mayo and his collaborators in the 40s. This doctrine stressed the central importance of interpersonal contacts and group relations to human needs and therefore proposed that these were more important than economic incentives in motivating workers. The human relations school of consultants sold management a social model of man as an interrelating being who instinctively created formal and informal groups with their own system of values which could be manipulated. Though the theory and its derivatives had a vogue among academics and international agencies, profit-seeking consultants, and other third-party outsiders to industrial relations, it had little real practical impact in industry. Too esoteric and abstract for practical management and too blatently paternalistic to lull the unions into acceptance, it subsided as fast as it arose.

Following Mayo's psycho-sociological model of man at work, arose the Kurt Lewin phase of working man as a self-actualizing, self-expressing, and self-determining being who was repressed by the hierarchical bureaucracy of the factory. Lewin and his disciples pointed out that because of such negating, inhibiting factors the workers were compelled to fight the system in defence of their personalities. They recommended that the bureaucracy be softened and that structures be adapted to people. The theory did not involve any revolutionary or drastic change in control and power, however, merely that such control be made more humane and more responsible and responsive to human needs. This central theme of the Lewin school was carried a step further in the 50s by McGregor. Management, McGregor charged, was still basically proceeding from the assumptions of Taylor's *Principles of Scientific Management* with its view of economically motivated man. Designating this set of assumptions Theory X, he charged that such a theory assumed in general that people inherently dislike work and try to avoid it, and that therefore they had to be controlled by threats and coercion to achieve the corporate goals. It also assumed that deep down people welcome direction as a substitute for personal responsibility and ambition. In opposition to this he formulated his Theory Y which posits that work on the contrary is natural to man, that his innate desire is for self-direction and self-determination in common commitment to functional objectives, that contrary to avoiding responsibility he seeks it to further his creative and imaginative faculties. Others developed variations of this self-determining social motivation around the central theme that the inhibiting bureaucratic structure of the working environment which stifles the self-motivated personality should be modified to create an integrated system in which superiors and subordinates interact through group concensus and goal setting. In this way a participative decision-making system could be evolved in which the managerial function could serve both to counteract the bureaucracy and to remove the antagonism of subordinates to the direction of superiors. At the same time this would emphasize the personal self-esteem needs of the individual and secure his commitment and motivation in the goals of the enterprise. But this phase has remained a characteristic of the 'think-tanks' rather than of the workshops, in the same way as previous theoretical insights.

The late 60s and early 70s saw the addition to management theory of the thesis that the way to organize the human factor in production is through job enrichment. Associated with the work of Professor Frederick Herzberg, this approach emphasizes motivation through the work itself rather than through improved interpersonal and social relations. It calls for increasing the complexity and the challenge of work to make it less monotonous and routine in order to satisfy the recognized human needs for self-fulfilment and self-motivation. Through 'job enrichment', greater responsibility and heightened recognition, the satisfaction derived from work will grow and with it the motivation of workers in the operation and production of the enterprise. Currently enjoying a vogue, job enrichment is being pushed strenuously by academic commercial consulting groups as a major means of breaking down the damaging contradictions between the bureaucratic organization and economic goals of the enterprise and the workers' social and psychological needs for self-fulfilment and satisfaction. At the present time it is enjoying a great press and a hard sell but is finding very few interested corporate takers.

Job enrichment has actually become part of a larger advocacy for new forms of work organizations. The purpose of such theorizing is to discover whether new forms of work organization can help provide greater involvement, heightened satisfaction, improved worker–management relations, mitigated stress and anxiety and, of course, as a result raise productivity.

Numerous experiments are being carried out in this area. In 1963, Philips, the Dutch-originated electrical giant which employs 80,000 in the Netherlands, began carrying out a programme of job restructuring. Changes are being introduced on the counsel of doctors and psychologists, efficiency experts and personnel technicians. The aim is to correlate workers' abilities and aspirations to the work function and to determine the effect on moral of different patterns of shift work and working environments. Under intense union pressure, FIAT began a similar experiment in Turino, Italy. Texas Instruments, Armour and several electronic firms in the United States have been experimenting with self-regulating work teams who plan both their own work system and job pattern as a complete work module. In Norway, experiments have been carried out since the 60s in four firms in the metal and chemical industries into such factors as job rotation, job enlargement, greater skills and the semi-autonomous work group with greater scope for organizing its own work than is normally the case.

At the instigation of the unions, the management of Volvo and SAAB – Sweden's two largest car makers – have experimented with various methods of job humanization over the past few years. Volvo has 3,900 workers (or 60 per cent of all personnel on the shop floor) directly engaged on the assembly line at its main plant at Göteborg. These people are increasingly becoming involved in experiments with 'industrial democracy', in particular self-government, job rotation and job enlargement. Self-governing groups are formed as teams of three to seven men at free stations along the truck assembly line. They organize their work as they think best, electing their own leaders and, if they wish, rotating the leadership. Each of the twenty teams is paid collectively and decides how to divide its earnings. When a new man joins the group, the company provides the money for his apprenticeship with the team.

Job rotation is practised by 700 workers, each of whom changes his job daily according to a fixed schedule and thus learns all the tasks performed by his group. However, workers who prefer the security of staying at the same job each day may still do so. Job enlargement enables workers to combine two or more elements of a job on the assembly line. This has been found particularly applicable in the painting shop.

It is hoped that from the employee's point of view, inter-personal relations will improve and work may become more varied and meaningful. The system aims also to simplify some management problems. Volvo maintains a permanent surplus of assembly line labour, to meet a worker turnover rate of 25 per cent and a sickness rate of 10 per cent (including casual absences from work). Worker versatility created by job rotation, it is argued, will make possible higher utilization of this floating labour, and reduce the disrupting effects of absenteeism.

Similar, if more limited, experiments are underway in the Netherlands Post and Telegraph, in the Alcan Aluminium Company and Domitar Paper Company in Canada, in British Railway workshops and in academic research projects in several American and British universities.

More pertinent, however, is the growing demand for reducing and downgrading work entirely. The rising interest in the four-day week, based upon the 10-hour day, already introduced in hundreds of American, and a handful of European firms, in the three-day week and even six-month working year, are manifesta-tions of a new trend of thought in industry on the problem of work alienation. Because of the costliness and the often in-surmountable complexities of any substantial reform of work organization, especially in the production assembly lines and in intensively rationalized administrative and information-processing functions, this concern proceeds from the premise that it is in providing more continuous free time away from work that the answer to conflict lies, rather than through job enrichment.

New, but largely academic, proposals are being advanced along these lines for contracting working time to provide for more continuous release from the stultifying routine of production on an increasing scale. The initial three-day weekend of a 10-hour, four-day working week would thus give way progressively to a nine-hour day, 36-hour week and move on towards an eight-hour day, 32-hour week, and perhaps eventually to a three-day, 30-hour week. Other formulae may be put forward involving new divisions of working time, such as seven days on, followed by seven days off, or one month on, one month off, etc.

Related to this line of thought are the experiments in a num-ber of companies permitting employees to compose their own daily and weekly shift patterns to suit their family and social requirements. Pilkington Brothers, the glass firm in Lancaster, England, is one of nearly a hundred firms in various countries, such as Sweden, the USA, Switzerland, Germany and Holland, experimenting with flexible working hours. There the scheme consists of a fixed number of weekly hours divided into core times of five basic hours a day during which the worker must be present and remaining free hours which he can make up to suit his needs. Of course, most of these latter programmes, for the most part initiated by industry in association with specialist consultants, propose keeping the overall hourly work week or monthly hourly total intact, thus even reducing wage costs through the elimination or reduction of daily overtime work which must be paid for at a premium.

HUMAN EFFECTS

All of these new approaches, whether they emphasize the need to modify work organization or to reduce the authoritarian bureaucracy of the productive enterprise, are defensive responses to the intensifying opposition in the factory and office and the receding commitments and motivation of workers. Participative management, human relations and Theory Y styles of super-vision, sensitivity training, or an even more recent call for maximizing a worker's psychological EGO needs, all aim at essentially changing the style and orientation of management to reverse the declining morale and rising mental and physical suffering of workers caused by the anachronistic, alienating work culture and which threatens the totems of productivity, growth and efficiency.

Already in the United States and the United Kingdom, one person in ten suffers from mental illness at some time during their lives. A report by Britain's Department of Health and Social Security shows that in one year 22·8 million working days were lost by men and women suffering from personality, mental and psycho-neurotic disorders, nervousness, debility and headaches. The report puts mental illness as the second leading cause of work absenteeism due to illness after bronchitis, but ahead of accidents and heart disease. In broad social terms and in respect of its egalitarian political democracy and social security system, Sweden has earned a deservedly eminent reputa-tion. With the highest wages in the world, except for the USA and perhaps the highest average living standards, together with the most extensive guarantees against work risks and general vicissitudes of life, the social system and trade union movement have been quotable examples of what should and can be achieved. Such a high level of living and social standards generally help to focus all the more clearly the modern dilemma of the 40-hour week's victory of machines over men. A government-commissioned report issued in May 1972 on the mental health of Swedish workers had a shock effect. It revealed a dramatic rise in mental hospital admissions over recent years, attributable largely to the pressures upon Swedish workers in their work situation. Long hours, extremely rapid work paces geared to machine speeds and efficiency routines in offices, with both husband and wife compelled to work, result in small children left with casually interested child-minders, whilst fatigue and exhaustion leave little force and spirit for family life and even normal sex relationships at the end of a 'normal' working day. This picture of disrupted family life in one of the best balanced societies at the macroscopic or politico-economic levels is a grim signal of an over-stressed, insecure industrial culture. Failure to reduce drastically the machine-induced stress and insecurity generally in factory and office work will cause further dangerous rises in mental illness.

Sociological studies have revealed extreme psychic disturbances, mostly of a neurotic character, among nearly three million married working women in West Germany. Around 2·4 million West German children suffer from parental neglect due largely to the overdriven physical and mental state of their working mothers who are deprived of both the time and energy to care adequately for their children. The New York Commissioner for Public Health recently stated quite seriously that no more than 20 per cent of the city's inhabitants could be classified as 'mentally fit'.

There is now convincing evidence that the human stress produced by the insecurity and repression of our modern industrial culture is a primary cause of the terrifying rise in the chronic diseases of middle age, notably of heart diseases. Modern analysis is challenging medical dogma on the main perils threatening men in their working prime. Though a century ago heart disease was virtually unknown anywhere in the world, over 700,000 people died of the disease in 1971 in the United States, and almost 200,000 of them were under 65. An alarming aspect is that the age level of the coronary stroke is dropping, reflecting its relationship to the industrial world's mechanistic aggression against the social and psychological needs of the person and particularly the destruction of his sense of security, skill and status in the social order. Today it is recognized that stress, which produces chemical changes in the body weakening and destroying the cardiovascular system, is very much a product of the industrial order and a consequence of the hierarchical bureaucracy's power to direct, oppress and finally reject the individual. This rising phenomenon will grow into a scourge unless the cause is checked at its source, not in man's internal organs but in the bureaucratic power structure of the factory-office jungle.

WORKPLACE POLLUTION – ANOTHER TARGET

Quite apart from the modern industrial disabilities induced by stress and tension a new awareness is emerging of the factory-level pollution which confronts workers. The growing concern is partly a result of greater knowledge of the toxicity and dangers to health of many traditional chemicals, processes and materials, and partly due to a feed-back from the largely middle class alarm of the dangers of polluting the total environment through air and water contamination by industrial effluents and particulates, especially hydro-carbons.

The well-promoted 'Club of Rome', MIT-scholared report on the predicament of mankind is an example of the concern being shown about planetary pollution. Its conclusion is that 'if the present growth trends in world population, industrialization, pollution, food production and resource depletion continue unchanged, the limits to growth on this planet will be reached some time within the next one hundred years. The most probable result will be a rather sudden and uncontrollable decline in both population and industrial capacity.' But no such concern is shown in the pollution of the working environment which has already claimed millions of lives, shortens the life span of industrial workers and maims, enfeebles, injures and impoverishes millions of others. Little wonder, for most of the leading spokesmen of the pollution crusades of the 70s are elitists, associated professionally in one way or another with the enterprises and industries most responsible for the pollution. For example, the Club of Rome is the brainchild and inspiration of a vice-president of FIAT, while one important US-based international institute for the environment has a co-president who is the chairman of a major American oil company and extensive relations with the UN environment program.

Nevertheless, the feed-back from the global concern with 'pollution' is awakening realization of the far more tangible dangers which stalk the workplace, as highly dangerous and toxic chemicals are increasingly introduced into industry. In a statement before the US Senate Labor Committee, the President of the American Chemical Workers' Union pointed up the hazards arising in the chemical industry out of constantly advancing and increasingly complex technology. He charged that these hazards range from outright killing and maiming by accidents, explosions, acids and corrosives and exposures to the insidious poisons which penetrate the body through the lungs and skin and cause cancer; chemically induced diseases of the liver, kidneys, lungs and blood and other chronic and frequently fatal diseases. 'Through the years chemical workers have sacrified health and lives for industrial production and profits. Diatomaceous earth and asbestos have killed chemical workers in the factories by producing pneumaconiosis and asbestosis. Betanaphthylamine causes cancer of the urinary bladder, new enzymes added to detergents are causing respiratory responses yet unknown. The chemical worker is hired and placed on a job which compels him to handle and breathe noxious fumes, mists and gases of chemicals. New chemicals and processes are introduced usually with no prior testing as regards worker safety or tested only superficially. Traditionally industry has dealt vigorously with a hazard only after tragedy has occurred: women radium watch dial painters in the 20s, fluorescent light blub beryllium workers in the 40s, the betanaphthylamine workers in the 50s, diatomaceous earth workers from the turn of the century until today.' The black-lung scourge of coalminers exists today as does the brown lung diseases of textile workers. Mercury was classified as a deadly, lethal substance half a century ago, but it still continues to destroy the brain cells of workers today. Despite a complete dossier, elad poisoning is widespread among those in factories processing the substances.

Only as late as April 1972 did the US administration order that priority be given to an investigation of five substances, long known to be dangerous, to which the lives of four million workers in the US are particularly exposed, which might affect some twelve million workers around the world: asbestos, cotton dust, silicium, lead and carbon dioxide. Asbestos provokes lung diseases and cancer. Cotton dust and silicium induce silicosis. Lead exercises a lethal action in the gastro-intestinal system, the blood and the central nervous system. Carbon dioxide can damage the brain and cause death. In the United States, more than 8,000 substances are considered dangerous, but only 500 of them are covered by health and safety regulations.

In view of the record this is hardly surprising, for the mores of the factory culture have always been particularly delinquent in regard to health and safety conditions. Work accidents due to deficient education outlays, safety standards and equipment, and neglect of proper construction safeguards in buildings and machines have always been excessive and the number is growing. The International Labour Office in a report for an expert committee on industrial health and safety stated:

'In the industrialized countries, notwithstanding the absence of criteria for detailed comparison between countries, the high incidence of occupational injuries is illustrated by the fact that it is estimated in round figures that every year one worker in ten incurs an accident of sufficient gravity to be reported to the authorities; that the working days lost each year due to this fact average 5 per cent; that the financial loss entailed by accidents not involving injury is 20 times that resulting from accidents or diseases involving bodily harm to workers. It has been estimated that in certain countries the over-all cost of occupational accidents and diseases amounts to between 3 per cent and 10 per cent of the national income. The resultant loss to the national economy far exceeds that attributable to industrial disputes. In the United Kingdom, the figures for industry, agriculture and commerce, taken together, show that in 1967 occupational accidents and diseases resulted in the loss of 23 million working days, as against only 3 million days lost through strikes. In the United States, the total cost of occupational accidents amounted in 1969 to $9 billion, while in the Federal Republic of Germany, also in 1969, the figure was DM 5·1 billion. To these detrimental effects, which can be measured in quantitative terms, must be added others – impossible to measure at present, but recognized to becoming increasingly widespread – resulting from the collective or individual tension created by poor working conditions and, in more general terms, failure to adjust the job to the man.

'In the meantime, progress in medicine has led to a gradually increasing tendency to apply preventive medicine to the whole population. Health checks permitting of early diagnosis of diseases make it possible, on the one hand to save human lives and, on the other hand to prevent illness from becoming chronic and to provide better health protection by putting a brake on the rising cost of medical care. To date, little has been done to co-ordinate activities of this kind with the work done by medical services in undertakings.

'As concerns the arousing of awareness of the importance of occupational safety and health matters, efforts appear to be marking time. A great deal still remains to be done to convince employers and workers that prevention is a factor in economic and social progress from which every undertaking and every worker can derive benefit. The public authorities, for their part, lack the resources necessary to enable them to put into practice a forceful prevention policy and methods geared to technological progress. In the Federal Republic of Germany, for instance, inspectors in the official services had time to spend only an average of 130 minutes per year on inspecting each of the undertakings directly liable to inspection under the official regulations.

'In the developing countries, the most serious problems, in terms both of frequency and of gravity, are encountered in undertakings in the traditional industries, craft workshops or family undertakings, where the lack of precautionary measures, defective equipment and archaic production process enhance the risks of serious accident with permanent effects. What is more, the public authorities are even more lacking than those of the industrialized countries in the resources necessary to enforce the legal provisions in this respect. Lastly, the vulnerability of the workers is enhanced by disease, malnutrition, inadequate medical facilities, poor sanitation among the population as a whole and the frequent unfamiliarity of workers with industrial techniques and conditions. Accordingly, all action in this field must be placed within the context of the country's general health policy.'

Belatedly the chronic malignancy of the factory culture has received official recognition. The age-old accusations of the working class against the polluted and destructive work environment was confirmed in the World Health Organization's Director General's report to its 1972 assembly. It showed that most workers work under unfavourable conditions and find themselves exposed to tensions and aggressions of all sorts beyond the factors which threaten the population generally.

The report insisted on the fact 'that despite gaps in current information, it can be certified that the incidence of occupational illness is often very high, notably due to the inhalation of dust in the mines, construction sites, foundries and other industries, and the exposure to toxic doses of chemical products, industrial solvents or other metals'. It estimates, for example, that 'fibrous pneumoconiosis strikes 25 per cent of all workers exposed to dusts' and that in certain developing countries 40 per cent of workers exposed to lead intoxication develop the lethal saturnism.

On the psycho-social plane, it referred to effects of advanced mechanization on tensions and nervous disorders: 'shift work, repetitive tasks and low job satisfaction', it rated, can generate 'fatigue, psychosomatic diseases and absenteeism'. 'Neurotic symptoms, digestive disorders, peptic ulcers and cardiac conditions' appear frequently among workers subject to mental and physical tension.

Further, certain illnesses traditionally classified as 'non-occupational' can be caused by chemical, physical or psycho-social factors present in the work environment. Epidemiological statistics, the report revealed, show that death due to cardiovascular illnesses is relatively high in the rayon industry, and that stomach ulcers are very frequent in certain industries in which workers are subject to multiple tensions.

Unfortunately the recommendation that the WHO accord more attention to programmes of industrial medicine, in particular to the study of the problems of workers' hygiene and to industrial medicine integrated in national health programmes, although a welcome departure from conventional diagnosis of the factory is a feeble palliative with no curative qualities. There must first be a total revamping of the economic and hierarchical structure of the enterprise, and priority given to the participation of workers in decisions on health and safety conditions at the place of work. Excising the sources of factory-induced tensions and diseases demands drastic surgery upon the total factory system. Social palliatives and partial treatments may relieve some of the most flagrant symptoms, but they cannot effect real and lasting cures.

Official figures put the number of British workers killed at work every year at around 1,000. About half a million are injured and 23 million working days are lost through accident and disease. A report of a government-appointed committee on safety and health (June 1972) highlighted the total inadequacy of the existing system of regulations. Over five million people, it discovered, work in conditions not covered by any safety regulations. The Chemical Workers Regulations date back to 1922, long before the development of modern chemical technology. Inspectorates were totally inadequate to carry out their responsibilities, scattered among different groups of statutes and government departments and restricted in the amount of penalties imposable. For example in 1970 the average fine imposed under the Factory Act was a decisively light £40. Among the principal recommendations for improving the poor state of health and safety in British workplaces was that workers should be granted legal rights to participate in safety matters.

According to an official survey carried out by the French Social Security Administration among 2,330,000 workers in the region of Paris, 36·2 per cent ceased work because of illness or accident during 1968. In about 28 per cent of the cases this involved absences of a maximum of thirty days.

Similarly, the US Occupational Safety and Health Administration has reported that of 29,505 plants and work-sites inspected during the year ended 30 June 1972, only 7,418 were found to be in compliance with the safety regulations. A total of 32,700 inspections were conducted, which found 102,861 violations of federal job safety standards. This means that in the US, three out of every four plants fail to meet legally set safety standards.

Despite widespread criticism of the generally poor health and safety conditions, industry and government continue more or less successfully to keep legal sanctions to a minimum. A case in point was the bitter protest of American trade unions in July 1972 against the removal of 'small business' from the eighteen-month-old Federal Occupational Safety and Health Act. Responding to a wave of pressure, the House and Senate voted to exempt at least 86 per cent of the nation's employees and fifteen million or more workers for at least a period of a year with the prospects for further extensions afterwards. As in Great Britain, and most other countries, inadequate funds and enforcement personnel threaten to debilitate the real effect of the measure. According to officials of the Department of Labour's Occupational Safety and Health Division, in the ten months ended 30 April 1972 only 5,791 workplaces inspected were found to be free of hazards – roughly three of every four checked were found to be in violation. During that period, 75,864 violations were charged against 18,500 employers. The workplaces checked employed 4·6 million workers. This confirms, the unions contend, that too few checks are made and that the record of violations shows the need for thorough enforcement.

Industry obviously has the message that regulation means money since the Wall Street Journal of 14 June 1972 spelt out very clearly the dangers at present in industrial noise levels:

'It has long been suspected that as many as 10 million workers may hear poorly due to excessive noise. Now some research links noise to such diverse ills as mental distress and heart disease. In Germany, a recent study of workers found that those subject to the most noise on the job suffered a higher incidence of heart disorders, circulatory problems and equilibrium disturbances. A number of medical men are certain that job noise is a factor in some neurotic and psychotic illnesses.'

However, in view of the difficulties of getting adequate government resources, both financial and personnel, for the task of controlling and enforcing regulations over such a wide range of different industries, and sizes of firms and plants, external enforcement is not likely to be successfully carried out. This further emphasizes the importance of worker control, exercised on a day-to-day basis at the work-site, to bring about any meaningful improvement in the elimination of industrial hazards to human health and safety.

One need not look far to realize why health and safety aspects have been so blatantly neglected for so long, despite the continued concern of the organized trade unions. Precautions cost money and may impair productive efficiency – both are immediate reasons for profit-oriented management to ignore the whole shameful area. The disability and death of workers in pursuit of industrial production has not been laid to the account of management in a way which would seriously impinge on profits, whereas money invested in process machinery and the negotiated piece-rates for its operation are a constant reminder of the high cost of a change of raw materials, the shutting down of a process or the slowing of operators by the insistence on safety equipment. When those who set the working goals and set up the economic rules are concerned only with the single aim of profit maximization for growth investment, there can be no other prevailing attitude. Only by his insistence on taking a hand in planning and management in the primary policy areas can the worker ensure that priority consideration (as opposed to lip-service) is given to the fundamental issue of his own well-being and safety.

POWER—REAL OR ILLUSORY?

But most of the prescribed doctrines and gimmickry proposed by management consultants have not proved and will not prove lasting. Emphasizing behavioural and socio-psychological features on the surface, even the schemes negotiated between management and unions in certain important firms based on the theories discussed avoid the taboo area of economic and material compensation. They are mainly designed by consultants to relieve pressure on the production sector and result in reduced wage bills through the elimination of overtime categories and improved efficiency.

They raise few questions about basic transformation of the enterprise and about its intrinsic power structure. The goals they set are those of better transmission and acceptance of management policies by workers and of mitigating their dangerous emnity to work and the enterprise leaving untouched the basic profit-maximizing goals of the concern itself. Having confirmed the growing difficulty of achieving worker compliance through external economic coercion and intimidation they propose, in different ways, to achieve the same end through drilling workers to greater self-control and self-commitment to the company's production. Such schemes are in no way facets of industrial democracy and if they are signals of change they are still extremely feeble. The worker comes under stress because he has little effective voice and power of decision in the industrial processes which affect his working life and derivatively his family and social life, and the fact has become too flagrant to be ignored or minimized by the tinkering of theoreticians. Almost all of the above doctrines and experiments from Taylorism through to job enrichment and EGO-building have been management-fostered and controlled. With the possible exception of the Norwegian and Swedish autonomous group, job enlargement experiments where unions participated from the outset, they have been developed independently and frequently in conflict with the trade unions. It could scarcely be otherwise for, although the more modern techniques stress the sociological and psychological importance of the work function and appear to recognize the intrinsic necessity for adult, healthy men and women to participate directly in the decisions and milieu which shape their existence, they are all merely new, more refined behavioral techniques for securing compliance to work and goals set by management, for management and under management.

In such 'participation' no transfer or sharing of real power over decision making and no really significant reform of the corporate hierarchy and bureaucracy is projected or even conceived. Job enrichment and job enlargement approaches may have inherent merit, but they will not get very far for they are costly and disruptive to capital-intensive, high technology industry. The industrial decision-making process is basically one of trading-off social and human costs against the rigorous imperatives of higher production and higher profits. In the factory and enterprise the pursuit of profit for investment is the motor of ownerless modern industry. As long as control over investment lies absolutely with management, the balance of power is critically weighted in favour of capital to the detriment of labour. Consequently, behind the rhetoric, models and humanitarian theology of the neoclassical and modern doctrines of management is the continuing attempt to integrate the worker into the company, thus weakening his militancy and his trade union loyalties. The strategies have been unsuccessful in the past and will be just as unsuccessful in the future. For they will continue to be rejected by workers and their unions who properly see in them only more sophisticated versions of age-old devices for manipulating and controlling the human side of industry for the benefit of the machine and for profits. The needs of the organization in such doctrines always take precedence over the needs of the human personality at all levels of organization.

Across the entire range of opposition to industrial democracy runs the common criticism that the system is inherently incompatible with optimum industrial organization and efficiency, that it is inefficient and costly. This proposition is generally based on one or more of the following three classical premises:

1. Collective, participative decision-making produces a form of conservative, slow-moving, consensus government which is unsuitable to modern industry where creative risk-taking and rapid decisions are essential.

2. Labour and capital are naturally exclusive if not naturally predatory. Any form of participation must therefore involve

surrender of basic rights and responsibilities of one side to the other to the detriment of the function of each, the success and the efficiency of the enterprise.

3. At the present stage of social development, workers lack the skill, education and natural intelligence to participate effectively in the decision-making process of industry. Their advent to top management and works management therefore makes for discordance and conflict with detrimental effects on production.

These premises spring from a total disregard of the ample evidence and from a self-serving wish to maintain and bolster cherished advantages.

The burgeoning groups of third-party hangers-on to labour–management relations have, of course, a vested interest in perpetuating the mythology of 'separate and unequal'. Labour lawyers, management consultants, international agencies and academics, by peddling their 'objective wisdom', have created a very lucrative tertiary service industry for themselves. Two-way conflict and the separation of industrial functions creates a wide, theoretical gap between management and labour which the 'neutralists' can occupy profitably. The mythology can best be exposed, however, by an integrated analysis of past evidence in the light of present change. Any argument that the workers lack education and culture is merely the obverse of an implicit assumption that top-level managers are, by contrast, specifically educated, cultured and leadership-oriented. This is demonstrably not the case. Most top-level managers are long on specialized experience in select fields and short on the general 'Business Administration' education taught at the multitude of university business schools, despite their need to be generalists by function. Less than half of the members of the executive boards of German industry have university-level education. The 'old School tie' and 'colours' won on the playing fields of Eton – the symbols of family connection and class privilege – have been time-honoured passports to the board rooms of Great Britain, rather than the cap and gown of a Bachelor's, Master's or Doctor's degree. Recent surveys in the US confirm that top management selection tends to revolve in cycles. Of twelve managing directors or executive presidents named in 1967 in the principal 100 firms, nine had engineering degrees and only two had general business degrees. During the last two decades the engineers have come to the command posts, reflecting the overriding concern with technology and productivity over this period. Over 50 per cent of the managing directors of the 500 principal US industrial enterprises received engineering and technical degree-level education, whilst only 9 per cent have degrees in economics or business administration. In the decade of the 1960s the prodigious boom of private business was fueled by soaring corporate profits and by depreciation allowances. This internal cash-flow seemed an inexhaustible source of capital expansion as inflation coupled to protected markets provided technically trained management with the means necessary for financing operations. But all this changed in the 1970s. The insatiable cash needs of the growth-hungry enterprise outgrew the rate of growth of internal funds. Corporations were hard pressed as investment capital became increasingly scarce. An already historically high and sustained rate of inflation has made it more and more difficult to raise prices and previous rates, even in highly monopolized markets. Finance has therefore moved from being a staff function into the centre of corporate decision-making and has changed both the pattern of corporate planning and the skills demanded of central management. The once lowly rated skills of the accountant have now become the critical skills for corporate survival. As a result, the financial officer has risen to a more exalted corporate position than the production or commercial specialist before him. Financial accounting has now become the key function of modern industry and its managerial proponents are the new crown princes of industry.

The next phase of significant corporate change will certainly be in the direction of increased social responsibility and greater concern with the social and personal needs of people both as workers and consumers. Narrow, profit-maximizing objectives will give way to the broader criteria of meeting social and human needs. It will be necessary to optimize real benefits to the wider community and to the workforce in place of the growth and dividends previously accrued for stockholders. This transition to social motivations will demand different outlooks, psychology and commitments on the part of directors and managers. The financial function will be superseded by the social function as the top priority corporate need and the financial wizard will need to be replaced by a person with new insights and wider understanding if the organization is to survive.

As most industrialized countries stagger from crisis to crisis, the bankruptcy of the economic traditions and rules of private enterprise are widely recognized if not openly admitted. A parallel crisis of confidence in the old objectives of productivity-centred management (cash flow, sales and output) has prompted demands for a new dimension of management responsibility in the social or non-economic spheres. No longer are corporate officers to be allowed with impunity to put high profits before the multitude of social priorities: controlling and paying for pollution; helping develop urban programmes to remedy the innercity decay and the spread of ghetto-life; financing and administering training programmes for the hard core unemployed; providing public and consumer representation on the boards of directors; supporting charities, educational and artistic organizations, etc.

The emergence of these social or non-economic values into the management consciousness will exert new pressures on corporate strategies. Any emergence into a 'post-industrial society' will take as its starting point a redefinition of the role and responsibility of the enterprise and its management. Social progress and the maximization of human benefit before that of economic growth will revolutionize management strategies and will demand new skills and values in meeting these objectives.

Such skills and values are precisely those possessed by workers and trade unionists. Their culture of humanity and their work experience are precisely what will be needed to formulate the new corporate strategies in which any benefits will be earned by the total social 'good' produced rather than by manipulation of the manufactured 'goods'. Practical work experience and shop floor culture will no longer be regarded as low-rating, purely instrumental factors; because they provide direct communication with the needs and wishes of *people* they will acquire a directive power over the patterning of *things* and will become the elements of estimable, sought-after top managerial skills.

This is an area where there are few available skills in traditional management. Certainly it is the field farthest removed from the special mechanistic capacities and experience of the financial officer. Conversely, it is precisely the field where workers and trade unions have skills. For centuries their collective efforts have been directed towards exactly such goals. Trade unions exist inherently to promote social change and have long traditions of fighting for the social transformation of society.

In fact, their entire concern is with enhancing the status of the working man and his family against the debilitating reduction

forces of corporate profit-maximizing. Whatever may be said of
the labour movement's academic credentials, few of which would
be relevant to the subject at hand in any case, its accumulated
experience of managing for social objectives is unique and
virtually inexhaustible.

Even the systems of decision making adopted in trade union
affairs are emerging as more advanced and up to date than their
extant counterparts in corporate society. The chaos and crises
of management systems is a popular best-selling theme. The
bookshelves of the world are laden with 'best-sellers' on the
neanderthal corporate leadership. This has spawned a vast body
of business-source literature indicting the current corporate
systems of decision making from *Parkinson's Law* through *The
Peter Principle* to Townsend's *Up the Corporation*; whilst the
demand for professional pundits such as Peter Drucker, John
Kenneth Galbraith and literally hundreds of others are indicative
of the general indictment. In the US persistent demands are being
made from within the system for 'public representatives to protect
the interests of the commonwealth' on corporate boards of
management. Most approaches seem to be concerned to find a
means of transforming blatant economic maximization to a
facade of social optimization without conceding any of the
essentials of power. Such criticisms will not therefore produce
much change, regardless of how profitably the best-selling books
perform for their authors. The common underlying shortcoming
is that the essentials of the management process remain basically
hierarchical and authoritarian, and consequently obsolete.
Today's corporate structure, with its line and staff functions, is a
cultural anachronism and its various processes such as linear
programming, systems analysis, management by objectives and
the countless derivatives are totally irrelevant to real efficiency
and the sacred economic goals of industry. The army of corporate
giants is led by a command of mental pensioners, patterned on
the heroes of antiquity and out of touch with present reality.
They are not equipped to grasp the fact that the authoritarian
style of leadership is no longer practicable. The speed of change
and the constant upending of values and goals no longer permit
the static rigidities of hierarchical forms of leadership. There are
no longer any immutable values in terms of the old objectives.
To adapt and create solutions in an environment of total dynamics
involving dialogue, negotiations and personalized group decision-
making, is the new requisite. It is precisely this type of democratic

collective process which is more to be found in trade union government or management, than in any other institution or social grouping. Dialogues, discussions, collaboration, voting, delegated authority are the parameters of the democratic system. They require that power be shared and that the relationship between superior and subordinate be reversed. Instead of the implicit recognition that ultimate power is vested in the superior, the lower echelons are cognizant that his authority is merely delegated and as such is subject to recall. These concepts are alien to the old line and staff principles of the corporate organization charts and cannot be kept in limbo through tinkering or patching-up of past mythology.

RETROSPECTIVE ON SELF-MANAGEMENT

The demand for self-management is trans-ideological and represents a threat to the continuation of entrenched power elites wherever they operate. The ground-swell is as strong beneath the centralized state-capitalist bureaucracies as it is under the privileged structures of monopoly capitalism. Just as the West German laws of 1951 and 1952 provided the catalyst for the thrust towards industrial democracy in the West, so the Yugoslavian law of 21 June 1950, making workers' self-management the official policy of the state and transferring all factories and undertakings to the administration of workers' collectives, marked a historic turning point in the theoretical and political evolution of socialism in Eastern Europe.

The promulgation of this measure finalized Tito's break with Stalin on the heresy of self-management which had been a subject of running controversy between the Soviet Union and the Yugoslavian leadership since late 1947. Whether the proclamation of the self-management principle issued from more prosaic power differences between Tito and Stalin's centralist megalomania as some sceptics in the West contend, or whether the widening Yugoslavian experiments with self-management, attacked by Stalin in June 1948 at a Communist Party council in Bucharest as a 'betrayal of socialism' and 'counter-revolutionary', was the direct cause of the rupture is of great historic interest. But much more consequent is the happening itself, for it introduced a major new, practical advance towards humanitarian or democratic socialism in the socialist bloc.

That the Yugoslavian experiment of self-management could become contagious to other parts of the area under Soviet hegemony was a very real threat to Soviet central authority. Events leading up to the Soviet occupation of Czechoslovakia provided dramatic proof of this. The decision of the Czech trade unions with government acquiescence to declare their autonomy of the party, create industrial federations and proclaim and utilize the right to strike called forth the first warning tremors of a possible impending political earthquake.

The announcement of the so-called 'Ota SIK reforms' was a second nail in the coffin of nascent Czech democracy. Confronted with virtual bankruptcy by the bureaucratic management of the economy, and especially by inept management at the enterprise and factory levels, a large group of leaders called for the application of certain reforms, submitted by Ota SIK, which were intended to reduce state controls over industry and to accord a large degree of autonomy to the enterprises. This would effectively diminish the massive power of the central planning authorities over production and was coupled with the highly radical proposal to establish Workers' Councils empowered to participate directly in the management of the decentralized concerns. These reforms were rapidly introduced and the previous directors, unionists and party officials replaced by union militants and officials elected directly by the workers. 70 per cent of those selected to serve on the management committees were technicians and highly skilled workers, which bespeaks a keen sense of responsibility on the part of the average Czechoslovak worker.

This maturity and developed social consciousness of the workers profoundly disconcerted the party bureaucrats and technocrats long accustomed to conceiving the work force in the classic hierarchical view as composed rather of incompetent 'masses' to be directed, led and managed from above. Equally disturbing to that elite was the noticeable improvement in the effectiveness of the planning and production of the economy under the new democratic base-managed enterprises.

Given the long tradition of opposition to managerial authority and the relatively advanced level of technological sophistication and culture, compared for example to that of the Yugoslavian working class at the time of the introduction of self-management, the creation of workers' councils obviously had a ring of permanency which would certainly resound through the other socialist countries. There is little doubt that the decision to invest the country militarily was prompted by the urgent need to forcibly stop the process initiated in Yugoslavia from gathering further momentum. The Soviets knew that a Czechoslovak team of experts had visited Yugoslavia to study its system of works' councils prior to the selective introduction of Czech self-management councils in 1968. Though a few enterprises continued to establish councils after the occupation in November 1969, many were dissolved, including one at the Pilsen Skoda works, which foreshadowed the end of the experiment and focussed attention on the role which it had played in the invasion. This decline of the main cause of the occupation was concluded by a government announcement in July 1970 that all the works' councils were to be abolished. Accompanying the announcement was an official statement to the effect that right-wing forces had been instrumental in passing the legislation which authorized the establishment of workers' councils in the full realization that their establishment 'would have deprived the Communist Party of its leading role in the economic sphere, liquidated the state's influence on enterprises, and legalized the transformation of the ownership of the entire people into group ownership'.

WIDER EFFECTS

Not only did this repression crush the self-management movement in Czechoslovakia, but it also had the intended effect of inducing party leadership in some of the other countries (notably in Rumania and Hungary) to exercise greater caution in pursuing similar reforms. Workers' assemblies in Rumanian factories had already begun active participation in management decision-making. The strength attained by the development in Rumania was cogently illustrated by the policy statement of President Ceaucescu to a meeting of the Central Committee of the Rumanian Communist Party in February 1971 that the earlier party orthodoxy, which held trade unions to be transmission belts for government economic policies and production plans, was a bureaucratic anachronism left over from the immediate post-war years. He said that trade unions must become a 'completely autonomous organization', acting independently and engaged in what he called 'a movement towards economic democracy in industry and other places of work'. To further such a movement, Ceaucescu proposed the establishment of committees and councils composed of trade union and worker representatives as a form of collective management in industry and other branches of the national economy. This, he claimed, was to be the principal means of extending economic and workers' democracy within the overall administrative authority of the state; in other words, the economy would continue to be based on socialist central planning. This emphasis on the secondary position of the new enterprise structures beneath overall state authority was intended to answer, in part at least, Soviet criticism that such reforms were really intended to undermine the socialist economy and progressively transform it into a capitalist market economy.

These principles began to be implemented through the creation of workers' enterprise assemblies with the right to audit, and, if need be, revise the policy of management. They were considerably strengthened in a draft 'Law on Organization and Economic Management', presented for discussion in October 1971. Article I of the proposed legislation states that 'State Socialist undertakings are to be directed according to the collective leadership principle through direct participation of the workers in the discussion and resolution of socio-economic developments as well as in the planning and carrying out of measures necessary for fulfilling the obligations of the plan and for improving the working and living conditions of the entire work force'. The proposals also call for changing the name of the workers' plant assemblies to Workers' Councils, and that of the leading administrative economic organs to Workers' Economic Commissions. They further specify that the top state economic executive and administrative bodies should include not only technicians and high-level experts, but 'elected representatives of the workers, including representatives of minority groups as well'. This current evolution towards greater participation of workers and trade unions in the decision-making process of Rumanian enterprises and the economy certifies to the strengthening of the self-management philosophy in Eastern Europe. Though promulgation of the new law has been postponed for a year to allow more time to consider more detailed proposals on the functioning of the plant committees in production and economic matters, its eventual introduction will provide a major new impetus to the extension of self-management in the socialist camp. Without question it will help to strengthen a similar process taking place in Hungary, though the advance there is more prudent and gradual to avoid provoking Soviet inter-

C

vention. Though still halting and confused as to the means and extent of transferring responsibilities and power from the bureaucratic centralism of the past to decentralized workers' participation at the enterprise and plant levels, the Rumanian and Hungarian experiments represent a trend towards the Yugoslavian model of self-management and a divergence from the centralized power structures operating most of the other Socialist Republics.

For political bureaucrats in the Soviet Union and the other East European countries any expression of workers' self-management which progresses beyond the formal, ineffectual form of representational participation through the party, the trade unions or official mass organizations, has become an ideological and political danger. It promises to be the thorniest of their internal problems in this decade, however, for it will sharpen divisions between different countries upon this fundamental problem of the structure and control of the economy and the roles of the party and trade unions.

A REVERSION TO 'ONE-MAN LEADERSHIP'

Following the Polish workers' protest movements in Gydnia and Stettin and the deposition of Gomoulka, for example, much discussion took place around the question of basic economic reforms and the transformation of workers' councils into effective instruments of participation in plant and enterprise management. But contrary to tendencies towards stronger democratic, collective leadership in Rumania and Hungary, a regression to the 'one-man authority' of traditional management principles seems to be taking place in Poland. Before the 1971 Party Congress, Prime Minister Jaroszewicz declared: 'We shall strengthen the principle of the "one-man leadership" and individual responsibility. The director of a socialist undertaking or concern must carry the responsibility for the entire enterprise. He should be supported by the council of the collective, inform it on the situation and its responsibilities and consult with it on important decisions, but the duty to take final decisions is his alone.'

As in Czechoslovakia, East Germany and Bulgaria, Poland has reverted to slavish alignment on the Soviet system of one-man authority in industry and a transmission belt role for the trade unions in relation to the economic dictates of the party. The authoritarian exercise of power towards centrally planned objectives which give priority to investment and industrial expansion over social expectations and personal consumption has always been a key feature of industrial and later political policy. The industrial system paralleled its military system of command and execution, from the top planning authority down to the individual plant. In the more than 200,000 factories and 100,000 construction sites of the Soviet Union the principle of one-man responsibility for final decisions prevails. The keystone of the organization is the centralized, lone exercise of decision-making power.

This subjection of social needs to economic growth was facilitated, as the Yugoslavian experience was hampered, by the limited attention accorded to the problem of the human personality in the production system in Marxist theory. Both Marx and Engels did refer in several instances (notably in their discussion of the Paris Commune) to the importance for the working class to safeguard itself against its own representatives and officials by making certain that all officials had to be elected and removable at all times. Lenin, too, affirmed that official positions must be stripped of every semblance of privilege. But from the perspective of Marxist-Leninist theory as a whole the subject was given only passing and incidental attention. One explanation for this is the underlying assumption at the time that economic power and ownership of capital were decisive whilst political power and authority were derivative. Concentration on the problem of the power of the state and of capital-owning classes to exploit workers, led to a theoretical concern with ownership and the possession of capital. Once capital had been socialized and the ownership of the means of production transferred to the party of the workers (the theory ran) the exploitative nature of the economic system would be finally resolved. The elimination of the class distinctions of capitalism under socialist state management would automatically produce harmony between workers and economic administrators, because they both belonged to the same party and to the same trade union. According to this doctrine, class antagonisms are by definition impossible, when both parties to collective agreements are of the same class and involved in the common general pursuit of furthering socialist production.

Historically, of course, things have not followed this theoretical framework. The building up of a vast socialist economy has produced a new stratum of bureaucrats and elitists who concentrate through their positions and functions enormous and unrivalled power. In many respects their position resembles that of the capitalist class they replace in the privileges accorded them and in their power over workers. In this instance, however, they claim to be exercising their power *on behalf of* the workers. The Soviet experience shows that the basic problem of the exercise of economic power and the parallel political and legal authority over the lives of others resides not in *ownership* but in *control*. Previous theory took no account of such a distinction and obsolete apostles of the old school consequently have no perspective on the important ownerless class of bureaucrats and officials who, through their effective control of the means of production, now possess the same power as owners. Under state capitalism, or absentee ownership by the party, the state- or party-appointed administrators are in an identical position to the professional managers of a modern capitalist enterprise who possess the real power through control of the means of production of an enterprise. The absentee capitalist owners, who are largely banks, fiduciary institutions, etc., have been uncoupled from effective control of production, other than to insist on its over-all commitment to growth, whilst the hoary myth of 'people's capitalism' through share ownership, is a non-starter in the face of the facts. Similarly, the theoretical 'dictatorship of the proletariat' is without a voice in determining the basic economic and social goals affecting working men and women.

Thus, there arose in centralized socialist societies conflict and tension between the administrators (or employers) and the wage earners, between the order givers and the order takers, as occurs in all collective undertakings based upon a hierarchical system of power. The traditional concepts of the class struggle and the doctrine of state property as the 'highest form of property in the transition period' were coupled with the need for 'iron discipline' in the party and for a transmission belt function to be assigned to the power institutions such as the trade unions, youth and other 'mass' organizations which would ensure that directives of the top party echelons would be enforced. This philosophy has now been challenged by the new socialist doctrine of self-management. Prospects are good that the old Stalinist precepts will progressively lose their potency and be replaced gradually, even in the USSR, by more democratic procedures, but it is most unlikely that demands will be ceded without struggle by those who have most to lose.

If 'one-man rule' is swept away in the changing industrial patterns forced upon the administrators, it would represent an ironic return to the original principles of 'all power to the soviets' of the days of the revolution, when the workers' factory soviets and the trade unions were upheld as the basic units of the transformation to a socialist economy. It is interesting that in regard to agricultural development the soviet has paradoxically continued to be the accepted form of economic and socialist organization. In the Kalkhozes and Sovkhozes, economic democracy exists for the anti-collectivist peasants, despite its denial to the industrial workers or proletariat. Lenin claimed in his work *The State and Revolution* that no revolution and no collective planning is possible without the direct participation of the workers' councils and of their representatives. Similarly in his famous Party Programme of 1919 he called for the trade unions 'to concentrate in their hands all the administration of the entire national economy', and proclaimed that the 'participation of the trade unions in economic management . . . constitutes also the chief means of the struggle against the bureaucratization of the economic apparatus'. But by the 1922 Congress of the Party under the pressures of Stalin and Trotsky, Lenin changed the perspective of socialism and all reference to trade union participation in management of the economy and enterprises was completely expurgated. Already, a couple of years prior, the operational maxim of one-man management had been officially proclaimed and the authoritarian hierarchical power in the factories was made the official system of industrial management. In this way, it established a complete identity with capitalist enterprise in all but the power and ownership by the state of the means of production. The incentives and criteria of operations also became comparable except that in the capitalist enterprise the criterion of efficiency and success was measured in terms of profits or money values, whilst in the socialist, state-owned enterprise the efficiency and success of the director was measured essentially in economic terms or in output. Work organization was almost identical, which probably reflected the deep admiration of the politically minded leadership for the professional and technical skills of capitalist management, an admiration which is apparent more than ever today.

In effect, the priority given to production over human labour in the name of efficiency meant imposing a rigorous work discipline, cost discipline and psychological discipline upon workers. The need to build up heavy industry, develop technology and amass large-scale concentrations of labour and capital understandably pushed the political leadership to emulate their capitalist rivals in the things they did best: namely, in concentrating massive capital to alienate workers from their human needs and aspirations by making them subservient to the dynamics of capital acquisition. As a result the hierarchy of the factory came to bear a faithful resemblance to any large-scale capitalist counterpart: director, sub-directors, department heads, technicians and engineers, foremen as order givers and work-group leaders, skilled, semi-skilled and unskilled workers as order takers.

DOMINANCE OF THE PARTY

And so the structure of the soviet factory has developed. The director's power to manage his factory is virtually unlimited within the prescribed administrative and legal obligations to the state, party and trade union. An important feature of this relationship is the effective interpenetration, or better, the integration of all the functions of responsibility within the party, which is in effect state, director and trade union. Over 95 per cent of the directors and sub-directors of Soviet factories are members of the Communist Party. Almost the same percentage applies to trade union officials at all levels. Their common membership and supreme obligation to the party of which they are the designated agents in their respective domains forges a stronger bond than the intrinsic differences and antagonisms existing in their constituencies. This is even further accentuated by the fact that, among workers, membership in the party is down around 30 per cent and in some very large complexes is as low as 20 per cent. These stronger common party ties have largely determined the historical relations between trade unions and management at the workplace, the only level where non-party people are involved. At all higher levels of local, regional or national economic administration the decision-making bodies are almost completely composed of disciplined party members. This helps explain why, although the right to strike is not forbidden by the Soviet Constitution, it has been exorcized as a virtual counter-revolutionary act by the director–union axis, who judge it inadmissible and inconceivable in state-owned industry of which they are the fiduciaries. Joint management–union committees, comprising 50 per cent representatives of the director and 50 per cent representatives of the union, do function in all factories. They deal with conflicts arising out of the application of the collective agreement bearing on the execution of the production plan, work organization, wage payments, factory discipline, housing and other public services. However, they are not base-influenced organs and function as paternalistic problem-solvers in the interest of the plan production. They have no rights or authority in economic and industrial spheres including work-load problems. In the non-economic area, however, the unions have an impressive and vital role in administering social services, health programmes, rest homes, vacation centres, educational programmes, etc. This dichotomy hermetically seals off the factory into the non-participatory economic sphere of the party-controlled hierarchy and the participatory social sphere involving the workers as trade unionists.

The core of Yugoslavian self-management is, of course, the decentralization of the economic system and the elaboration of a system of workers' control. This creates for the workers and trade unions a direct and decisive economic authority in the enterprise. Supreme authority for economic and industrial decision-making therefore resides in the workers' collectives or councils at the base and makes the top echelons of elected or appointed executives subject to the will of the numerically greater majority. It is both the theoretical negation and the political challenge to the one-man management principle and to the separation of economic from social functions in the factory. It is also the anti-image of the centralized state apparatus. Already the Yugoslav unions report that over 70 per cent of national revenue is distributed through the self-management institutions and only 30 per cent through state institutions. Crucially, it is through the same process of decision-making power that the allocation between funds for investment, reserves, wages and social spending on education and housing is made.

Perhaps the most important aspect of the incipient conflict is that today pressure is increasing upon all industrial systems to decentralize and to substitute more flexible and more socially responsible objectives for the narrow economic production maximizing of the Soviet system and the profit maximizing of Western enterprises which are both based upon the authoritarian form of organization transmitting power-from-the-top. The surging technological revolution is antiquating both types of management and making new participatory systems essential. The debacle of traditional management is reflected in mounting social crises and rising protests from the workers, which will not be stilled or avoided with palliatives. The enterprise today is a profound structural and moral organism. Its economic-maximizing functions can no longer be imposed or presented as beneficial or socially desirable. The factory and, indeed, the enterprise itself, must be considered in terms of its contribution to the total social environment. Not only does it produce goods and services for the external collectivity, it is also subject to increasing demands that its internal functioning be structured according to democratic and human principles which guarantee to its workers an opportunity to enhance the higher faculties of man rather than diminish them.

This common demand ties the co-management or co-determination movement in the West to the self-management movement in the East. It is what makes them distinct but related forces of the widening revolution of self-determination. It will also, predictably, be the prospect drawing bureaucratic socialist managers and capitalist managers closer together to preserve the economic production-profit type enterprise from which their privileged-class interests derive. Rockefeller and Brezniev are historically condemned to be partners in each other's joint enterprises.

THE GATHERING MOMENTUM

The rate of build-up in the West, especially in Europe, around the demand for industrial democracy has been breathtakingly swift. Probably no other movement in industrial relations in modern times has acquired such momentum and made such progress so rapidly. Today, in one form or another virtually the entire trade union movement in Western Europe (excluding the dictatorships of Spain, Portugal and Greece) has adopted the aims of workers' participation in the decision-making power of industry. By the end of 1974 it is expected that the trade unions will have succeeded in introducing in ten countries either through legislation or collective agreements, or a combination of both, new systems which grant workers a substantial say in the decisions that control their working lives, and by 1976 or 1977 the thrust will most likely overtake those who remain. At that point the first important phase of the modern industrial revolution will have been reached and the process of restructuring industrial society into a social and democratic system based upon socialized enterprise and a more democratic work environment will have truly begun.

It is not being excessively optimistic to predict that within a decade the movement will expand with equal speed to certain countries in Latin America, Africa and Asia and will be seriously demanded by a number of the major unions in North America as well. As the articles by Leonard Woodcock and Henry Lorrain clearly indicate, though through seemingly conventional collective bargaining procedures, the widening content of American agreements will extend over many aspects of managerial prerogatives and decision-making power and confer much of the substance if not the forms developed elsewhere. Proposals have already been formulated by the Canadian Labour Congress and by the associated New Democratic Party to make it illegal for management to refuse to bargain collectively on any aspect of management authority and prerogatives. It is, nevertheless, certain that the effects of radical changes in the structure of the enterprise, and of its permanent transformation on a global scale will demand correspondingly radical changes in the philosophy and practice of North American unions. Less emphasis will be placed on purely negotiated terms at fixed periods within clearly marked areas of negotiable and non-negotiable items and there will be a greater insistence on participatory forms of joint labour–management decision making on a continuing basis, especially upon joint decision-making power at the board level in the area of national and international investment strategies. For ultimately it is upon the investment function that wages and job security depend. Collective bargaining or other forms of negotiations, whatever they are called, which fail to deal with the accumulation and dispersal of capital assets on a global scale will progressively become ineffectual and dysfunctional.

THE FIRST INTERNATIONAL INITIATIVE

How rapidly in fact has the claim for industrial democracy developed? In 1968 the ICF decided to convene the first world trade union conference on industrial democracy in Frankfurt, Germany. At the time there appeared to be very little support among most trade unions for the principle and even a great deal of open opposition. In part, this was due to reservations regarding the applicability of the German co-determination model to other countries. Opposition also came from the more politically conservative wings of the movement who, as in most other matters, do not favour serious changes in the status quo. Surprisingly, one of the loudest and most persistent arguments of the most conventional sections of the movement, which was also the most integrated, the most responsible and the most comprehensive of the problems of capital and capitalists, was that participation would mean integration and responsibility and surrender or restriction of the union's paramount right to defend the interests of its members.

Not surprisingly, an identical position was adopted by the self-styled 'left radicals' for diametrically opposed reasons. Doctrinally committed to the primacy of the party over the trade union and accepting the subservient role of trade union action to the electoral and policy strategies of the political wing of the movement, the switch in emphasis away from bureaucratic political action towards direct participation in economic decision-making by workers constitutes the replication of original sin and therefore integration and support for the capitalist system. It is axiomatic that this position is held by nearly all party-dominated organizations, such as the Communist Party-dominated unions in Italy and France, sympathizers with the Stalinist-socialist model, and others tied traditionally to parties of a pluralist and denominational character, such as the Christian Democratic parties in Italy and Belgium.

One of the principal aims of the 1968 ICF Conference was to overcome the semantic differences impeding the movement and to unify ICF affiliates around the generic concept of industrial democracy at all levels of industry, which could embrace the different specific national schemes from Yugoslavian self-management through co-management on supervisory and executive boards to advanced joint decision-making processes at the workshop level. Instead of an attitude of opposition, the conference adopted a resolution in favour of industrial democracy and for international co-operation by a unanimous vote – the North American delegations being among those in favour. This was a major breakthrough and maked the start of a profound change in the attitude of many national trade union organizations. For example, before this meeting the leaders of the American AFL–CIO, of the British TUC, of the Swiss Federation, of the Dutch, Belgian, Italian and French national centres, rejected the notion of participation out of hand as something in which the workers had no interest. Most of them have turned completely around since then and have come out in support of some form of industrial democracy.

The articles in this book illustrate the progress registered since 1968. In a number of countries ICF affiliates took the initiative in advancing demands for participation and co-determination both within their own industries and within their national centres. European affiliates in the Nordic countries, Ireland, the United Kingdom, Switzerland, Austria, Holland, Belgium and France in particular assigned a top priority rating to formulating and implementing action programmes. From this risorgimento in Europe, the elan carried over continental frontiers into the developing regions. On the African continent where interest in co-operative and workers' self-management had been introduced, but was limited to Algeria, Mali, Guinea and Egypt, it now includes Tanzania, Zambia, Libya, Kenya, Tunisia, and others. In Latin America, Bolivia, Peru and Chile moved forward towards workers' participation. And affiliates in Japan, India, Indonesia, as well as other parts of Asia, launched study and action programmes for achieving industrial democracy in their industries: chemicals, cement, rubber, etc.

Simultaneously, European unions in the public service sector, transportation industry, service and newspaper industries made dramatic gains towards co-determination in matters affecting the lives of employees and which were previously beyond the scope of their involvement and control, such as hiring and dismissals, work classifications, career and training opportunities, etc. The following random examples help to illustrate the range and diversity of the new forms of industrial democracy being introduced.

SOME RANDOM EXAMPLES

A major experiment in one form of industrial democracy at the plant level is being carried out in four plants of the Herya installations belonging to the giant Norwegian Norsk Hydro Company. The plants are involved in chemical production and employ 6,000 people. The experiment from its beginning was planned and implemented in full and equal co-operation between the local Herya union, the Chemical Workers' Federation and LO.

The aim of the experiment was to determine whether freer,

more democratic forms of work involvement and design would contribute to greater production and job satisfaction than the traditional line authority of industry.

The hypothesis motivating the research group states that a worker is capable of increased production and that his job satisfaction can be increased if he is allowed to participate in areas of responsibility larger than those he encounters in a narrowly prescribed job. The research group verified the beliefs that most workers find their jobs monotonous, and that they insist on not taking responsibility for anything that happens on either their own jobs or those of their fellow workers.

The hypothesis was that if rigidity of work and attitudes were changed, and if workers were allowed to participate in industry on a wider scale, then the work force would be happier and more productive. Subsequently the plan made a careful selection of groups of workers, trained each individual in all the jobs within the group, and conducted seminars to explain the meaning of the new approach. The technique was straightforward: instead of being held responsible for a prescribed job, each worker was invited to participate in and hold joint responsibility for the total operation, functioning at maximum output. This meant he he would ensure that the group as a whole would work more efficiently, not because each individual worked harder, but because he was able to exercise his abilities more widely. It was expected also that he would find his sharing of responsibility more challenging than work in isolation.

Many problems arose, not only with workers who were apprehensive about pay, but also with foremen who had to be retrained or re-educated. When the workers assumed responsibilities for a group of activities, the foremen had to co-ordinate the work of the groups. Top management, although willing to co-operate, had to change its attitudes towards workers' responsibility.

Because of the many unknowns in the experiment, the group made mistakes, but there was ample evidence to demonstrate the benefits of the new approach. The workers in the four firms selected for the experiment developed a new attitude towards their work; they were highly motivated, interested in what they were doing. The productivity of all four undertakings rose by from 5 to 20 per cent – a result attributed solely to the experiment.

The employees of Sweden's National Tobacco Company,

Svenska Tobaksbolaget, were given a voice in management in the course of a programme which began in 1970. The initiative for the experiment came from the national trade union federation's (LO) industrial democracy committee, with the purpose of demonstrating the feasibility of workers' participation at various levels of management.

The experiment was planned in two stages. The first consisted of a thorough evaluation of the firm's situation and was carried out with the assistance of various experts. Thus a number of areas for participation were determined. The second stage – the putting into effect and evaluation of participation – was subject to the decision of workers and management acting together. Initially, two Tobaksbolaget factories are taking part in the experiment with others expected to follow.

Municipal workers in gas and electricity plants of the city of Kiel in the Federal Republic of Germany in 1970 won the following rights: co-decision on all appointments, transfer and dismissal of staff; fixing overtime, vocational training and reclassifications; modifications in existing or introduction of new work systems; full information on investments, nationalization measures and financial situation of enterprises; also the right of each Enterprise Council to two full-time representatives with leave of absence from work at full compensation and to paid services of outside experts and specialists in agreement with the employer.

West Germany's PTT (Post, Telephone and Telegraph) administrative council of twenty-four members is composed of seven representatives of the workers, and seven representatives of management, with five representatives of the Bundestag (parliament) and two economists proposed by employers and named by the President of the Republic, one financial expert, one press attaché, and a chairman elected by the council. The workers' representatives (six of whom are members of the union) are elected by the workers. The council is the supreme policy-making body in all management, administration and personnel matters.

In a parallel case, the top administrative council of the Swiss PTT (Post, Telephone and Telegraph) under the terms of a new statute approved by Switzerland's National Council or Senate on 1 July 1970 includes four trade union representatives among its fifteen titular members.

An agreement was reached is mid-1972 on workers' participation between the Swiss employers' associations in the metal and

and machinery industries (ASM and VSAM), the foremen's association (SSC) and the commercial employees' union (SSEC). An expansion of employee rights to participation will be sought through the establishment of representative organs in larger enterprises, or wherever the employees wish it. A particular importance is accorded the availability of *information* on operations.

Areas of discussion for the new committees will be jointly decided. Thereafter, managerial decisions in these areas will be subject to questioning. On certain matters, to be decided, mutual agreement will be necessary for action to be taken. In certain areas, the employee bodies will have autonomy.

Germany's fourth largest bank, the union-owned Bank für Gemeinwirtschaft, early in 1971 altered its statutes to provide parity co-determination for its employees. In the modified statutes the 21-man member administration council consists of ten representatives of the owners (individual DGB trade union federations), ten representatives of the employees, of whom three are trade unionists from outside the bank, and a jointly elected independent chairman.

Private Swedish banks now have sixteen state-nominated members on their boards of directors, two in each of the major banks. For example, in the Stockholm Enskilda Bank, one of the country's largest, the two are Rudolf Meidner, a top economist of the Swedish LO Central Union body, and Mr Rune Johansson, President of the Social-Democratic parliamentary group.

Late in 1970 a scheme for appointing broad-based Management Boards for each of the fourteen nationalized banks of India was approved by the Indian parliament. Representation on the boards was given to bank employees (both blue and white collar staff) as well as to persons representing the interests of farmers, workers and artisans. Both workers and officers of the banks are entitled to have one representative on each board, which is required to meet at least six times a year. Selection of the worker-employee directors for each bank is made by central government from a parcel of three names furnished by the predominant union or predominant federation of unions in each bank.

Sweden's major automobile firm, Volvo, doubtless in anticipation of legislative enactment, in 1971 decided to co-opt two representatives of its personnel, one operative and one employee, for its administrative council. To start with they were accorded the status of substitute members without voting rights, but the aim is to have them accede to full titular membership and voting rights following their election at the first general stockholders' meeting. An identical formula has been adopted by several other Swedish enterprises.

Early in 1972 British unions negotiated an important incursion on the established British industrial tradition of 'managerial prerogatives'. After three years of unsuccessful discussions for a national agreement with the Engineering Employers' Federation, the unions succeeded in negotiating an agreement with British Leyland Motors giving the unions the right to reject any operational change put forward until agreement is reached through the negotiating machinery. A similar accord was negotiated in the Pilkington Glass Company. Under these schemes prior consulation is to take place before any change goes through in working practices, production processes, transferring workers, etc. In the event of a dispute over such changes, the practice will revert to the status quo and only be made applicable after satisfactory agreement has been reached.

In January 1971 General Motors, responding to attacks by activists and charges of social irresponsibility and civic neglect by the union, appointed Dr Leon Howard Sullivan to its 'blue chip' board of directors. Dr Howard, a Negro, is considered a 'public board member', representing the general interests of non-management segments of the community.

Important changes were made in the system of worker directors in the nationalized British Steel Corporation early in 1972, to help infuse new vitality into the scheme which had begun to lose interest for the unions. The experiment, initiated with the nationalization of the industry in the 60s, provided for sixteen employee directors on the advisory committees of divisional boards of BSC. They are appointed by the General Director after consultation with the Trades Union Congress (TUC). The new changes are designed to bridge the gap which had grown up between the worker directors and the unions by permitting them to hold union office while serving on local boards – a function specifically excluded previously – and providing greater consultation between the BSC executive and the unions in the industry.

Following a walkout of its 104 musicians in support of demands not only for higher pay, but for a voice in picking a new maestro and more participation in the administration of their orchestra, the management of the Cleveland Symphony Orchestra agreed that players' representatives would sit on the committee to choose a conductor. In addition, principal players would sit in on auditions for potential new members and in the planning of the concert season, programmes, etc.

More and more newspapers and magazines across Europe are becoming co-managed as staff participation in editorial policy and management expands: *Le Figaro*, *Le Monde*, *L'Express*, *L'Observateur* in France; *Der Spiegel* and *Der Stern* in Germany; the *New Statesman* and *Spectator* in the UK; *Europeo* in Italy, and numerous other important commercial publications in Sweden, Denmark and Austria. At a protest convention of American journalists held in New York in April 1972, one of the few things that the mostly radical but eminent journalists could agree upon was that participation by working journalists in the management of newspapers and other publishing undertakings was fundamental to reorganizing the ailing industry and to improving the inadequate printed information services provided for the community at the present time. Though it has run into strong opposition from management, the American Newspaper Guild Union in its 1972 negotiations with leading Chicago dailies, the *Chicago Daily News* and the *Chicago Sun-Times*, demanded a voice in the news and editorial policies of the papers. Its demands were for one-third of the votes on the board which sets editorial page policy, and the right to claim space to rebutt the management viewpoint if the employees' viewpoint is unanimous in opposition, plus power to veto the selection of department heads and one-third representation on a labour–management committee which would set policies on news coverage.

These limited examples of advancing rights of joint decision making and co-determination in the vital process of industry life could be extended almost endlessly. The process of contesting absolutism and bureaucracy is penetrating most of society's institutions: religion, education, welfare, politics. All are under critical pressure. At the end of this process of increasing co-management and joint participation between working people and centralized power is of course the ideal of self-management and ego-involvement. But there is no absolutely final stage of perfection for a dynamic process has begun which will trigger continuing change. The important thing is that the process has begun and has already acquired sufficient strength and momentum to beat off attempts to arrest and suppress it. It is equally important that the goal of individual participation or self-managing systems should not be lost sight of or replaced by an alternative form of institutional or representational participation which merely returns to the point of departure under a new terminology and ideology.

The other articles of this volume, both by their detail and through the authority of their authors, clearly and dramatically help point up the very substantial progress which is being made in different countries. They also make plain that in the West the campaign is advancing on both levels of industry: at the workplace and in the boardrooms. This extension through the entire line function of management is perhaps the most important feature of the current thrust and the key to its revolutionary nature. This does not represent a series of fragmented and isolated incursions into management prerogatives which are easily assimilated and neutralized. The industrial democracy of the 70s has evolved rather into a total system, gradually extending its influence to all decision-making power in industry. As such, it is not as readily open to attack by the anti-bodies of the corporate self-immunizing defence system.

FROM WORKPLACE TO BOARDROOM AND BACK

By and large, the postwar works' councils, enterprise committees, etc., have been a failure. This is as true for Latin America and the other regions in which they were created as it is for Western Europe. The aim to make these councils organs for controlling the management of the enterprise did not succeed. In most countries, the attitudes of the workers and unions towards them grew from sceptical to hostile, even where participation in them continued: as in France, Italy, Belgium, Holland, Germany, Switzerland, and elsewhere. Reasons for the failure are multiple, but the most important cause was that most works' councils were created by legislation and remained formally independent of the union. This arrangement provided for systems of consultation but gave almost no rights of participation in the taking of decisions. This facilitated management's strategy of turning the councils into simple instruments of social relations, dealing with canteens, vacation camps and the like, with no real voice in economic and production matters. Obligations to submit bona fide financial data and other important information to the councils were universally circumvented. In nearly every case the enabling legislation limited the scope and authority of the councils by failing to specify the concomitant responsibilities of the enterprise or holding company boards of directors to supply information and consult with the councils.

The new drive, as expressed formally in the great majority of the national demands of unions for democratizing industry, is for the right of workers' representatives to participate directly, usually on a basis of parity, in the decision-making process at plant level on questions of economic production as well as personnel problems, whilst mere rights of consultation are recognized as insubstantive. At the same time, there is an effort to establish the right of representative participation by the workers at the board or top management levels, whether on a minority basis or parity basis. This symbiotic extension of participation at the centre and at the local level creates the link-up between, for example, promoting the workers' voice in the elaboration of investment and production plans and maintaining direct involvement in their effective application at the workplace. This critical innovation stands out cogently in most of the following articles, which deal with systems currently in force or shortly to be introduced. Like the double helix of life's basic molecule, DNA, this is a double-stranded, integrated form of participation which has become the fundamental molecule of the new form of participation, unlike anything previously known.

This two-level participation also gives a new reinforcement to worker representation on the different boards, executive or supervisory. Even where such representation is minority or less than parity, the fact that it is invariably linked to greater rights of co-determination at the factory level contributes to reciprocally strengthening the real power of both. Formulation and implementation of policies likely to affect the workers on the shop floor cannot be withheld from them. Nor, inversely, can the dissatisfaction which may arise from their application fail to be faithfully transmitted to the central boards and dealt with by joint management. Consequently, one of the most glaring shortcomings of the conventional system of communication in the enterprise, the unidirectional flow of information through a hierarchical command chain, is significantly reduced. For, even if the minority position does not permit an equal balance of power when it comes to the decision taking, the managing majority does not have the additional advantage of a monopoly on the true facts and relevant data at either level. Another gain for workers in the enterprise is that, even with a minority participation, their presence on the board enables them to take part in future planning and to be fully informed of long-term investment programmes and projected changes in the overall operations. Under the traditional systems of authority, workers were seldom aware of the long-term plans of the company and usually learned of their effects only when it was too late to do anything about them except to argue for slightly improved monetary compensation for a totally disrupted life. Naturally, the propensity of top managers will be to limit the practical expression of such new rights to a minimum. This is an instinct common to all politically oriented authority. However, the formal framework for getting at the facts and exercising control over policy making and over executive management, even in a minority situation, is a crucial first step towards parity and eventually to self-management forms of participation. Coupled with parity rights of decision making over the broad range of direct and indirect consequences on the shop floor, this move represents an important advance along the new super-route to industrial democracy.

MANAGEMENT AND ABILITY

As formal systems of industrial democracy begin to emerge, the centre of gravity of the opposition is shifting. A growing intellectual scepticism questions workers' capacities to run industrial enterprises at all. Much of this obstructive theorizing is, of course, merely a second line of defence following the global breaching of management's primary defences. Its scope, however, is broadened by the criticism of groups and interests normally favourable to the cause of labour but now concerned with apparent and real threats to their existing interests, roles and functions within the overlay of professional intermediaries, consultants, researchers, legalists, conciliators, experts, etc., which has encrusted around the labour–management interface. There is growing unease among such people that these roles and functions will be significantly curtailed.

The question of the ability of workers' capacity to manage industrial enterprise predictively will become the focus of much of this new opposition. Less emphasis will be put on the displacement or corrosion of the traditional role of trade unions, and more placed on the assertion that workers are not in any case qualified by training, capabilities or, implicitly, by intelligence to participate effectively in management. The inclusion of workers' representatives on the boards, for example, will be held divisive, controversial and unviable. It will be claimed that such representation will make management inefficient and disturb balanced decision making within the enterprise.

Although the capacity of workers to participate effectively in decision making is a vast and complex subject, it is not a fundamental or critical one. Any general questioning of this capacity is not only tendentious but also abstract and irrelevant. It would be a little more pertinent to ask how equipped workers are at present for different levels and functions of management, each of which admittedly requires a different mix of knowledge, aptitudes, skills and experience; or to question perhaps whether workers have the education and training to perform efficiently through the different line and staff operations. Even more practical, however, is the question of what systems are available to permit workers to acquire the necessary theoretical and operational skills in a continuing and permanent way. These problems, of course, have little to do with workers' intelligence or IQs as a general proposition. The basic conceptual and political capacities are demonstrably as abundant within the working class as within other groups, and the range between high and low degrees of intelligence is probably just as wide as for other groups. In terms of numbers alone the store of intellect is of course infinitely more abundant. In fact, the entire industrial system, from operating the drills and equipment for extracting basic raw materials from under the earth's crust, through building machines and instruments in the transformation industries, to assembling typewriters, calculating machines and sophisticated computers in the service sectors, is manned and operated by the cerebral and muscle capacities of workers.

As we have already discussed, the system is largely run by the order *takers*, implementing the directives of a small minority of order *givers*. Although the position of the order givers in the pyramids of power is situated high above that of the order takers, this does not indicate a superior level of intelligence or possession of a more vital social skill. *Different* intelligence and skills certainly, but not superior.

The management function is increasingly concerned with policy setting the nearer one approaches the boardroom. In practical terms this implies the formulation of overall objectives, principles and procedures into a system which regulates the interactions and relationships of the working parts of the group or enterprise. Integrating the various partial sectors of the policy structure (sales, production, finance, shop floor operations, administration, etc.) into an overall coherent organization therefore requires a certain type of perceptual, judgemental and manipulative ability. As policy is established at organizational points near to the boardroom it is at these points that policy-related ability is found. As policy is imposed upon a larger working force such ability is automatically associated with skills in wielding power and authority. The skill is acquired from the function or role of the policy position, regardless of the innate or personal intelligence of the person occupying the position. Even a modest or diffident personality possesses and exercises strong and important policy-power by virtue of his role as manager. The purpose of strategic policy is to secure the transfer of ideas into action. The process of policy making is through analysis and research, defining procedures and techniques and checking and adjusting results. It is a pre-action phase of operations. The predominant skills are those of perception, assessing the impact of managerial information input and judgement; these are exercised in projecting a set of co-ordinated responses appropriate to the task. To a very considerable degree these skills or faculties are based upon experience and practice.

Most of the data manipulated is in the form of symbolic logic or transmitted knowledge. It is not direct knowledge or experience. All policy-setting functions are supplied with symbolic information through verbal and written reports, statistics, charts, accounts, computer print-outs, or other abstract conceptualized information, relating to the organization. All managerial positions have this type of information fed into their policy slots. Such data collection has little to do with the intelligence or skill of the occupant of the position or his direct skills in carrying out his role. But possessing this symbolic information, over the entire range of the policy sector he manages, is a fundamental prerequisite of any action he may take as a manager. It is analogous to the relationship of a car driver, pilot or musician, to his car, aeroplane or instrument for example. The act of driving, piloting or playing requires at least the presence of the vehicle or instrument. Stated otherwise the transfer of knowledge *of* or *about* a particular activity into an action or performance requires hardware and software support and the development of operational skills. Equally with policy management, only in the presence of the necessary symbolic knowledge and through its utilization and manipulation can managerial action be carried out.

Any question as to whether workers can participate effectively and efficiently in management is therefore meaningless in a situation where the symbolic knowledge and data, which is prerequisite to management decision making or action, is denied them. Once this information is available the major impediment to efficient worker participation will have been removed. It follows that any personal efficiency derives from and is a function of carrying out the role of management, for only then will information and data be provided. Workers must first be involved with and assigned the role of policy management before they can begin to perform, either excellently or poorly. To argue workers' alleged incapacities as an excuse to keep them out of the role before they have exercised the role is therefore a non-sequitur of most blatant proportions.

Disparagment of workers' acquired skills is symmetrical to discounting their innate intelligence for the order-giver role. Skill is essentially the ability to change, modify, adjust, transform and replace malfunctions or disturbances of a system through appropriate and continuous responses. Workers universally apply such disturbance-correction response patterns in all the countless vocational and administrative tasks they already perform in keeping the economy running. Transferring such patterns of skill from one segment of activity to another is not as complex, nor as difficult as some assume; especially when the switch is from the action-based skills to the perceptive or conceptual ones. The manual skills, visual skills and oral skills of a mechanic or electrician, for example, are more readily adapted to the response patterns of management skills than vice versa.

What is essential to such a transfer, however, is that direct experience or knowledge is acquired in the learning process. Without this direct knowledge there can be no effective transfer of skills and responses. It is the reason why one cannot learn to drive a car, pilot a plane or play the piano by reading or hearing about them in books, pamphlets and conferences. Although symbolic information may facilitate perception and comprehension, skill in performance cannot be acquired without the direct experience of driving, piloting or playing. While practice does not necessarily lead to skill or proficiency, skills cannot be acquired without it. Therefore, it is fatuous to argue that workers do not possess management skills before they are given the opportunity of learning such skills through direct experience. Skilled responses are a result of active participation, and they cannot be developed without it. Prior lack of direct skills is a totally invalid argument for opposing worker participation in management.

Beyond the central question of workers' capacities and skills for performing managerial roles, which cannot be seriously disputed at this stage, remains the secondary but nevertheless significant question of their capacities for undertaking specific managerial functions in the different sectors. Here too theoretical arguments and empirical data confirm the fact that there is no fundamental reason why workers should not make efficient managers. Historical evidence conclusively proves that it is the distribution of economic power which regulates and maintains the relationship between order takers and order givers. In virtually all phases of management there are sufficient specific examples of effective worker participation to prove the overall ability of workers to participate throughout the entire range of functions.

Plant-level management roles from the foreman up through the supervisory hierarchy are generally staffed through promotion of workers, some of whom end up as works managers. At this level practical direct knowledge of the work processes coupled with vocational and technical education and on-the-job training uniquely qualifies workers for plant-level management functions. The great majority of shop floor management are 'up from the ranks'. In situations calling for collective participation through elected representatives, as for plant committees, workers' councils or other forms of joint decision-making bodies at the level of the plant or place of work, active workers fill the local trade union positions in numerous countries: the Nordic countries, West Germany, Austria, Holland, Switzerland, Peru, Chile, Yugoslavia, and elsewhere.

Worker participation, through trade union channels, in national economic planning and programming, surely an exalted form of the top-level management function, is already very extensive. This is true both in respect of participation in central planning agencies operating at the political and/or technical level and for sectoral planning bodies, specializing in planning for sectors of industry or for particular spheres of the national economy. Though such bodies usually have only advisory roles to government and rarely have executive power, they are usually involved in the elaboration of fundamental economic plans throughout the entire planning process. Thus they not only contribute to the elaboration of plans, but are actively engaged in the process of implementation, control and evaluation. One form of this economic management is the consultative economic and social councils existing in various countries such as France, United Kingdom, Belgium and Italy and a number of African countries (Algeria, Tunisia, Senegal, Ivory Coast, etc.). Examples of predominantly technical planning bodies consisting of trade unionists as well as employers and government officials exist in Holland, Belgium, Ireland, Sweden, Chile and Columbia.

Public bodies and agencies created for the purpose involving occupational organizations, notably trade unions and employers, in vertical or sectoral planning and policy are even more extensive than central planning agencies. Such bodies exist for dealing with employment problems (Sweden, Holland, FR of Germany, United Kingdom, Austria, Israel) incomes problems (Yugoslavia, FR of Germany, Israel, United States, United Kingdom, France, Italy) and industry problems (France, United Kingdom, Belgium, Italy, Israel, India, Japan).

Vocational and continuing training is another area where trade union participation in management functions is being exercised widely. Joint participation by workers and employers in vocational training programmes extends from national, regional and industry-wide schemes to programmes to meet training needs arising in specific branches and local situations. In over a dozen Western countries trade union representatives participate in boards responsible for apprenticeship, craftsman and journeyman training, as well as planning and implementing vocational training programmes as part of employment policies and active manpower programmes. In addition trade unions in a number of countries operate their own independent vocational training schools for their members. In Israel, for example, the Histadrut carries out a large part of the total vocational training activity of the country in its own schools. The West German DGB also operates over a hundred vocational training schools. The trade union centres of Sweden, Norway and Denmark maintain numerous vocational and technical schools. The Austrian Chamber of Labour, which is entirely staffed and administered by the trade unions, plans and carries out most of the vocational training programmes in the country.

But perhaps the most conclusive demonstration that workers can provide the necessary managerial know-how and skills when required is the success of most union-owned industrial enterprises which are independent of state, private or other outside bodies. As Itzhak Ben Aaron's article points out, the Histadrut controls 25 per cent of Israel's total GNP. Some of the branches, like the Solel Banel Construction Company, have important ramifications overseas. Solel Banel contractors, engineers, architects and construction teams are building everything from housing projects to government buildings and communications systems around the world under technical assistance agreements. Most of the country's social security system, health insurance, pensions, retirement homes, medical services, clinics and so on are managed directly through Histadrut agencies and divisions.

In the Nordic countries, worker control and participation has had a long tradition. There is virtually no state planning or policy board, no agency in the manpower and social areas which does not have trade union representation. Social insurance and unemployment insurance is administered directly through the unions, and some of the largest life insurance companies are union-owned. Co-operatives in wholesaling, retailing and even production which are organically integrated with the trade unions have long been a distinctive feature of the Nordic economy and constitute an important segment of the distribution system.

Successful directly owned and operated trade union enterprises are numerous. Union-owned travel companies (union-owned Reso is the largest travel company in Sweden), hotels, construction companies, publishing houses and co-operative banks are to be found in most of the four Nordic countries.

In Holland and Belgium union-owned or union-associated enterprises, either in conjunction with co-operative movements or in Socialist Party institutions, have been built up over the years. Holland's social insurance system and communications networks provide for tripartite participation between union, management and the administration. In Belgium, mutual clinics, retail co-operatives and travel agencies have been built up over the years by the unions. Britain's co-operatives have annual turnover surpassing £1,000 million and employ some 280,000 people. The 500 retail co-operative societies represent nearly 10 per cent of all retail trade in Britain.

The amount of union-owned industrial enterprise in Austria has grown steadily over the last decade. Beyond the comparatively widespread representation enjoyed by workers in all state boards and agencies dealing with planning and social problems, the Austrian Trade Union Congress – öGB – has full control over major life insurance, travel, credit, publishing and recording, construction, pharmaceutical, paper, retailing and other undertakings. The success of most of these ventures is a clear answer to charges that, in Austria at least, the workers are not capable of managing industrial enterprises.

The German trade union Bank für Gemeinwirtschaft was created for the purpose of serving workers and the social economy. Its capital, like its board of directors, is provided by the affiliated industrial unions of the DGB (German Trade Union Congress). It makes a profit, but intentionally keeps this small. It deals in all areas of banking in close co-operation with the unions. The B f G has grown into the fourth largest commercial bank in Germany and about the fortieth largest in the world outside the United States. Its assets have grown to nearly $5,000 million and it is clearly outstripping the big three private West German banks in its rate of growth, with the increasing probability that it will soon become as important, if not as large. It has foreign branches in London, Israel and Vienna, and does extensive business with the East European countries, notably the Soviet Union. In other countries it has joint ventures with national union-owned or co-operative banks, as in Switzerland, Holland and Luxembourg. The Bank für Gemeinwirtschaft is an important partner in the operations of Volksfürsorge, a leading union-owned insurance group which controls the largest number of insurance companies in Germany. It is similarly participating in a recently created travel agency which will combine the activities of smaller agencies which until recently have been operated by the individual affiliated unions.

But by far the most rapidly expanding branch of the German union-owned industries is Neue Heimat, the nation's largest residential construction company. The aim of this enterprise is to favour the construction of low-cost housing for German workers and over the years Neue Heimat has built more than 400,000 houses or apartments inhabited by more than one million people. Currently it spends almost $500 million a year in all forms of building, including an entire university, supermarkets, department stores, schools and modern hotels. On the planning boards are new hotels in Monte Carlo, Paris, Hamburg, Frankfurt and Amsterdam. In partnership with an American group, Neue Heimat will shortly move into the US, to build co-operatives, housing developments and apartments in at least three different cities. The combined management and technical resources of such a company are enormous, making it the biggest of its kind in the world. Such management efficiency enables it to carry projects which would cripple most private construction firms. Near Munich, Neue Heimat is building a new town known as München-Perlach, which will provide housing, mostly in modern, high-use apartments of revolutionary design, for 80,000 people. Its foreign activities, carried out by its subsidiary 'Neue Heimat International', have built 10,000 dwellings in France and Italy, 2,200 homes in Israel, residential centres in Kenya, Ceylon and Ghana, as well as over 3,000 housing units in Canada and Venezuela.

The above are only selected examples of worker-owned and managed industrial enterprises. They are far from exhaustive. To the list could be added the second-largest supermarket chain and leading life insurance and banking companies in Switzerland, the Amalgamated Garment Workers' Union Bank in New York with the largest number of individual deposit accounts of any bank in the United States, and increasing numbers of workers' banks, construction companies and numerous other enterprises in different countries of Latin America. Further demonstrations of workers' capabilities to manage successful companies are provided by the numerous companies both owned and run by the employees working in the plants. The Scott-Bader Commonwealth, an expanding chemical and pharmaceutical firm in the UK, is one example. It has acquired nine subsidiaries, all managed directly by the workers, and is now involved in a foreign joint venture in Sweden. The leading Danish Ceramic Company is similarly a directly worker-owned and run enterprise. Other examples exist in Germany, Austria and North America. Although they may not all be as important in their respective national industries, nevertheless as pilot projects or test cases they are worthy contributors to the overall picture of existing workers' control and ability in managing successful companies within the private market economy. In view of this record, charges that industrial democracy will not work successfully because of the incapacity of workers and trade unions to manage efficiently fall completely flat.

Unquestionably, the swift extension of different schemes of participation places a heavy obligation upon the unions and upon governments in respect of education and training. The principal and irreplaceable method of training in workers' management is, of course, active participation in the process itself. This has been the experience in Yugoslavia over the years. But such practical, direct learning requires support by complementary continuous training courses, seminars and the like. In Yugoslavia, where nearly 300,000 persons are active members of workers' councils, practically all important industrial undertakings organize courses and seminars for members of workers' management bodies. Such training is assisted by union-organized and worker-university training programmes. Over two million persons attend special courses for adult workers in the space of a year.

In the West the trade unions conduct extensive training programmes, mainly for training militants and leadership in collective bargaining, political action and union administration. Most of the largest national centres and industrial unions carry out permanent training programmes and devote a considerable part of their resources to them. Central residential colleges are maintained by most major confederations: United States, Canada, France, Italy, Germany, Sweden, Denmark, Norway, Austria, etc. Over 1,000 attend the central courses of the DGB in Germany every year, whilst Sweden's LO has two resident colleges with a capacity of 360. International trade union organizations have set up general resident colleges in Africa, Asia and Latin America. But by far the major share of training is carried out by the individual national federations. Many have constructed spacious and modern residential training centres for membership training. Large American unions like the Automobile Workers', Machinists, Ladies' Garment Workers, Steel Workers, Teamsters and many others have similarly built or established important resident colleges. The major industrial Swedish, German, Austrian, Swiss and Belgian unions in metal, chemicals and public services, to cite only a few, all maintain their own resident colleges at the core of important training programmes. The Swedish Chemical Workers' Federation reported that nearly a third of its budget was allotted for membership training.

Thus the task of providing for training in management participation will not mean starting from nothing for many unions. It will be rather a question of adding the necessary courses and instruction to existing programmes. Increasingly, unions are winning provisions in collective agreements for the release on full pay of workers elected to co-management committees to attend special training courses. In Austria, Germany, Holland, Sweden, Norway and Switzerland, for example, agreements provide for such release from work for a certain number of hours each year to attend courses which will equip them better to carry out their responsibilities under the new co-management systems recently introduced in those countries. Much of this instruction is devoted to management training as well as to economic and industrial subjects.

An interesting initiative has been the establishment by the German DGB in Bad Zwischenahn of a management academy. Inaugurated in September 1972, the academy provides three-month courses in middle- and lower-level management for workers participating in co-determination bodies at either board or shop floor levels. It will be extended eventually to include top-level management training as well. The Swedish LO has prepared a crash programme for training around 2,000 workers in relation to the new responsibilities which they will accede to under recent legislation effective from 1 January 1973. Similar efforts have been organized in Norway, Austria, Peru and Switzerland. These activities corroborate the thesis that when workers' control or participation in management decision-making becomes a reality, parallel training and education efforts in the sphere of management will be automatically undertaken by the unions. As long as effective participation is not a practical proposition, the trade unions will not devote any worthwhile effort to what would be largely a theoretical and wasteful exercise. Along with this heightened training effort by the unions themselves, at all levels of organization, will come a greater demand on the firms and the state to help provide the necessary training and instruction. The Swedish LO has declared, 'it is disappointing . . . that only a small proportion of the State's total educational resources is being used to rectify the educational disadvantage of workers' representatives in dealing with these highly trained specialists. In this way the state, albeit unintentionally, is helping to widen the gulf between management and workers as far as their scope for looking after their respective interests is concerned. This [industrial democracy] then should be taken as a challenge to the state to examine how the educational system might be reformed so as to assist in bringing about greater industrial democracy and a more equal division of power between the sides of industry.' The growth of industrial democracy as a practical and practised feature of industry will not remain a limited and isolated process. The statement of LO is typical of the overall demands which unions will make upon all institutions, private and public, to transform education systems and philosophies. The education process must be made compatible with the need to redistribute power between private management and workers in order to achieve the balance and equality which industrial democracy needs in order to work.

Industrial democracy is no longer a theoretical or conceptual issue, nor yet a system which operates in one or two isolated instances. It has become a practical and power-motivated reality in a number of countries, and its rate of expansion is accelerating. As workers require first and foremost to learn managerial knowledge and develop skills through actual participation, this practical advance is altering all the parameters. New efforts to provide training and support for workers in the performance of their tasks will be forthcoming and training and education will be transformed into a permanent and evolving support system for primary learning by actual participation in management decision-making problems.

The articles which comprise this book, both by their substance and by the authority of their authors, constitute an impressive criterion of the progress which industrial democracy is making and will continue to make. All of the contributors are activists and practitioners of power. Among them are leaders of some of the most powerful and influential trade union organizations in the world. All of them are progressive leaders, with impressive credentials of achievement. They would all identify themselves as socialists of one brand or another. Several lead national centres in countries where national centres possess real effective power in dealing directly with employers and industry such as in the case of Israel, Sweden, Norway and France. Others lead the largest industrial unions in countries where such real power is vested in the unions and not in the national centres, such as applies in the case of the United States, Canada, United Kingdom, Germany and Switzerland. Together the organizations they lead constitute an impressive and influential cross-section of the power of organized labour in industry to effect change and to transform a delinquent and obsolete industrial and social order. That they all have committed themselves to the achievement of industrial democracy is the greatest guarantee that it will continue its present momentum. The following is a short list of some of the specific advances made since 1970 up to the summer of 1973 provided as evidence of this momentum.

Date	Country	Form	Features
1970	Peru	Law on Workers' Estates, workers' assets and participation at Board level	Workers to gradually acquire shares up to 50 per cent in all enterprises. Two workers on Board in public enterprises; one in private firms.
1971	Chile	Law on workers' participation in nationalized sector	Workers' representatives appointed to nationalized sector's boards of directors, steel, copper, etc.
1971	Yugoslavia	Constitutional amendments on Workers' Self-management	Direct ratification of decisions on shop floor rather than through elected Workers' Councils.
1973	Austria	Legislation on Plant Committees applicable to all of industry	Plant Committees' representatives given right to information and discussion of economic situation, investments, etc., disputes subject to arbitration. One-third workers' representatives on Supervisory Boards.
1971	West Germany	Law on extended co-determination rights for Works' Councils	Increased trade union rights and influence in plants. Law extending supervisory board representation to 50 per cent for all industry projected for 1975.
1971	Holland	Law on Works' Councils	Works' Councils elected by workers except for President. Prior council approval of all changes in working conditions, consultation on all major decisions, right to outside consultants and financial data. Directors' appointment must be approved by Works' Council.
1972	India	Policy position adopted by Indian Cement Workers	Call for co-determination rights to be extended throughout all levels of the Cement industry.
1972	Belgium	Law on Works' Council information	Management to inform Works' Council on receipt, use and benefits of all state aid. FGTB seek Workers' Control at all level of industries.
1973	Norway	Legislation on company assemblies and management boards applicable all large firms	Enterprise Assembly of minimum 12 members with one-third workers' representatives – elects 5-person Management Committee with two workers' representatives.
1973	Sweden	Legislation all industry	Two workers on single Board of Directors – Extensive advances shop-floor decision making through joint Union-Management Committees.
1973	Ireland	Irish TGWU resolution to TUC Congress	Demands 'democratic' control by workers over the utilization and allocation of investment funds.
1973	United Kingdom	Policy Report adopted at TUC Congress	Advocates 50 per cent workers' representatives on Supervisory Board of two-tier system – rights of control and information on investments, production, etc.
1974	Denmark	Legislation industry wide	Two workers on Board of Directors, one operative, other salaried employee – vast extension of co-decision on work place conditions.
1974 (estimated)	Luxemburg	Legislation applicable all large firms opposed by unions	Creates two organs mixed enterprise councils with 50/50 parity and administrative Councils with one-third seats for workers. Unions demanding 50 per cent.

Chapter 2

Federal Republic of Germany

OTTO BRENNER

Late President, Industriegewerkschaft Metall
Late President, International Metal Workers' Federation

BASIS OF CO-DETERMINATION

The subject of this book is a world-wide phenomenon. Everywhere in the world – both in the East and in the West – working people are fighting for greater influence over all aspects of their work and over the economy itself. The definitions used or the methods adopted may not always be the same, but there is probaby agreement about one thing: we all want to get away from a situation in which every job belongs to some private or public owner and every worker is regarded by this owner as a saleable instrument of production.

The ways by which this general objective is to be achieved may differ from one country to another. Different stages of development may also give rise to different priorities. The degree of maturity of the workers likewise plays a not unimportant role.

We have learned from long experience that the question of giving workers and employees a decisive influence over economic decisions – and that implies influence for their organizations – arises everywhere sooner or later and must find a response. Once again this response should be made in the clearest possible terms, with arguments that the majority of the population can understand.

It is not always easy to make oneself understand and to understand what is said beyond one's own frontiers. There are not just language difficulties to be overcome. Quite a number of concepts have to be explained: some talk of 'joint consultation', others of 'economic democracy', 'workers' control' and 'self-government' have also found general acceptance. In some cases these describe stages along the road towards the general objective, in others they describe the objective itself. For this reason we should not be hasty or superficial in our judgements, but in each case ascertain what the term really means. In other words, we must ask ourselves whether apparently different concepts in fact have the same or a similar meaning.

In our country, the Federal Republic of Germany, the term *co-determination* has been generally used for a long time. It is more than half a century old and refers to the participation by workers on an equal footing in decisions at all levels of the undertaking and the economy as a whole.

The German trade unions call for co-determination because they take the view that political democracy by itself is not enough to overcome the absence of freedom and the relationship of dependence that exist at the workplace. Moreover, absence of freedom in economic life – as we in Germany have repeatedly had occasion to learn – represents a constant threat to political democracy. It is all the more dangerous because the pressure that it continually exerts is usually not recognized in time.

In other words, the German trade unions' demand for thorough-going democratization at the workplace and in economic life, with equal participation of the workers in decisions at all levels of society, is based on the conviction that a truly democratic system can only be brought into existence when working people settle their own affairs not merely as citizens through parliament, government and administration but also by having the right to influence the economy directly through the trade unions that represent them: in the plant, in the management of undertakings, in sectors of industry and the economy as a whole.

Democratization of economic life would also make a decisive contribution to transforming the economic 'subject' of today into a free economic citizen. This alone is enough to make it important to concentrate all our efforts on creating the conditions in which this aim can be realized, since there is no other way to move forward into the future and since accommodation to existing, out-dated social structures is an obstacle to progress.

D

HISTORICAL DEVELOPMENT IN GERMANY

To be sure, opposition to a state of dependence which was felt to be contrary to dignity existed before modern industrial society came into being but such resentment has, undoubtedly, become stronger since then. The struggle for democracy in the economy and at work has developed an explosive force such as was experienced previously only in connection with the fight for political freedom. The situation that has evolved in Germany can, however, only be understood against the background of specific experiences which I can only sketch here in general terms.

The first German parliament which met in 1848–9 in Frankfurt-on-Main even at that time discussed regulation of industry in the German Empire. Factory committees and factory councils were proposed. The first general German workers' organization, the General German Workers' Brotherhood, which came into being during that period, even went so far as to call for the free election of foremen and supervisors by those employed in the factories. The failure of the 1848 German revolution, however, put an end for a long time to all efforts to introduce democratic elements into working life.

It was only towards the end of the nineteenth century that new opportunities arose as a result of economic growth and strengthening of the labour movement. In 1890, Kaiser Wilhelm II expressed the wish in his February message to Imperial Chancellor Prince Otto von Bismarck and Minister of Commerce Berlepsch that the condition of the working class should be improved. It was the growing influence of the labour movement that compelled him to voice this opinion.

The Emperor expressed himself in favour of worker representation in undertakings to present the workers' views in negotiations with the employers and the government and put forward the idea of an international conference concerning legislation for the protection of workers.

In 1891, workers' committees were legally recognized in an annex to the industrial regulations, though it is true that it was left to the undertakings to set them up. Nevertheless, in the tense situation of the First World War, even the authoritarian monarchic state had to pay more attention to the workers. As a result, the law concerning patriotic auxiliary service came into effect in 1916. For the first time this made it obligatory to set up committees of workers and employees in undertakings. This law was not the result of any intention to promote workers' liberation. However, the imperial government was obliged to take measures in favour of the workers and to make concessions to them. The trade unions were therefore successful in having provisions included in the auxiliary service law that gave workers and employees certain rights to participation.

With the end of the First World War and the revolutionary appearance of the workers' councils, the struggle for greater worker influence received fresh impetus. The republican constitution of 1919 legally established the right of workers and employees to co-determination. Article 165 states: 'Workers and employees are authorized to co-operate on an equal footing with employers in regulation of wages and working conditions as well as in economic development as a whole. Organizations on both sides and their agreements are recognized. Representation of workers and employees is legally recognized for the purpose of promoting their social and economic interests.'

This article of the constitution formed the basis for the Works Councils Law of 1920, which for the first time established participation of workers' representatives in the supervisory boards of limited companies.

However, the Works Councils Law only provided for a rather limited right to co-determination in the undertaking. While it constituted progress as compared with the previous situation, it soon became apparent that the Republic did not have a really democratic basis. All attempts to democratize the economy were abortive. The Nazi seizure of power in 1933 put an end to all the legal rights of workers.

It was thus necessary to draw lessons from this experience at the end of the Second World War in 1945. The new German trade unions which were no longer divided, as they had been before 1933, according to ideology and political party, did everything they could to supplement formal political democracy with democratization of the economy.

The first tangible success of these efforts was the agreement obtained by the trade unions within the framework of the reorganization of the German coal and steel industry by the occupying powers. This first resulted in the appointment on 1 March 1947 of labour directors and equal workers' representation on the supervisory boards of four iron and steel undertakings.

At the end of the Second World War, even the representatives of industry expected they would lose their domination permanently. Since they wanted to save what they could, they offered the workers and their trade unions co-determination in the responsible bodies of undertakings in the coal and steel industry. By these concessions they hoped to prevent a fundamental reorganization of their industry including, in particular, its transfer to public ownership.

As soon as the industrialists were back in the saddle, however, they did not want to hear anything more about this. By 1950 the co-determination that had been established by collective agreement in the iron and steel industry was already in danger. Controversy about this question rapidly developed, with the overwhelming majority of the population supporting the trade unions' position.

It was necessary in 1950–1 to exert considerable pressure on parliament and on the first Federal government led by Konrad Adenauer to establish co-determination in the coal and steel industry by law. It was only after a ballot of miners and steelworkers gave an overwhelming majority in favour of strike action to preserve and extend their right to co-determination that this legislation was adopted. It not only guaranteed co-determination in responsible company organs in the iron and steel industry but also extended the right to coal miners. The result of this campaign was the law on co-determination in the coal and steel industry.

The next legislative phase came in 1952 with the law on company organization. Unlike the law on co-determination in the coal and steel industry, this lays down how workers' interests are to be represented inside the undertaking, including the rights of the works' council. The law also includes provisions about the presence of worker representatives on supervisory boards of companies which are not covered by the law on co-determination in the iron and steel industry.

The 1963 basic programme of the German trade union federation states: 'The trade unions fight for the extension of workers' co-determination. By this means they want to achieve a restructurization of the economy and of society which will enable all citizens to participate on an equal footing in economic, cultural and political decisions.'

Co-determination therefore does no mean that the workers and their trade unions are being incorporated into an economic system that they fundamentally oppose. There is no question of ambiguity or loss of the unions' autonomous function. Three points make this clear:

1. Though co-determination, the workers and their trade unions participate directly in the decision-making bodies of the production process. They thus obtain not only improved opportunities for information and control but also for actual intervention on behalf of the workers.

2. Through co-responsibility, which is inseparable from co-determination, the workers are in no way committed to the existing economic system. On the contrary, this rather lengthens the list of goals to be attained. Co-responsibility does not commit the workers' respresentatives to the welfare of the industrialist, as is often falsely asserted, but to the welfare of the industry. Above all, it commits the workers' representatives to the welfare of those employed in the industrial undertaking. This is a most important point, which corresponds to the intention of the constitution of the Federal Republic of Germany which establishes a state based on democracy and social justice. Moreover, the participation of workers' representatives in the undertaking – that is, in matters concerning production – does not affect the legal position of trade unions with regard to collective bargaining. There can therefore be no question of the trade unions' freedom of action being restricted.

3. Like all other models that propose democratization of the economy, our demands regarding co-determination relate to the economic system as a whole. We have never left any doubt that co-determination in the undertaking must be integrated into a complete concept of co-determination at all levels of decision.

Therefore, no one can claim that the form of co-determination that exists, or is called for, in the Federal Republic of Germany will restrict the strategic range of trade union policy.

When we call for extension of co-determination today, this does not mean that we have made our peace with existing conditions. Co-determination is a promising tool for changing these conditions. It is the appropriate instrument for removal of arbitrary authority and unnecessary subordination and for reducing the employer's power to take decisions without reference to other people's interests.

GERMAN TRADE UNIONS' CLAIMS FOR CO-DETERMINATION

The German trade unions' position with regard to co-determination centres on the demand for extension of equal co-determination to all major companies. We regard the responsible bodies of these companies as the core of the planning and decision-making establishment of the capitalist economic system. For this reason, they form the obvious point at which the trade unions can exercise control and countervailing power.

From the institutional standpoint, the concept of equal co-determination provides the assurance that policy decisions in the undertaking can no longer be taken unilaterally, and solely in the interests of shareholders and their representatives. When the supervisory board is composed of equal numbers of workers and shareholders' representatives, under a neutral chairman, this makes democratization of company policy possible from the standpoint both of personnel and of production. In these circumstances, the workers' representatives cannot be placed in a minority position by the shareholders' representatives, as regards either the appointment of the board of directors or the approval of important policy decisions such as increased investment.

In this connection, it is important to be clear about the structure of workers' representation on the supervisory board. In our view, the workers' representatives should include persons both from inside and from outside the undertaking, because we believe that the nomination by the national trade union organizations of workers' representatives from outside the undertaking will contribute to independence in company policy.

The appointment of a labour director who cannot be removed without the consent of a majority of the workers' representatives on the supervisory board creates a situation in which the workers' interests and views are at least listened to and discussed on a permanent basis by the board of directors. Furthermore, the appointment of a labour director means that in the major companies in the Federal Republic of Germany today, the labour and personnel department stands on the same footing as the commercial and technical departments.

From the standpoint of substance, the concept of equal co-determination contributes to democratization of company policy in two ways. On the one hand, it constitutes a guarantee of protection for the company's employees in the event of economic fluctuations, dismissals for structural reasons or plant closures. If manpower planning is from the outset placed on the same footing by the management as the planning of investments and profits, it becomes possible to authorize dismissals only subject to social conditions. In addition, co-determination in the undertaking breaks new ground from the standpoint of company policy in general. It provides positive examples of company policy in social matters and this stimulates the imagination of those who are employed. It helps them to feel independent, more self-confident and reinforces the trade unions for new efforts.

Experiences in the coal and steel industry have shown that industrial democracy and economic growth are not contradictory objectives. In spite of this, our demands with respect to co-determination have not yet obtained support from the legislative bodies. Only the Social Democratic Party has so far agreed in principle with our position and has prepared a draft law. However, this party does not yet have the necessary parliamentary majority. For this reason, we regard it as our priority task at the present time to persuade growing sectors of the population to support our demand for equal co-determination in all major companies.

Any success in this political strategy, however limited it may be, will make it more difficult for the parties represented in parliament to go on ignoring our legitimate demands.

Our objectives with regard to co-determination are, of course, not limited to the level of the undertaking. We know that industrial democracy must cover the workers' immediate field of experience and that it must be visible in those parts of the undertaking of which each individual is aware. This is why we demand the extension of co-determination in the framework of a revision of the law on industrial organizations. It is a condition for 'grass-roots' participation in co-determination. At the same time we are quite aware that consideration of co-determination policy must today look beyond national frontiers. Capitalism has long since taken steps to organize itself at the international level. In the wake of the multinational concentration of industry and European integration there is a clear trend towards an international approach to planning by private enterprise. The EEC Commission is now engaged in preparatory work on a new multinational legal structure – the European company. The aim of that legislation is to supplement national company law and make it easier for companies to make multinational arrangements inside the European Economic Community.

We should welcome it if there were a European company law which would serve as an instrument for the adjustment of corporation structures to the conditions of a wider market. But we still call for workers' participation within the framework of this new form of corporation. It is the essential condition for co-determination in decision making. From the trade union standpoint, the concept of industrial democracy therefore includes participation by the workers and their organizations on an equal footing at all levels where economic decisions are taken. Co-determination in the undertaking must be accompanied by a solid infrastructure at the plant level and an effective superstructure at the international level.

The present position of the German trade unions with regard to co-determination is set out in the 'DGB Proposals for Amendment of the Works Constitution Law' issued in March 1970. In the first place we demand that the scope of action of the works' council should be extended and its legal position improved. The following proposals for amendment are particularly designed to extend the possibilities of action of works' councils. The 'peace pledge' accepted by works' council members is made less absolute: they are expressly authorized to engage in trade union activity within the plant. In principle, the independence of works' councils from the trade unions remains intact: the works' council shall in future carry out its tasks in close co-operation with the trade unions represented in the plant, and with their support. The ban on activities on behalf of political parties is lifted: in the past it was all too often used against the works' councils and the workers themselves and transformed into a general ban on political activities. The conflict about whether improvements in collective agreements are or are not permitted under the works constitution law may be ended by a single legal provision: more favourable rights for workers and their representatives may be agreed upon under the Works Constitution Law. To achieve a better legal position for works' councils is the aim of a whole series of amendment proposals, which aim at having the works' council participate on an equal footing in decisions on social, personnel and economic matters. The works' councils' right to co-determination in social matters is intended to become more far-reaching by having its powers extended to cover matters relating to the individual workers. Their right to co-determination in personnel matters is to be extended by transforming their present right to consultation into a right to equality in decision making. Appointments, assignments, transfers, ordinary dismissals of individual workers and extraordinary dismissals of office holders in the plant should in principle depend on the agreement of the works' council.

The works' councils' rights to co-determination in economic matters are to be modified in two ways. First, the right to information now possessed by the economic committee is to be transferred to the works' council. In the past these joint economic committees either never came into being or, with very few exceptions, were of no practical significance. For this reason, management should now be obliged to inform the works' council in good time, regularly and in detail on all matters of this nature, and to submit the relevant documents. Secondly, the works' councils' right to co-determination in planned changes in operations should be extended. Among the examples of changes in operations are explicitly listed such questions as changes in organization of the plant, or in its objectives or in its equipment, the introduction of new processing methods, or a change in ownership.

To reduce the risk of alienation at the plant level requires not only greater rights for the works' council but also new forms of communication. This is also true with regard to the works' councils' contacts inside the plant. In a corporation composed of legally independent undertakings the top management often takes decisions on social, economic and personal matters that are binding on the management of individual undertakings. To prevent the right of plant representatives becoming purely formal as a result of mergers and concentration, the DGB proposals for amendment of the Works Constitution Law foresee the possibility of establishing by collective agreement a works' council at the level of the corporation.

Furthermore, our reform proposals set out two ways to achieve better communications between the works' council and the workers. The first introduces, in addition to the former workers' meetings at the plant level, smaller meetings – for example, for individual departments in the plant. Experience has shown that particularly in major companies, the general workers' meetings do not deal adequately with the problems of smaller groups within the whole. Secondly, the individual worker's situation should be improved by extending his right to be heard. Before a decision is taken on social or personnel matters, the works' council should hear the point of view of workers affected by the measure.

The new Federal government has made reform of the Works Constitution Law one of the points in its official programme. On 29 January 1971 the government draft amendment of the Works Constitution Law was presented to parliament. In certain points it falls short of the justified demands made by the trade unions. Thus it would be detrimental to the trade unions' right of access to the plant, as compared with the present legal position. The category of executive and supervisory staff who are not covered by the Works Constitution Law is so widely defined that the principle of a single representation for all employees by the works' council is seriously breached. At the same time, the right of workers and salaried employees as distinct categories are so widely defined that the works' council could be split and its position weakened. We expect the Federal government to take our apprehension on these points into consideration. However, in principle we recognize that the government draft makes important improvements with regard to certain points as compared with existing law and on other matters makes it possible to utilize more easily particular existing provisions.

I have already stated that the trade union concept of industrial democracy is not restricted to co-determination at the plant and company level, but must include the higher levels of economic decision-making. This raises the complex problem of co-determination beyond the company, covering the whole economy. According to the DGB's 1963 basic programme, co-determination in the plant is to be realized through bodies in which workers have equal representation. At the beginning of March 1971, the DGB put forward an integrated scheme for co-determination in the national economy. Under this, economic and social councils with equal worker representation should be set up at the Federal, Land and regional levels. These bodies should be given extensive rights to information, advice and consultation. Their competence would cover all areas of national economic, financial and social policy affecting worker (and employer) interests. The regional economic and social councils would take over from the existing 'chambers' (chambers of industry, commerce and handicrafts) the responsibility for structural policy and vocational training, and the chambers would lose their status under public law.

At the same time our ideas about co-determination cannot lose sight of the fact that capitalist company and corporation planning is increasingly international in character. National frontiers have for a long time been too narrow for today's giant corporations. Management has already recognized and made use of the new freedom of action that has arisen as a result of European integration. It is therefore all the more important for the trade unions to make their influence felt at the international level. There are two lines of action which the trade unions must follow.

In the first instance, we have created new opportunities for exchange of information and co-ordination in the European Confederation of Free Trade Unions and international trade secretariats. In addition, the member unions of the ECFTU have developed a common position concerning co-determination in a European company. The starting point for the discussion on co-determination at the European level was the common dissatisfaction with the unilateral authority of capitalism and the authoritarian decision-making structures in all member states of the Community. So we soon reached unity on objectives inside the EEC. Industrial democracy has been and still is a common demand of the entire European trade union movement. However, there are differences about ways of achieving it. This is mainly due to differences in national experience, but also to differences between unions. The latter arose less as a result of disagreement on principles than of misunderstandings and lack of information. In particular, two reproaches were levelled against us.

First, some of our foreign colleagues took the position that worker participation in capitalist decision-making was equivalent to integrating the trade unions in the capitalist system. In response we pointed out:

- that we have not forgotten that trade unions from their origin have been anti-capitalist;
- that we have not concluded a permanent peace treaty with the existing economic system;
- that we do not regard co-determination in the undertaking as a means of adapting to the present system, but as an important measure of protection against unilateral, profit-oriented management decisions.

Secondly, some of our foreign colleagues took the mistaken viewpoint that co-determination in the undertaking was the bureacratic alternative to political mobilization of organized workers. We have always replied:

– that in our view a move into the centres of economic decision-making – that is, the boards of companies and corporations – is important but we should not for this reason abandon our fight for an effective infrastructure in the form of co-determination in the undertaking;
– that improved contacts between those employed in the plant and their representatives in the various bodies is one of the most urgent aspects of co-determination policy.

Today these regular discussions about co-determination problems have brought their results. We are now united in a common endeavour inside the EEC. This came about in two stages. In 1970 the Executive Committee of the ECFTU took a majority decision to campaign for worker participation in the boards of European companies. It decided on a detailed set of demands on worker participation in European companies. These concentrate on three points which should be made obligatory in the law establishing European companies:

1. The supervisory board of a European company should be composed as follows: one-third representing shareholders, one-third representing the workers, and one-third representing the public interest. The shareholder representatives would be elected by the general meeting, the worker representatives from lists presented by the trade unions through the central works' council. These two groups would together elect the remaining third by co-optation. The responsibility of the supervisory board is to appoint and supervise the board of directors.
2. To ensure proper representation of worker interests in matters affecting all or a number of plants belonging to a European company, a central works' council would be set up. This would be chosen by plant representatives on the basis of lists presented by the trade unions. Its competence would vary. We have thought of giving this central works' council co-determination rights with regard to specific social questions and the right to be informed and consulted on economic questions.

3. The board of directors of the European company should include one member who is responsible for personnel and labour matters.

In June 1971 the European Economic Commission submitted a draft of a law on European companies which also dealt with the question of worker participation. This draft from the Commission itself has accepted the principle and goes far beyond the lip-service that was previously paid. The European company law is not to be a substitute for national company law. But it is to create a new international law for mergers, for establishment of a joint holding company and for creation of joint subsidiaries by companies in the different EEC member states. Three measures are included with regard to worker representation:

- the European company has the power to bargain collectively;
- elections to a works' council for a European company by representatives of individual works' councils at the national level, the trade unions being able to present candidates;
- one-third worker representation in the supervisory board, the Commission taking the view that the shareholders should have a two-thirds majority.

The Commission's proposal is thus based on existing law. Of course, it takes as its starting point the legal situation in the Federal Republic of Germany which has gone much further with respect to co-determination in the undertaking than its neighbour countries. The Commission's attitude is not due to lack of imagination but rather to an estimate of the real political possibilities within such an international body.

I doubt whether it would be tactically useful to reject the Commission's draft out of hand. If we enter into discussion with the Commission this does not mean that we accept their position unreservedly but that we consider it as a basis of discussion.

The draft law would create two kinds of new rights to co-determination in the supervisory boards of European companies. In the first place, in the other member states of the EEC co-determination provisions would become obligatory, even when they do not exist at the national level, whenever a European company is established there. In the second place, the European Commission provides that worker representatives who do not belong to the company can participate, and this is also valid for the Federal Republic of Germany. In our Works Constitution Law this is an optional provision.

I therefore repeat that we maintain our aim of parity with shareholders. But we are ready to discuss matters with the Commission because we recognize that they have tried to find a sensible solution. This is important because so far there has been no positive response to our claims from the employers' side. This survey of our idea of industrial democracy cannot be dissociated from the trade union movement's overall strategy. This is based on the idea that social change is one of our most urgent objectives, but we place no hopes either in romantic social Utopias or in a sudden collapse of the capitalist system. We know that every single step forward in the tough world of our present society requires struggle. We rely on finding increasing support for our demands among public opinion which is at least to some extent politically aware and is learning gradually to understand where its real interests lie. However, now as always, our strongest weapon is the solidarity and strength of the organized workers in the trade unions.

Chapter 3

Federal Republic of Germany

KARL HAUENSCHILD

President, Industriegewerkschaft Chemie, Papier, Keramik
President, International Federation of Chemical and General
Workers' Unions

IG FARBEN–FROM DECARTELLIZATION TO CO-DETERMINATION–A CASE STUDY

The conclusion of the Second World War with the unconditional capitulation of the Nazi armed forces raised the problem of the responsibility of German industry and its management in preparing and supporting Hitler's war. Representatives of German heavy industry stood beside political figures of the Third Reich in the dock at the Nuremberg Tribunal. The victorious powers had to face the prospect of administering the economic, social and political life of the German Reich that they had destroyed, until such time as a new German State emerged to take over this task.

In the Berlin Declaration of 5 June 1945 the allies took over state power in Germany. The occupying powers set themselves the task of reorganizing political and economic conditions in Germany. Part of this reorganization was the demand that the IG Farmen firm should be decartellized.

Since it was founded by merger 1926, IG Farben had grown into the biggest industrial undertaking in Germany. In 1938, it was responsible for 25 per cent of world chemical production (in 1932 this figure was as high as 32 per cent), and for 57 per cent of German chemical production. Turnover rose from 1,029 million Reichsmarks in 1926 ($410·8 million) to 3,115 million Reichsmarks in 1938 ($1,246 million). In comparison, turnover of other world leading companies in 1943 was:

Dupont de Nemours – $612·9 million.
Standard Oil of New Jersey – $1,302·8 million.
General Motors – $3,796·1 million.

In 1943 IG Farben employed 199,500 people, while Dupont, for instance, employed 63,200. As a result of its intensive research effort, IG Farben at that time controlled 40,000 patents (including about 30,000 foreign patents) and about 26,500 registered trademarks (including 22,000 outside Germany).

It was obvious that the future development of such a gigantic undertaking could not be allowed to remain with the former management – some of whom were being politically charged – nor could it be left to chance.

Immediately after the occupation of Germany and quite independently of one another, the military governors of the occupying forces confiscated all IG Farben assets. Their legal basis for this was Control Commission Law No. 52 in the American Zone and General Instructions No. 2 of 5 July 1945. The grounds for the confiscation measure were announced as being that 'IG Farben had played a prominent role in building up and maintaining German war potential and had aided Germany's striving for world domination.' The aims of confiscation included: compensation to devastated European countries and members of the United Nations; destruction of all installations that had served warlike purposes; redistribution of ownership and control of confiscated factories and installations that were not destroyed or dismantled.

In the Potsdam Agreement of 1945, the allies laid down principles relating to the political and economic treatment of Germany. Article IIIb, paragraph 12 of that Agreement states in this connection: 'In the shortest practicable time, German economic life is to be decentralized with the aim of eliminating existing over-concentration of economic power, as particularly represented in cartels, combines, trusts, and other monopoly groups.' The preamble to Control Commission Law No. 9 further states that the law was issued, among other reasons, 'to render impossible any future threat by Germany to its neighbours or to world peace'.

The German trade unions, in particular IG Chemie-Papier-Keramik (Chemical, Paper and Ceramic Workers' Union), were from the outset in accord with the occupying powers' attitude towards decartellization. In a statement concerning the reorganization of IG Farben in October 1949, the trade unions laid down the following principles in this regard:

1. Concentration of economic power in the hands of cartels, trusts and monopolies must be destroyed and any renewal prevented.
2. Technical progress, which particularly in the chemical industry is mainly due to joint undertakings and co-operation between firms, must be maintained.
3. Consequently, reorganization must be carried out in such a way as to satisfy these two principles.

In their statement, the trade unions complained that German public opinion had so far been poorly informed about the decartellization measures and that German co-operation had remained unsatisfactory.

The essential feature of this reorganization was said to be 'the integration of organized labour into the supervision and management of the new companies'. Such democratization of the boards of the new companies was required in view of the very small degree of control a shareholders' meeting could have, since ownership of shares was so widely split and scattered. Democratization would be the best guarantee against any misuse of industry for private ends. One of the essential purposes of the reorganization was to bring the leaders of major industries under the control of democratic bodies to which the management was accountable and from which it was to receive a mandate in legitimate fashion. A further demand was made that the workers be integrated into management and supervisory bodies, in the same way as they had won this right in practice in various forms in the iron and steel industry.

From the outset the employers raised a storm against such a proposal. At the beginning of 1951, the 'Working Group of Employers' Associations in the German Chemical Industry' expressed its opposition to the introduction in the chemical industry of the right to workers' determination in accordance with the model of the coal and steel industry.

At that time trade union, employers and the Federal government were represented on a so-called 'combined IG Farben Advisory Committee', which dealt with the occupation authorities, represented by the Allied High Commission, and whose function was to prevent dismemberment of the German Chemical industry to the point where future international competitiveness would be diminished, thereby placing workers' jobs in danger. The trade unions were finally unsuccessful in convincing political groups, including both Federal Chancellor Adenauer and the chemical industry itself, to back their demands for co-determination. However, the intensive efforts made by the German trade unions, the assistance they received through their earlier international contacts and their political weight with the allied authorities made it possible to prevent IG Farben being split up into unviable small undertakings. Without the support of the workers and employees and their organizations the later economic growth of the chemical industry in the Federal Republic of Germany would have been impossible. The fight carried on by the workers and their trade unions to maintain the industry's capacity to operate effectively, which often led to open confrontation with officers of the allied occupation authorities, was thus a success from this standpoint.

However, the demand of the workers in the chemical industry for co-determination remained unfulfilled. Anyone who goes through the history of the IG Farben decartellization affair will find no pretext for accusing the trade unions of lack of understanding, insufficient technical knowledge or an inadequate sense of responsibility which might be taken as a disqualification from fulfilling their functions under co-determination. The example demonstrates rather that the trade unions are praised and their help is sought when that strategy seems useful, but that immediately afterwards the 'boss' attitude returns when the economic situation is considered to be stable again. If, at a time when everybody was needed for reconstructing the production facilities that had been destroyed, the workers and employees in the chemical industry had used their power without taking account of the economic consequences (a threat which the employers are now brandishing to scare people), they would have been in a position to obtain co-determination in the chemical industry against any opposition.

The demand for control by the workers over economic power is as old as the history of the labour movement itself. The use of steam power for industrial production, organized division of labour (as a precondition for rational exploitation of new discoveries), and the unimagined increase in productivity of human labour (as the result of changes in production techniques), have all led to developments that brought strong reactions from the workers. Capital accumulation on a previously unknown scale existed side-by-side with unimaginable misery among the working class. The army of unemployed who were displaced from their jobs by machines grew immeasurably. Anyone who still had a job was subject to competition from his workless comrades and had to allow the boss to dictate his working conditions. Demands for the elimination of conditions that violated human dignity became intense. In view of the workers' political impotence in the middle of the nineteenth century, there was only one plausible solution – elimination of private ownership of the means of production and the transfer of private enterprises to public ownership: namely, total nationalization.

In the 'Communist Manifesto' of 1848, conclusions were drawn from a situation in which 'capital is concentrated in the hands of a few, while the great multitude is starving'. The basic concepts of the 'Communist Manifesto' served for many years as an incentive for strengthening a political labour movement, and also as the basis for further theoretical considerations. By the start of the twentieth century, the material and social situation of the working class had improved, but oppression and injustice still reigned. At that time there was lively discussion inside the German Social Democratic Party as to whether the aims set forth in the 'Communist Manifesto' should be achieved by revolutionary methods, by general socialization of the means of production or whether the workers should construct the new society by evolutionary methods, by strengthening and expanding their organizations (parties, unions, co-operatives), by striving for better education and training, by obtaining greater influence in the state and the community, and thus finally bringing more freedom and justice into all aspects of economic and social life.

It was not a coincidence, but a consequence of the growing importance of the organized labour movement, that caused the catholic and evangelical churches to take up labour questions at that time. The social encyclicals of the popes aroused world-wide attention. In 'Rerum Novarum' (1891), Leo XIII dealt with the question of the private ownership of the means of production. He came to the conclusion that the transformation of private property into common property would not improve the situation of the working class. In 'Quadragesimo Anno' (1931), Pius XI stressed the direct unconditional responsibility of the state for looking after the general welfare of its citizens.

The voluntary organizations of workers and employers were assigned the task of bringing the different points of view of the two groups closer together. This encyclical favoured property formation for wide population groups as the means to achieve common ownership of the means of production. The level of wage incomes and the will to save on the part of the worker were described as decisive factors in property formation. Similarly, 'Mater et Magistra' (1961) from John XXIII devoted long passages to the situation of workers in employment and contains general indications of the need to assure 'co-determination', without defining the concept of co-determination in any detail. The same Pope in 'Pacem in Terris' reaffirmed the responsibility of 'public authorities' for the general welfare and stated that participation in public life in the formation of political policy and the promotion of the general welfare was the right and duty of every capable person.

In the evangelical church there is no central body that can lay down a definitive policy on social or political questions. This has often given rise to the impression that the evangelical church has no opinion or commitment with regard to social problems. In fact, at the time when monarchs ruled in Germany, the evangelical churches were 'state churches' and consequently their representatives allied themselves with the rulers and their system and defended existing conditions. In practice, however, representatives and institutions of the evangelical church have often taken a stand on conflicts in state and society. For example, in the resistance to the Hitler regime, men and women of the evangelical church sacrificed their lives or their health along with catholics, social democrats, communists and liberals. At the world church conferences after the Second World War, Christians from different social and political systems have come together for discussion. Because of the varying composition of the participants, any definitive statement about a particular social system was impracticable. Nevertheless, the question of 'Freedom and Justice' has always been at the centre of discussion at the world church conferences. In 1948 at the Amsterdam Conference, 'freedom of mankind' was affirmed to be the principle of a responsible society in which people 'know themselves to be responsible for justice and public order and in which those who possess political authority or economic power are responsible to God and mankind for their exercise'. If you like, that is another definition of the concept of co-determination and co-responsibility. The Amsterdam Conference also dealt with communism. Communist parties are denied the right to demand unconditional obedience from their members, since the conference believed that this right belongs only to God. At the same time, the conference expressed its opinion with regard to 'unbridled capitalism' which has the tendency to create great and burdensome inequalities. Mention was made of the danger that economic decisions would mainly be to the advantage of those who manage industry rather than for satisfaction of human needs.

The evangelical church in Germany (EKD) has taken an outspoken position in a statement on 'property formation in social responsibility'. The statement notes that the distribution of property in Federal Republic of Germany since 1948 does not correspond to the requirements of justice. The owners of property rights over the means of production had been granted lighter tax burdens in the interest of economic reconstruction and thus had had their capacity to accumulate property unilaterally strengthened. The question of workers' ownership of the means of production was raised, but confiscation was ruled out as a solution of the problem. The evangelical church conference of 1950 in Essen also dealt with the workers' right to co-determination. It spoke of extending the scope of the Works Councils Law of 1920 (at that time the Works Constitution Law of 1952 had not yet been adopted.) The aim of co-determination was seen as being to overcome the employment relationship and to establish the worker as a human being and collaborator. The idea of self-government with adequate worker representation should be put into practice with much greater effect than had so far been the case.

The standpoints with regard to co-determination inside the democratic parties in the Federal Republic of Germany have developed along different lines. The CDU in the British zone still spoke of it in 1949 in its 'Ahlen Programme' and said that the capitalist system had become unjust to the interests of the German people and that there should be a radical reorganization of the economy. Subsequently, the CDU moved further and further away from this position. At the present time only a dwindling minority of this party favours workers' co-determination.

The Social Democratic Party has unanimously expressed itself in resolutions in favour of co-determination in major industries on the model of the coal and steel industries. However, in existing conditions in the German parliament, the SPD–FDP coalition has no majority for this. The possibility of passing a law against the opposition of the FDP with the votes of a minority of the CDU–CSU opposition is only a theoretical one. In the first place, it is not certain that the 'left wing' of the CDU–CSU would break party discipline, and furthermore in such a case the future existence of the coalition would be in danger, and with it all the other points in the government's programme, not least the conciliatory foreign policy of the socialist-liberal government.

What does exist in present circumstances is the hope of growing awareness among progressive, social-minded forces of the need for workers to participate in the decisions that daily affect them. It seems as though there is a growing recognition among wide circles of German public opinion that a man who is a free political citizen can no longer be kept as a voiceless subject in the economic system.

One of the essential reasons for the demand for co-determination in the chemical industry is the growing concentration of economic power in this sector. Taking part in this process of concentration – sometimes in union with German companies – are firms whose headquarters are in countries whose governments once had the aim of 'destroying the existing over-concentration of economic power'. In most of these countries there has recently been intense discussion about co-determination in industry and this demonstrates how necessary and urgent the demand is, and also indicates that a process of learning has been going on.

In a democratic social system it is a principle that no member of the society should be subject to a decision if he does not participate in its conception and control. This principle has so far not been put into practice in one important sector of society – namely, the economy. As long as this is so, we live in a 'partial' democracy. A society which denies its members reforms in this area is in danger of placing in jeopardy more than the much-vaunted 'managerial freedom to take decisions'. The alternative to co-determination in industry is not just maintenance of the status quo. Even supporters of 'private enterprise' and the 'market economy' must recognize that highly technical industries in the industrialized Western countries cannot be left to the free play of economic forces. Even competition as a regulatory factor is losing its importance with world-wide concerns, market and price agreements and many other manifestations having increasingly monopolistic consequences.

Total elimination of private ownership of the means of production, which is still being put forward as the only real solution by left-wing groups is only apparently a practical solution. In the first place, it is impractical because confiscation without compensation of all private ownership in the means of production cannot be carried out in a democratic society. Guarantee of property rules this out, and financial resources for compensating owners of capital do not exist in over-extended state budgets. Furthermore, a modification in the weight of authority in industry would not make co-determination superfluous. Even in state-controlled, nationalized undertakings, the workers' subordinate position is not eliminated.

The realistic, practical way would therefore be to strengthen the state-controlled sector and also take steps to create real competition by built-in control mechanisms both within and outside the undertaking which replace the authoritarian rule of the manager by the joint authority of capital and labour. The longer this solution is delayed, the greater the danger that in the discussion of this subject certain groups will gain influence – groups which offer themselves as the workers' allies in the co-determination question because they want at the same time to gain their sympathy for their dubious political ideas.

Anyone who opposes workers' co-determination in industry is also opposing an important and urgent measure for stabilizing and developing a democratic social order.

Chapter 4

France

EUGÈNE DESCAMPS
Secretary General, Confédération Française Démocratique du Travail assisted by Bruno Dasetto, Bureau de Recherches et d'Action Economiques

France is thoroughly adapting and overthrowing its way of life and of work, in its towns and its undertakings, by developing a form of economic domination which is slowly pervading every physical and psychological sphere. The pressure is on from 'them' who want to move us into the era of production, commercialization and profit. At the same time, although we recognize the open struggle in the revolt of little Vietnam, of those who are fighting for bread and for freedom in Latin America, Spain, Greece and Palestine, of our young workers and students agitating for civil and social rights, mankind is being trodden down, crushed more subtly by the factory in which he works, the town in which he lives and the objects that he consumes. Society is changing, man's techniques and potentials are developing at an amazing rate. Yet he is suffocating, for nothing is being done *for* him while the time hastens on when nothing further will be done *by* him. He is becoming the survivor of another age and, for the younger members of society, he is, in some cases, becoming the witness of another dream that some Frenchmen called 'Little France' – the land of small towns, small farms, small employers and small dishes!

Our right-wing rulers tell us of the 'New Society'. This is a reality, we see it daily being built before our very eyes. But although we were led to understand that 'they' wanted to build *our* new society, it is in fact *theirs* that 'they' are preparing – the society of the big undertaking, the big computer, the big bomb and the big boss. We are beginning to realize that we shall have to build our own society – of joy, liberty, solidarity – the society of the people for the people. We shall call it 'democracy'.

This time trade unionism is in a good position. Although the economy is the new modern oppressive power, acting through the undertaking and its managers, we do at least know it well, having suffered it for quite some time. As the influence of huge trans-national undertakings increases with their proportions, the banks and the governmental administrations merely accentuate their profit-making and oppressive character which we have to suffer in our workshops and offices. We are in the lair of the cyclops whose single eye is fixed on the money bags.

Undoubtedly, during their century of existence, trade unions have improved the lot of the working masses by wresting more time and money from the employers. But when it comes to economic democracy, that is to say the amount of weight that we have acquired in the decision taking of the economic machinery in order to set it to work for society as a whole, our successes are but modest. The following text will describe the institutions of French economic democracy both in the undertaking and in society, for we make no distinction. Looking back over our shoulder, these results are not negligible, but they are limited when it comes to real decision taking which, alone, is the basis of democracy.

If, instead of casting our glance backwards, we take a look both at the tremendous international, military, financial and economic build-up, and at the mass of technology which is just waiting to be put to work for mankind, we can see that we are far from being a match for the problems which face the workers and the people. We must, therefore, find some way of giving back to downtrodden humanity the will and the energy to make its society flourish. This is the aim of the new prospects for an economic democracy which the CFDT is proposing to its political and trade union partners and to workers in Europe and throughout the world.

THE INSTITUTIONS OF ECONOMIC DEMOCRACY

Powerful mass movements in France, in 1936, 1945 and 1968, have produced a fairly good democratic facade in which can be

recognized certain legal institutions, many examples of concerta-
tion and some satisfactory jurisdiction. When mention is made
of us in documents, we give a good impression among Western
nations and it is not rare for us to be taken, and for our leaders
to be quoted, as models. It should also be realized that we often
play a pioneering role in the legislative field. This is true of
spheres as varied as those of working hours, recognition of trade
union branches in factories and the 'mechanism' of indicative
planning.

We shall see later what is to be made of the realities hidden
by this facade, which we shall consider first of all. We shall take
a quick look at the main institutions of French economic democracy, beginning with that which is nearest to the workers, the
undertaking. However, we will consider the democratic situation
as a whole. Otherwise, we may seriously contradict ourselves
by isolating one institution or another, especially if we wish, in
good faith, to enlighten our friends, our brethren in other lands
and all those who are interested in what goes on in France,
in order to help them understand what our trade unionism
involves. For this reason, we shall also consider economic
democracy outside the undertaking. This is further justified by
a social paradox, which is known in many countries, namely that
trade unionism was recognized by the nation before it was
recognized by the undertaking. It took almost a century to pass
from one to the other!

THE DEMOCRATIC INSTITUTIONS WITHIN THE UNDERTAKING

Democracy is exercised by means of three mechanisms which
we intend to describe successively, i.e. representation, negotiation and, finally, supervision and corrective action.

In France the history of democracy within the undertaking
means nothing unless taken together with the history of trade
union law within the undertaking. It would be as well, in order
to analyse the various democratic institutions, to consider them
from the standpoint of December 1968, when trade union
branches within the undertaking were legally recognized.

The oldest institution is the *délégué du personnel* (shop
steward). He made his first appearance during the 1917 war
effort and again during the activity of 1936, and it was only in
1946, after the Second World War, that he was finally enshrined

in the law. The procedure for election of shop stewards constituted the first trade union victory in that candidates are put up
for the first ballot on a proportional basis, by the most representative trade union centres. They may also be accompanied
by a member of their union in their dealings with the management. The number of stewards may vary from one in undertakings with 11 to 25 wage earners, to 9 in undertakings with
500 to 1,000 wage earners, plus one further steward for every
500 wage earners over 1,000. They enjoy special protection in
the case of dismissal (this provision is unfortunately not very
effective), and fifteen paid hours per month to carry out their
functions.

This minimum facility and protection was to become the first
trade union stronghold within the undertaking which made it
possible to protect militants from the very active and expeditious
repression which, even now, has hardly disappeared. Of course,
the object of the law was not to root the trade union in the
undertaking. The Act merely gave stewards the right to make
a personal or a collective complaint, initially, and it did not take
the place of the privileged channels provided by the undertakings' own hierarchic structure and, in particular, of the supervisory staff. It took much militant effort for the stewards to
become anything more than mere secondary 'letter boxes' and for
them to be able to rely on trade union policy and strength in the
undertaking. This evolution which was made necessary by
the repression of trade unionism, was not purely positive. On
the negative side it obliged the stewards to fulfil two kinds of
function: firstly, there was the spontaneous expression of the
workers' difficulties and secondly, recruitment and the definition
of trade union policy. This double function resulted to a certain
degree in an administrative bottleneck owing to the greater stress
laid on the latter of the two. This bottleneck partially explains the
revolt of certain classes of workers against the trade union
structure during the uprisings of May 1968.

The second institution, the *factory committee*, grew from quite
a different idea. The principle of such an institution was prepared during World War II by the National Council for the
Resistance (Conseil National de la Résistance) on which sat
both the CGT and the CFTC. Its aim was to confer upon the
workers such responsibilities as would raise them above the
station of pawns to which they had been confined previously.
The idea was to give them a hand in the running of the factory

on an equal footing with the suppliers of capital, especially as many of the latter had chosen to collaborate with the enemy. Although the Act of 22 February 1945 did grant the factory committee the right to take a hand in running the social side of the enterprise, it did not, unfortunately, give it any right to act in an informative or consultative capacity with regard to problems concerning the technical, economic and financial side. Furthermore, this consultative role was construed idealogically as a desire to co-operate, which neither the traditions of the French working classes, nor the events of the War, nor the separation of the world into antagonistic blocs, made very realistic. Frequently, however, owing to the lack of jurisdiction over the concrete problems of the undertaking, which was due to the inability to enter into contracts, the unions intervened through the stewards on the committee to change it from a co-operative and informative body to one in which the power of the employer came under fire.

The very reserved attitude of the employers when it came to handing out information, even to their own shareholders, must also be remarked upon. Only very recently have the more dynamic among the French employers changed their attitude, partly following the creation of the trade union branch within the undertaking which helped to relax the atmosphere in the committee, and partly owing to the demands of modern management in the big monopolistic economic institutions. Without taking any stand on the future of this institution, it was almost stopped dead by the events of 1968. Factory committees existed in only a third of the establishments concerned and 50 per cent of those that did exist worked badly.

It should be noted that the factory committee (or where there are several branches, the branch committee and the central factory committee) is made up as follows: the factory manager or his representative, acting as chairman, and a staff delegation varying from 3 in factories with between 50 and 75 wage earners to 11 in factories with more than 10,000 wage earners. Apart from this, each representative trade union centre can send a delegate appointed from among the staff to act as observer on the factory committee. He would enjoy the same protection and the same working facilities (twenty hours per month) as the other representatives of the wage earners.

We should mention also a change in the electoral system arising from the political strength of the managerial staff.

Traditionally, elections are held in two groups, i.e. blue and white collar workers – engineers, managerial and senior supervisory staff. However, if the managerial staff and the engineers account for more than 5 per cent of the total staff, they may form a special electoral group.

Since the law was changed in 1966 and following the 1959 and 1967 Ordinances on the financial and active involvement of the workers, the 1969 employers–union agreement on work safety and the 1970 agreement on training, every effort has been made to revitalize this institution. It is, however, too soon after the failures of the first twenty years to pass judgement on a possible new start. This is particularly so as problems have continued to develop meanwhile. The shift of decision taking in the undertaking beyond national frontiers, the change of the controlling bodies from limited companies to holding companies, makes it necessary for the international trade union movement to perfect new and, let us hope, more efficient institutions.

In 1947, the factory committee was joined by the *health and safety committee*. This committee is composed of the factory manager, the departmental manager, the doctor and the labour welfare officer, plus 3 staff representatives in undertakings with less than 1,000 wage earners or 6 in those with over 1,000 wage earners. This committee looks into cases of accident and illness at work, ensures that the health and safety regulations are applied, and informs and educates the staff. It may be helped in its work by appropriate organizations from outside the undertaking. To date, this institution has been endowed with widely varying degrees of importance. It is quite likely that the increasing pressure being brought to bear on the wage earner by the ever-faster pace and the very rigid organization of work, may accentuate the political nature of this institution. This is all the more likely as the wage earners are reacting energetically against the deterioration of their working conditions which form part of an increasingly frustrating and wearying urban life.

Even though the right of association has been recognized in France since 1884, trade unionism did not win official recognition in the undertaking until 27 December 1968. Quite obviously, the 1968 Act radically changes the social complexion of the undertaking. In particular, it enables the institutions that we have so far mentioned once again to take up their proper functions of representing the claim of one side while informing the other. It will be up to the union branch to prepare claims, to negotiate with the employers and to act as a link between the workers within the undertaking and the community outside. This Act at last recognizes the right of the union to hold meetings, to spread information and to collect subscriptions within the undertaking, even though, during this first stage, this is still only allowed outside working time. What is more, the union branch has the right to negotiate, that is to speak as the power of the workers within the undertaking.

This Act is the outcome of a long series of struggles mainly, as can be seen from May 1968, on the part of the CFDT. In most undertakings, trade union branches had taken shape well before the Act was passed. Furthermore, these branches have met with considerable success since the Act came into effect. At the beginning of 1970, there were more than 10,000 branches in the 28,000 undertakings concerned. These covered more than 90 per cent of the undertakings with more than 1,000 wage earners.

This victory might be considered to mark the end of the evolution of workers' representation in the undertaking. This is not so straightforward, however. The latest movements have given birth to new forms of organization in the undertakings which take the shape of committees for action or units of political parties that can be very aggressive at times. This heavy-handed incursion of politics into the undertakings, especially the larger among them, may result in a greater realization of the need for a more radical transformation of the institutions of the undertaking in order to achieve more effective democratization. Whatever solution is eventually found to this situation, it is more than likely that trade unions will, in one way or another, have to take it into account.

The French undertaking would, therefore, appear to be relatively well endowed with means for democratic expression. This impression is even more striking if we add to the picture the part played by wage earners on the board of directors of large public and nationalized undertakings. We must not forget that in France reality may be a world apart from the texts written on the subject or speeches made about it. The textbook versions often present a purely theoretical interplay of forces and that which is said is, after all, just a passing word. We might say that while, on the one hand, all of these institutions can work together properly only in large undertakings, on the other hand the mechanism, and perhaps also the spirit of negotiation is generally poorly developed. For this reason, having outlined the representative institutions we must now discuss *negotiation within the undertaking*.

We should say straightaway that, among other things, the process is not very highly developed in the undertakings themselves. Some attempts have been made of course. One of these was in 1955 when, under pressure applied by the non-communist trade unions, Renault, a nationalized undertaking, negotiated an agreement which, in the minds of its promoters, was to have served as a model for all other undertakings. This example was followed in particular in the metalworking industries in which trade union pressure was especially strong, but there was so little enthusiasm elsewhere that it was necessary to take legislative measures in order to spread the effect of more favourable provisions, especially those concerning paid holidays. In fact, negotiation within the undertaking has always been considered by the employers as a formality or as the specific application of broader negotiations carried out in connection with a particular trade or region, or else it has concerned the application, for better or worse, of the interplay of political forces as set out in an Act of Parliament.

This lack of negotiation has not been limited to private undertakings. It should be stressed that it also existed in a far more compelling way in public undertakings and in the civil service which, under the protection of the Ministry of Finance, felt the need to settle the matter centrally. This austerity, softened by trade union action over the past few years, serves as a background to the current preparation of the technical methods and procedures which are to provide the bases for the conclusion of contracts within these undertakings. There are still important problems to be solved. The first concerns the right to strike, the second relates to the nature and quality of the information supplied and the third to the possibility of a national reorganization in which intolerable inequalities and disparities might be avoided.

Here again, after May 1968, much remains to be said. Here and there, the establishment of some kind of direct democracy is beginning to be noticeable, especially where problems concerning working conditions are concerned. The workers manage to reach their own decisions and impose them on the employers without, apparently, having to resort to negotiations. It was unquestionably in anticipation of the swelling thrust of participation engulfing industry in Europe that the French government introduced new legislation in 1972 for worker participation at the board level.

This legislation encourages the reorganization of the enterprise to provide for both a supervisory board and an executive board, instead of a single administrative council. This is apparently intended to bring it into line with the German, Dutch, Austrian and other systems, as well as with the projected statutes of an eventual registered European company. Two representatives of the personnel may be elected to the supervisory board, one by the employees and one by the supervisory personnel (technicians and cadre) with full deliberative and voting rights. In view of the obvious tactical aims of the measure, it is not surprising that it was immediately criticized by the trade unions as 'partial and limited' and designed to integrate the workers into the existing system rather than to initiate real participation in management. The future will show what such practices are worth. Once again, their existence cannot fail to have an effect on trade union practice.

At this point we should describe the instruments of supervision and corrective action. In fact, even if we take a modern view of democracy based on the utmost freedom of expression for existing factions, we cannot disregard the right or the facility to have the agreements which have been signed implemented. It is, in fact, up to the courts to state clearly how that which we in France consider the source of law is to be applied (i.e. Acts of Parliament, collective agreements and work contracts) and to explain and interpret those laws which are not always explicitly defined. Arbitration meets with little success in France. Neither employers nor unions would like to submit to a man or an institution symbolizing equity. We still prefer to solve our conflicts directly when they concern economic and social problems that fall within our competence, and if they do not, we go beyond the area of our conflict to appear before our tribunals. That is why joint disciplinary commissions have so far met with limited success in undertakings, there being only a few exceptions, mainly in the civil service.

We have two possibilities for legal intervention. Firstly, the normal courts, both those of Appeal and that of Cassation,[1]

[1] There are twenty-seven regional Appeal Courts in France and one Court of Cassation which is in Paris. The role of the latter is to annul any improper decision of an inferior court, it takes no decisions of its own accord.

which have recently been provided with a special chamber known as the 'social chamber', and which provide the normal channel for collective conflicts and especially trade union action. Secondly, we have the 'Tribunal des Prud'hommes' which is the only French legal institution composed jointly of elected trade union and employers' representatives. But the trade unions are being allowed to put their grievances before it with increasing frequency. Furthermore, it should be stressed that the first part of this procedure is of a conciliatory nature and that in 30 per cent of all cases it succeeds.

No false conclusions should be reached about this for, despite the goodwill noticed among certain sectors of the legal profession, lawyers cannot correct the rules according to which a society is organized. The judge is powerless, sometimes voluntarily so, in the face of the law of property and the disciplinary power of the employers. There is no disciplinary law. Judges refuse to ascertain whether the misdeed committed is in proportion with the sanction decided upon by the employer. All they are concerned with is that the misdeed and the sanction both appear in the regulations of the undertaking. Furthermore, the forms, content and procedures of law are the direct outcome of an essentially rural and bourgeois form of civil law which is at odds with modern society and the new relationships between social groups. That is why collective law resulting from collective agreements and trade unions cannot be easily and efficiently applied. The amount of red tape, the lightness of the punishments imposed upon the offending undertakings, and the partiality of the law all go to make the French legal machine an excellent means of defence for the employers. We are having considerable difficulties in building an independent body of law and jurisdiction. It would even seem at present that the government plans to forbid trade union representatives to exercise the right to defend employees before a 'revised' form of tribunal which, furthermore, would do away with the election of the 'Prud'-homme' judges. This is an example of how fragile democracy really is in our country and how important this legal battle is.

At this point we can define the basic grounds for our concept of economic democracy which, for us, goes beyond the undertaking to encompass the whole population of the country. We shall return to certain characteristics of French society. Let us here consider only that which is relevant to the point under

E

discussion. On the one hand, the difficulty of negotiating with the employers has obliged the trade union movement to rely on forces outside the undertaking. On the other hand, the undertaking or the profession is too narrow an area for the achievements of certain requirements of the French trade union movement. This is the case with employment security problems and with the reduction in the disparity which goes beyond the active population to encompass the young and the underprivileged classes such as the old, the disabled, the sick and others. We shall not refer any more to the links between overall economic policy and the concrete situation in the undertaking. Suffice it to say that our daily experience, together with the ever-present experience of certain Western European countries (Spain, Portugal, Greece), proves that economic democracy cannot exist in the undertaking, or anywhere else, unless democracy has first been established at the national level.

THE INSTITUTIONS OF ECONOMIC DEMOCRACY AT NATIONAL LEVEL

As soon as we cross the threshold of the undertaking the climate changes and trade unionism and trade unionists assume their rightful place in the nation. They are recognized everywhere; in fact their rights and their word are too highly respected. There is no problem of representation here. The right of association was re-established in 1884 and included in the 1927 Labour Code, having previously been abolished by the French revolution and the Napoleonic Code. Nothing, however, was finally achieved. The great trade union federations were disbanded by the Vichy regime on 4 October 1941 only to reassemble and operate in secret. Not until 1945, with the victory of the allies and the resistance, was freedom for trade unions written into the preamble to the Constitution which was carried over into the 1958 Constitution in this respect. French trade unions are grouped into confederations which include both industrial federations and regional unions. They are based on a tradition of trade and inter-trade groupings. However, for historical reasons there are still a certain number of corporate and independent unions. Of these, the most important are the 'Confédération Générale des Cadres' (General Confederation of Managerial Staff) and the 'Fédération de l'Education Nationale' (Federation of National Education).

There will, however, be some people who will not fail to be unfavourably impressed by the multiplicity, or what we call the division, of French trade unionism. Apart from the fact that this situation is not limited to France, it can be explained in four ways. The control exercised by communist militants over the most important French trade union – the CGT, the division of the world into antagonist blocs, a very slow progression of the Christian masses towards socialism and a situation wherein the interplay of strength and of mentalities does not allow for compromise, suffice to explain, for the most part, why there exists the 'Confédération Générale du Travail' – CGT (General Confederation of Labour), the 'Confédération Générale du Travail – Force Ouvrière' – CGT–FO (General Confederation of Labour – Work Force), the 'Confédération Française Démo-cratique du Travail' – CFDT (Democratic French Labour Con-federation), the 'Confédération Générale des Cadres' – CGC (cf. above), the 'Fédération de l'Education Nationale' – FEN (cf. above) and the lingering remains of confessional trade unionism in the 'Confédération Française des Travailleurs Chrétiens' – CFTC (French Confederation of Christian Workers) which, in France, is called the CFTC – Maintenue'. In reality, the careful observer will note that the CGT and the CFDT hold sway.

Although the problem of representation hardly ever crops up, the negotiation problems already mentioned occur at col-lective level. But whereas in the undertaking the difficulty has so far lain in the rivalry between the trade union partners, the difficulties outside the undertaking concern the nature and scope of the obligation of the trade union and, to an extent, that of the employers. The right-wingers and the milder reformists seem to expect the trade union partner to guarantee social peace once he has obtained a 'good agreement'. This is a serious political misunderstanding into which even some of our friends are wont to slip. On the one hand, and this is the traditional view, the French trade union movement is basically a disputing body. If there is to be social peace then it depends upon the workers' being heard and heeded and the trade union is only their mouthpiece. On the other hand, it would seem that an organization constructed to work from the bottom up is expected to do an about-turn and impose the rulings resulting from negotiation downwards upon its members. A reversal of attitude is by no means impossible and the French trade union movement has, on all great national occasions (Resistance, Algerian War), been able to show its sense of responsibility, unlike other social groups. But the procedure to be used is very different from that imagined by those who have but one habit, that of commanding and of being obeyed and understood by force.

Having said that, the fact remains that economic democracy outside the undertaking depends on three negotiating mechanisms. The first is the collective agreement which is supposed to settle work problems in an industry or at regional level. For some time now, there has been a noticeable shift of interest from the collective agreement to the general agreement. The second mechanism is that of settlement which, in practice, is becoming more and more like consultation, the most familiar examples of which are the Economic and Social Council, the French Planning Commissions and, for example, the 'Commission Supérieure des Conventions Collectives' (High Commission for Collective Agreements) of the Ministry of Labour. The third and last, though not least, of these mechanisms is parliament and the executive which occasionally give the workers or the employers advantages that they have not requested, such as profit sharing for example.

Collective agreements, as we know them, date back to 1936, to the Popular Front and the Act of 11 February 1950. These provided industrial sectors or regions with an official agreement between the employers and the representative trade union organizations. They were the equivalent of a statutory schedule and their application was to some extent guaranteed by the courts and the Ministry of Labour. The Ministry could, on the advice of the High Commission for Collective Agreements, decide upon an extension which, after 1967, could affect both the undertakings in the sector or region concerned and those in neighbouring areas. Collective agreements must contain provisions concerning remuneration and working conditions. Until recently, however, such procedures were far from successful. There were many reasons for this. Because the employers' organizations were so dilatory, the trade union movement has always been necessary in order to ensure that the agreements were applied in the undertakings. As a result, trade union repression has resulted in the unions being very poorly represented in small undertakings or certain sectors of trade. On the other hand, the employers acquired the habit of negotiating to establish minimum acceptable conditions for the small undertakings to leave a completely free hand for the larger among them. Such an agreement was, therefore, totally lacking in interest to the majority of membership as the advantages obtained were often inferior to the actual situation of the workers in the dynamic under-takings. Some of the new and important areas such as working hours, training and safety were not included, thus making agreements unsuitable for modernizing labour law. Finally, as they were not contracts, the absence of a specific duration, coupled with the general lack of interest, meant that they expired, rarely to be renewed. The gains of May 1968 obliged the partners to take another look at the whole set-up. Only the future will show whether these agreements will enjoy a new lease of life after the legislative modifications at present being carried out come into effect.

To give the complete picture, we ought to mention three special collective agreements. These are the three national inter-occupational collective agreements which were signed by the employers and the big workers' trade union confederations and the managerial staff unions. That of 31 December 1958 established supplementary unemployment benefits to be paid out of funds run on a joint basis, and those of 13 March 1947 and 8 December 1961 established supplementary retirement benefits for managerial staff and wage earners.

Since 1967, but particularly since the strikes and negotiations of 1968, a new trend has become evident. The National Council of Employers and Trade Union Confederations, encouraged by the public authorities, are preparing procedures for *general agreements* concerning specific problems which will be negotiated at successive levels. The most important of these agreements cover, among other things, under-employment, security of employment, the monthly payment of wages and trade union law. For the time being these procedures do seem to be satisfactory in principle as they facilitate contact with the government. They allow representation at each level to play its part, while not excluding trade union action and occasionally strike action to blast through the obstacles set up by the employers to limit the scope of the agreements.

It is apparent that, side by side with these existing joint institutions, there exist instruments for settlement, consultation and study which look like the left-overs of a past age or the embryo of a tripartism to come. Such institutions are found at different levels of French social life and include the Economic and Social Council and the Planning Commissions.

Let us dwell a while on this famous French-style indicative planning. Let us recall that the original feature of this planning is that it groups, within a large number of commissions, all those factions and persons having something to say on a given subject. The original idea was to re-muster the war-torn population in order to rebuild both the French economy and, to some extent, a liberal nation. The institution was to reach its height during the IV Plan, around 1963-4, when it appeared to the nation as a truly innovating force as opposed to the parliamentary institutions on the one hand and the traditional ministries and their administrations on the other. This was a momentary period during which people thought that the Plan was going to free French society. Thereafter the conservative political powers, adopting a defensive attitude to the ideas expressed, *inter alia*, by the CFDT, once again took matters in hand. A minister was appointed to supervise the Plan Commissariat and the decision-taking procedures were institutionalized. That was the end of the enlightened technocracy. Since 1965, the Plan was to follow a political-cum-administrative ritual which deprived it of much of its interest as it appeared more satisfactory as a political philosophy than it was in practice. From that time on, the Plan was carried out in five stages:

(a) the examination of needs;
(b) the discussion of broad outlines in parliament and in the Economic and Social Council;
(c) the government decision;
(d) the preparation of a detailed Plan;
(e) the vote on the plan by parliament on the advice of the Economic and Social Council.

In fact, experience has left the bitter taste of failure in the mouths of those who had nurtured certain illusions regarding the softening up of the political structures through the intermediary of the economy. The Plan has stumbled on three types of problems: the transfer of economic decision-taking beyond national frontiers; a considerable revival of the influence exercised by private industry which left the social objectives of trade unionism with only a narrow margin for manoeuvre; and the refusal by all parties concerned to accept any formalized and accepted incomes policy. Therefore, when the CFDT officially withdrew from the Planning Commissions after the government had made its choice in September 1970, it made it quite clear to public opinion that something basic had changed in the nature of French planning and the balance of social relationships.

It would be a serious mistake to imagine that structures resulting from the principle of settlement are totally useless, but it would also be dangerous to think that they still offer a possible solution for our yearning for democracy. At the very most, they may remain the dream of an administrative and technical concept of democracy.

Lastly we shall deal with what was, and still is, the key to French economic democracy both within the undertaking and outside, that is *parliament* and the *executive*. Nowadays, no one is any too sure whether the executive power lies with the *government* or with the *President of the Republic* with regard to any given economic or social question. It is not so much the presence of the state which can create problems as its considerable power and the importance of its role in French trade union strategy. At this stage we can offer two explanations. The former concerns the influence of Marxist and communist ideologies on all left-wing mass movements. This ideology proposes that the move towards socialism would be facilitated by conquering the state machine through gaining a parliamentary majority. In this case, strength and attention are concentrated at this level. The second reason is that left-wing influence was, until the advent of Gaullism, always stronger outside the undertaking than within because of its predominant composition of civil servants and teachers. Parliament and government, therefore, appeared to be the best counterweight to the war that the employers were waging against trade unionism within the undertaking. This attitude persisted until 1968, that is, until the political left wing was able to cherish the hope of returning to power through the traditional channels. This situation becomes all the more paradoxical, especially for a Frenchman, as it has always been a principle of our trade unionism to keep at arms length from the parties in power or those likely to come to power. But this is still only a partial explanation and it would, no doubt, be advisable to look deeper into the Frenchman's concept of the state. We might effectively ask why the violent conflicts of May 1968, concerning the recognition of trade union law, the reduction of working hours and the increase in wages, had to be settled on the premises of a ministry in the presence of the then Prime Minister, Mr Pompidou.

The consequence of such a state of affairs has undoubtedly been a number of impressive legislative breakthroughs which make it possible for the employers and the government to act as the champions of social legislation in many areas on international bodies. Unfortunately, the facts are quite different. If the trade unions do not exert pressure to force the undertakings to comply with the law, it remains a dead letter. In the final analysis, the actual situation of the workers depends upon the real strength of the trade union movement. Consequently, when it comes to social legislation, participation in decision taking and profit sharing, some undertakings (occasionally large undertakings and even in the key industries) are lagging decades behind an institutionalized democracy which could, at times, appear as one of the most modern in the Western world.

There is yet another paradoxical aspect of French institutions. France is perhaps one of the rare countries in which the executive and its parliamentary majority try to impose a concept of economic democracy, of which none of the partners in the economy want any part, for a wide variety of reasons. This is the case when the workers are offered a financial interest, a share in the profits or a shareholding, which are the all-time utopias of the system. Public opinion, the workers and others concerned have, for a long time now, been fully aware of our views. There is no question, as far as we are concerned, of our settling for a share in the financial gain of the undertaking. We feel that the wage should amply fill this role and we are hard put to it to understand why they want, on the one hand, to give us an interest in the profits while on the other, they offer us absurdly low wages with a mass of productivity bonuses and anti-strike perks. We want to take a hand in decision taking, we want effectively to raise the standing of the working class within the undertaking. Experience has shown us that the direction and scope of decisions are not changed by a handful of shares nor by profit sharing, albeit in accordance with very modern methods. Furthermore, we consider that our status as workers is more than sufficient on its own and it embodies all the rights that they pretend to offer us in dribs and drabs. We will not exchange our dignity for freedom or a load of stock exchange gimmicks.

It is probably just as paradoxical that the same majority, the same government, offers the workers a financial interest in the undertaking with one hand, while with the other, by means of the 1967 Ordinance, it deprives them of control over the Social Security funds which it entrusts to the employers!

To conclude briefly this short description of the institutions of French economic democracy, we would point out that a certain degree of success on the part of those who represent the workers and the trade unions was offset by the absence or failure of negotiating procedures until 1968. This absence of democracy results in considerable disparities, each of which acts as a brake on the development of social progress, because any progress must now imply serious upheavals in the democratically most backward sectors. We will try to give some explanation of this somewhat unsatisfactory situation in order to convey a better appreciation of how the CFDT trade union position has built up into an ideology which alternately surprises, enthuses and disturbs international circles.

SOME OF THE BUGS IN FRENCH SOCIETY

Particularly for the benefit of foreign readers, there follows a quick survey of some of the familiar bugs of French society, a knowledge of which may help in understanding the underlying reasons for certain trends which may seem surprising at first sight.

Our first bug is *administrative centralism*. France is an old country, built from Paris outwards, in which Paris-made decisions frequently override local powers and particularities. Through all regimes – monarchy, empire and republic – can be found one constant factor, the elevation of France, the nation and state, above all its component parts. France is one and indivisible – it could not exist otherwise. There is no doubt that the implications of such a forced unification, where uniformity has not been achieved, have been well tempered at national level. But there are still provincial reactions, at times violent, which relate far more to the present than to the past. It is true that authority in Paris and the Paris region has taken advantage of its role as capital in order to increase its political and economic sway, to the detriment of certain other regions. But there are other, more important consequences. First of all there is the slow build-up of a centralized administration which likes to work unaided, which is happy to set itself above the citizen and which feels deeply and in good faith that it is the standard-bearer, the body responsible for the public weal. This administration busies itself in the social field, either to promote procedures which are sense-less except as far as it is concerned, such as settlement procedures, or to step into the shoes of the social factions while, at the same time, spontaneously injecting a few shots of social justice.

This system does, of course, have its advantages. It never-theless has the disadvantage of destroying all democratic be-haviour and attitudes which, from the point of view of the centralizer, can only cause reactions which might endanger national unity. The citizen has gradually become accustomed to not being able to change anything in his immediate environ-ment without applying to a 'préfet' or a minister. And when this citizen loses interest as a result in the whole process, complaints are heard that the masses are losing their sense of politics and the state machinery's role as substitute is strengthened.

Our second bug is *civil war*. It is quite true that civil war no longer involves deaths but there has been too much of such activity throughout French history for its influence to go unfelt. Each group still has a faithful and astonishingly vivid memory of all the massacres and all the extortion to which it has been subjected: the Cathares massacre, that of the Protestants, the execution of the Royal Family, the confiscation of the goods and chattels of the clergy, the terror of the guillotine, the massacre of the 'Commune', the repression of the trade unions, the hecta-comb of World War I, the capitulation of the Vichy government, General de Gaulle's appeal and the Resistance, the loss of Indo-China, the independence of Algeria with the advent of the Vth Republic, the general revolt, the terrorism of the 'Organisation de l'Armée Secrète' (OAS – Secret Army Organization) and the anti-terrorism, all of which led to the attempted assassination of de Gaulle and the execution of Bastien-Thiry. French history is also riddled with revenge and diehard hatred which divide this society more effectively and deeply than any democratic front and which sometimes form the substance of our politics. And when our dead are no longer sufficient for our needs, we take those of others. Czechoslovakia and Vietnam both provide grist for our mill when it comes to settling our debts.

We do not understand placid societies. Dare I say that they appear strange to many Frenchmen and that some of our left-wingers view them with a measure of disdain. We consider that a victory proves above all that we were intellectually right. But the losers often have the same attitude. It will be understood that to play politics and find compromises under such conditions is no easy matter. Such proceedings may, at times, even be totally prevented by the lack of general awareness. In such a case, it is very much better to pretend to do nothing if one is really forced to act. The balance of strength and of the problems within the nation is such that politics have, in a way, become Victorian. Let us refer to a few remarks made by a well-informed commentator about the French political left wing. In his opinion, the reason why the left follows a right-wing policy once in power, and why it is perpetually disappointed by its leaders, is mainly that it is not really interested in politics but rather in utopia, in ideology and in the romantic sensations of great historical commotions caused by the fusion of the working class masses. Situated as it is beyond the realms of reality and possibility, with the exception of the Communist Party, this left wing will probably never become a political alternative but merely an alternative to politics.

These bugs are made all the more effective by the international struggles in which the big nations are involved. Natoism, communism and Maoism are all aggravating the deepest of the old wounds. Consequently, although for the time being the greater part of the strength of the working classes is very definitely left wing, the parliamentary scene is blocked by a dominant majority party which serves to shield private interests and a technocracy of public and private administrations.

Finally, we should also mention the fact that France has had to cope with serious and occasionally painful problems in recent history. We had barely completed our reconstruction when we had to shed our Empire. Hardly had we finished with the quarrels of decolonization and welcomed the repatriots from North Africa, but we had to strengthen our productive machinery to meet international competition. The past thirty years have been hard.

FROM THE DEMOCRATIZATION OF THE ECONOMY TO DEMOCRATIC SOCIALISM – REFLECTIONS OF THE CFDT

Born of the development of the French Confederation of Christian Workers, at its 1964 Congress, the Democratic French Labour Federation has, since 1945, been moving towards the ideas and aims of French socialism from which it had been seperated by its origins. In 1970, the CFDT officially opted for socialism.

During this development, the political scene was gradually being monopolized by Gaullism. Social democracy was no longer a credible alternative to the regime. It was not until 1965 and 1967 that the different shades of socialism formed an alliance in the 'Fédération de la Gauche' (Left Wing Federation) and that the communists were able to kindle a spark of hope for victory which very slowly took shape at parliamentary level.

The events of May 1968, which brought the French left wing face to face with its responsibilities, also brought to light a split in the non-communist left-wing ranks which meant that it was impossible to put any political alternative that was not dominated by the Communist Party. After this failure, the regime was able to prepare for the elections which were to encourage a strengthening of the right wing in parliament.

The ideology of our confederation was to harden. It was to swing the idealist thoughts about the democratization of the economy which had filled the years 1953–62, in favour of democratic socialism. In the field, this operation was, since 1966, to go hand in hand with joint activity carried out with the CGT which, seriously upset in May 1968, struggled painfully back to its feet.

OUR CONCEPT OF ECONOMIC DEMOCRATIZATION (1960)

Concerted economy, democratic planning – these terms attempted to define the conditions necessary to stir and guide the economy towards economic progress and the proper solutions to the problems of the time – population growth, under-employment, equal sharing. We had decided to attain an economic regime, the development of which would be organized with the needs of the greatest number in mind.

Our trade union organization could not agree to the concerted economic prospects put forth by the senior civil servants. We felt that although agreement between the representatives of public or private capital and the heads of the big administrations could prove fruitful, it would not coincide with the real wishes of the workers. As we said at the time, the workers could not fail to lose out of the concerted economy were to be no more than a chamber orchestra in which the private technocrats were to play the violins, and the state technocrats the flutes, while the market economy wielded the baton. The rest of the story was to prove that we were right to think that it would be in vain to demand great efforts from the workers without letting them participate directly in what was going on.

Technical development, the concentration of economic power, the size and urgency of the needs to be met both in France and in the world at large, called, in our opinion, for a planned economy based on democracy. We wanted such an economy to be run in a rational manner by the community, with its eyes open, in such a way as to ensure that the needs of the largest number would be met. Having, on principle, repudiated Soviet bureaucratic centralization, we set forth what we called *democratic planning* in which the planning, implementation and techniques should leave as much leeway as possible for freedom of action. At the time, we went a long way in imagining what the operation and methods of such a system might be like. Maybe we underestimated the technical and political conditions necessary for such an undertaking; unless, at the time, it struck us more as a democratic variation on the concerted economy than as a revolution yet to be carried out. Be that as it may, the result of this ideological work is that we know perfectly well where we want to go even if we are not sure how to get there. Maybe we have broken the back of the job.

We have thought about definition of economic democracy. And now that we are discussing the democratization of the economy, we know that it is not just what goes on in the undertaking, but also what is happening in the country as a whole where all citizens and all political factions must, within democratic institutions, put the economy to work for the greatest number. There are, therefore, three facets to this democratization:

- a guarantee of human rights at work – right to a wage, to security, to a job and to education;
- a share in the responsibilities of running the economic system within the undertaking and in the national economy;
- a participation in democratic planning and in all the political institutions in the country.

At one time, we envisaged a division between the executive and the legislative within the undertaking. The preparation, implementation and perfection of long- and short-term aims and their supervision, required the workers' representatives to sit on the joint boards (the legislature). The technical, administrative and financial management constituted the executive power. But this view did not take us very far from the theories of self-management or co-management, which are strictly limited to the economic field. As far as we were concerned, it was a clear case of once again setting the economy to work for mankind. This was particularly so as the gap between the owners and the wielders of power in the undertaking was widening. The only aim shared by the old and the new power was the quest for maximum profit which was given pride of place among the other aims of the economy.

For the trade union movement and for socialists who follow the Christian and Proudhon traditions in particular, an economic democracy is an economy which aims, above all, to satisfy the needs of mankind in a responsible society. That is why we want the workers to have real responsibilities whereas the capitalist and soviet regimes simply dream of integrating them in the undertaking. The worker must not cease to be a citizen because he enters an undertaking. Nor can the undertaking become shut in on its own interests. For this reason, we believe that the democratic institutions must form a continuous web rising through all significant levels and starting, of course, with the undertaking, passing also through the industrial sector and the region to arrive, finally, at the state. The existence of a non-technocratic economy must depend on the existence and smooth running of this democratic web.

It was with this in mind that, in 1960, I said, 'A working class without responsibilities will never give of its best. Factory managers controlled from afar by boards of directors, can, without greatly endangering their situation, make mistakes which harm the workers and their families. Similarly, where industry is concerned, mistakes in management could harm the nation. Worker participation and control, provided that they cater to the demands of justice and dignity, will also be far from negligible elements in the progress of economic activity.'

The CFDT was neither heard nor heeded until May 1968. Now many political or industrial leaders would like to turn the clock back, once again to hear this kind of talk. As a result of the conservatism of the employers and the demands of the workers and the students, we have progressed, leaving others to dwell on opportunities lost. Having made it clear where we wanted to go, now, after our 1970 Congress, we almost know how we are going to get there.

WHAT 1968 HAD TO OFFER

The events of May 1968 managed to blow sky high many of the political ideological effigies which had, until then, been erected. Gaullism had considerably cut down on democratic life so that the powers-that-be shed little light on what they were doing for the benefit of the masses who were considered as being passive. As one journalist put it, 'France was getting fed up'. The undercurrent in the universities, the sudden revelation of police repression and the many social disputes which had built up, were to rouse the workers who sprung into action with surprising and unexpected vigour, determination and responsibility.

This explosion caused no problems for the CFDT. Workers and students both moved spontaneously towards broader democratization which we wanted and for which we had trained and fought hard. But it appeared to be necessary to revise our ideology in order to include the outcome of the May events, in other words, the requirements and possibilities for responsibility, equality and decentralization. At another level, the continued absence of political negotiation under the Gaullist monopoly caused such a block that it resulted in politics within the undertaking crystallizing into action groups and party units that were, at times, anti-trade union. So much so, that after May 1968 the various factions within the undertaking frequently changed. Since then, there has been something other than trade unionism in some big undertakings which has forced that very unionism to go a step further in the political field or else to become simply a negotiating machine.

At the same time, trade unionism was to be confronted with new problems which were situated beyond its traditional field. French trade unionism has always taken a very broad view – the CGT protested against the Marshall Plan and we protested against the war in Algeria and agitated for decolonization. With the running of the Social Security funds as a starting point, we dealt with health and hospitalization problems. We did not, however, take an active enough part in a certain number of new problems such as housing, education, town planning and the deterioration of the environment, and we left the main responsibility for these problems to others. Now we must tackle them head-on, for they would appear to be of direct concern to the workers. This is particularly necessary because the solutions to these problems often come up against the same interests and forces as we have to combat in the undertakings. We are convinced that they will not be satisfactorily solved unless we also become involved.

DEMOCRATIC SOCIALISM BASED ON SELF-MANAGEMENT

In view of this situation and the way in which our earlier proposals were received, it has become clear that our demand for a democratization of the economy will have to be based on three requirements, i.e. public ownership of the main means of production, democratic planning and self-management.

The public ownership of the main means of production strikes us as a necessary condition if decision taking in the undertaking is to be exercised in a democratic way. This, in fact, makes it possible to hand management over to democratically run, decentralized bodies – undertakings, boroughs or regions – which, depending on the case, are the most appropriate to ensure that the task of management is handled to the general good. This will also enable us to move closer to our socialist and communist brethren. But we are also aware that this socialization does not sufficiently guarantee the practice of democracy. We know the economic price that had to be paid and, even more, the restrictions imposed on freedom and on collective and individual responsibility as a result of the right of public ownership exercised by a state or party bureaucracy.

Likewise, the state should not exercise direct management. Its job is to implement democratic planning which will allow the economy to satisfy the needs of the greatest number. This would be done by means of different methods of supervision and encouragement, many of which the French government already possesses and which simply need to be put into effect. This concept of the Plan, which the CFDT has been propagating for more than ten years, is now generally admitted by most workers. Although it is up to the country's political leaders democratically to decide upon the objectives of the Plan, they must not go beyond the general outlines and they must ensure that they are effectively in the national interest. It is the job of the undertakings to achieve these aims under the best possible conditions and to decide on their general policy in the light of the goals and aims set down by the community.

Lastly, self-management for us means that all the workers in an undertaking would take an equal and effective hand in determining their activities and the organization of their work. Basically, it implies that the persons in authority would be elected by the workers themselves and that decision taking would be effectively decentralized when it came to their actual application. Naturally, under present circumstances, there is no question of the trade union movement and the factory trade union branch in particular, becoming a business management body. Our experience and our temperament lead us to believe that the trade union movement must safeguard its role of encouraging democracy, training men, supervising decisions, protecting the workers, regardless of the degree to which society has been democratized. The trade union movement must remain, as far as the workers are concerned, a guarantee of liberty, and, if necessary, of revolt against any economic management systems that might be diverted from their aim.

Consequently, as a result of our 1970 Congress, our concept of democratic socialism went far beyond our old ideas of economic democratization. The main differences are in the public ownership of the main means of production and trade, an effective and highly decentralized redistribution of power and increased trade union autonomy resulting, in particular, in the refusal of the trade union movement to have anything to do with management by workers, regardless of the virtues of the existing system.

PRINCIPAL OBJECTIVES AND EXISTING MEANS

None of us believes that such an aim can be achieved overnight. It will take us a long time to get where we want to go. We must also take account of opinion, political changes and trade unions in other countries. This will call for perseverance, but we are determined to go on to the end. Experience shows that our ideas are catching on among the workers. We must also be ready, when the time comes, to help them build up the framework that they want for their community. For the time being, we are working to explain, to disclose democratically our lines of activity and thought to the workers, trade unions and political parties. It will be up to them all to help to enrich a still far from perfect model and to create the conditions propitious to its implementation.

AN IMMEDIATE AIM – DO AWAY WITH UNILATERAL DECISIONS

First of all, workers must no longer be regarded as cogs in the economic machine, but they must be allowed their say at all levels of society from the undertaking to the government. Taking this from the point of view of the undertaking, it means a generalization of *negotiation* by the signing of *undertaking agreements* which are more than just simple extensions of a collective agreement. Such agreements should not cover simply real wage structures and rates, working hours, collective agreements, but also general rules of the work contract such as the conditions for the taking on and dismissal of workers and the content and conditions relating to vocational training. An effective system of supervision, too, should exist in the undertaking.

In this respect, we should clarify what we mean by negotiation. We made this quite clear after the Prime Minister, Mr Chaban-Delmas, had tried to put before the country a wage agreement which had been signed in a nationalized undertaking, claiming it to be a contract for social peace and a revolution! As far as we are concerned, negotiation is one instrument among many, an extra means of broadening freedom and of repulsing the pressures which management try to apply to the workers, while at the same time obtaining and guaranteeing social advantages for them. Consequently we could not agree that, through undertaking agreements, our most basic trade union rights, and mainly our right to strike, should be questioned in an underhand manner. We are, and we intend the trade union organization to remain, a weapon to defend the workers.

Our second aim is to bring about a change in the hierarchical operation and authority in the undertaking. We will no longer stand for those in the higher wage brackets helping themselves to an excessive slice of the payroll and thus to an oversized portion of well-being and advancement. But we want to go beyond this and, in that respect, May 1968 proved that we really could do so. We want to transform the relationships between man and his place of work, starting with the way in which orders are given. We can only do away with the arbitrary elements if we change the way in which the administration of the under-taking operates and, to start with, the way in which its members are selected and appointed. The hierarchy must not be used by the management as a weapon against the workers. We intend to change things and to establish a system whereby all the employees will have a say in the appointment of this hierarchy, just as we intend them to have a say in the aims and methods of the undertaking.

TWO COMPLEMENTARY INSTRUMENTS – TRADE UNIONISM AND POLITICS

First of all, it is up to the trade union system to involve all workers, white and blue collar, highly skilled and technical, regardless of sex, age and nationality, in the struggle for demo-cratic socialism. We must, therefore, democratize our own trade union life in order that the trade union branch in the under-taking may be an example of the sort of democracy for which we are striving. The work of the branch must not rest on the shoulders of a single man, of a leader, but must be the work of a team which is democratically elected and run, which consults regularly with the workers, even in the backwaters of the under-taking, in order that they may all feel that the trade union is first and foremost their own.

It is also the trade unions' job to standardize the behaviour of the stewards in the various representative institutions within the undertaking. The trade union section must take the lead in de-fining the plan of action, in assessing the balance of power, in negotiating and in organizing the workers. It is there that the types and forms of action to be taken should be planned. It should form the basis of trade unionism rooted in the hopes and problems of the workers.

As we see it, the shop stewards should present the workers' problems as they see and live them. They should become the persons who disclose the life of the undertaking both to the management and to the trade union branch while, at the same time, continuing to supervise the application of the regulations and agreements.

The factory committee, for its part, should basically be a clearing house for economic and social information, an embodi-ment of the workers' right to be kept informed of the present and future activity of their undertaking. It should be here that the situation is analysed with a view to criticism, but under no circumstances should it be a negotiating body.

We also feel that the health and safety committee could play a more dynamic role. The workers do, in fact, want to change their working conditions and such change is brought about as a result of their own initiative. At the present time, safety takes second place to the quest for maximum profits, whereas we intend that it should become a permanent requirement in the undertaking. It might, in certain cases, be up to our brethren on the committee to take direct action, thereby exercising their capacity for self-management in a limited, though essential field.

We should, finally, impose negotiation and democracy on the civil service. To start with we must make a careful distinction between two realities that some people would like to see confused for their own ends, i.e. the state as a public body and the state as an employer. An end must be put to the conservatism and paternalism of the leaders and the heads of departments, and all the instruments of democracy in the undertaking, all trade union rights, including the most precious of all in its totality, namely, the right to strike, must be introduced. We have to see that all places of work are bathed in the same light of freedom, responsibility and dignity.

In the knowledge that trade unionism alone cannot change the methods and objectives of a company, especially if, as we believe, democratic socialism is the only correct path to democratization in the undertaking, trade unionism must work hand-in-glove with the political parties having the same general trends as itself and should not delude itself that it can act as a substitute for them. This gives rise to many problems in a country like France where we do not have party–trade union relationships as our British, German and even Italian brethren have managed to create.

What is more, we do not have a big labour or social democratic party with an eye to a governmental majority or leadership which is able to federate most of the left-wing elements. And in a country which tends rather to accentuate its ideological differences, the main political opposition is the Communist Party – a situation which makes things a bit difficult for the democrats.

That is why trade unionism exists, to a certain extent, with a number of traditions and requirements. Although it agrees to be politically committed to help, for example, in the revival of a socialist left wing in France, it will not become integrated in a party, a state or an economic policy. Its autonomy does not prevent it from having political preferences or from being in sympathy with one experience or another, but it feels that it is its own affair how far it goes in its commitments to events over which it intends to continue to exercise complete control insofar as those events affect it.

Lastly, trade unionism must learn to co-exist in the undertaking with political movements. Our idea of a true democracy makes it almost inevitable that the two types of organization should exist side by side in the place of work. This is especially true as the economics and politics of the undertaking and the state are daily becoming more intricately intertwined. We would also do well to think about the responsibility of each of these organizations when it comes to setting off any given type of activity, although we cannot, out of hand, exclude the possibility of political organizations deciding to indulge in political activity within the undertaking. We must learn to take our trade unionism out of the undertakings and to join battle in other fields. We will find other allies such as parties, associations and committees whose traditions, language and operational methods will frequently differ but with whom we shall have to launch joint campaigns. The November 1970 agitations which were organized in Paris at the request of all the left-wing parties and the regional CGT and CFDT groups to protest about the shortage of public transport facilties, was a first and important step in that direction. The mobilization and socialist organization of consumers and users will undoubtedly be one of the prime tasks of the next few years. Let us say that, for the time being, by eliminating the concept of the leading party and that of the enlightened vanguard and the temptations of a trade unionism which claims to be sufficient unto itself, we have mapped out a field for research and action.

UNITE THE WORKERS OF EUROPE AND THE WORLD

We have over the past few years made considerable progress both in the international organizations and in the big undertakings. To give but one example, we would mention the March 1970 clash in the Liquid Air Co., when, at the request of the CFDT/Chemical

Industries, and thanks to the International Federation of Chemical Workers, the German, Belgian and Italian trade unions refused to allow the undertakings in those countries to make deliveries to the customers of the Liquid Air Co. We are very pleased by this development, for we feel that, at the present time, professional action, directly affecting the workers in the undertakings, will be the prime mover in creating an awareness in those workers of the European and international proportions of their main problems.

We think that we must continue and develop what is currently being done. Contacts must be increased, regardless of the nature of affiliations with international confederations, in order that men may come to know and understand one another. Joint aims must be defined in the big social groups and the uninspiring, slow and costly job of confrontation, not with the upper echelons but with the workers who are the driving force behind our movements, must be encouraged. By working ceaselessly for a powerful European trade union movement, we shall unite mankind, draw together its ideologies, define its aims, activate and direct its activities and try to change the balance of power in the economy. This joint activity of European trade unionism should prepare the way for the kind of Europe that is possible, that of the people, and, in the final analysis, that of socialism and democracy. Faced with the dominating trend of the big employers and the banking groups, European trade union activity offers a guarantee of democracy. But let us also get it into our heads that we shall not build a workers' Europe unless a European brand of left-wing socialism also emerges in the political field, which is solidly based on the needs and hopes of the greatest number, and whose aim is a thoroughgoing social change.

Logic here leads us to include the Third World in our plans, not as a generous extension of our ideas but rather because it offers a key to the future. In the years to come, international trade union solidarity will require a minimum of links and common aims in order to carry through the struggle against the big multinational undertakings and the dictatorships that they encourage throughout their business networks. This struggle is not 'something else', 'another type of problem', it is exactly the same struggle, to which the immigrant brethren in each of our countries bear witness. The CFDT cannot avoid this problem since it is so central to our discerned role which, in the undertakings and various trades, is to shake the mass of workers and French and European public opinion into awareness. This is of particular interest to the French, who having been the first to broadcast liberty, equality and fraternity, are now among the most prosperous vendors in the world of arms, most of which are brought against oppressed peoples.

Finally, the main concern of the CFDT is to achieve true democracy. We want to give freedom of speech and action to as many people as possible and immediately so to those with something to say and do. We want the workers to be free and to be able to see this freedom materialize in their acts – man was made to create. In witnessing the implementation of the most formidable conditioning machine man has ever known, and drawing strength from the tremendous scientific and technical boom, we realize with concern that man is being manipulated by the economic machine and its undertakings from birth to death, from sunrise to sunrise and from East to West. In fact, a few groups of men are taking advantage of power and the possibilities of our civilization.

If we wish, once again, to sway the course of history as we have done in the past, we shall have to start by coming into line with the modern world. This 'new Rome' has three characteristics. The first is a realization of potential in human and natural sciences and techniques; the second, a draining of the contents of the formal existing structures (and these include the undertaking, the occupation, the region and the nation, all of which are but facades for power), and the third is an awareness that, although this power is still economic, it is above all political in the deepest sense of the term. The economy ceased long ago to be a secondary power which needed only to be compensated to keep it on the straight and narrow for the common good. Whoever is in control of the economy now has total power.

In the face of economic conditioning, we must win back our right to be heard by means of better training and the use of independent and modern information handling and diffusion systems. The mobility of capitalism must be matched by trade union mobility. Our occupational branch structures and national confederations in some cases hold us back and it is time that we reviewed our tools in order to stand up and face the big multinational undertaking and monetary power. Finally, we must match conservative political power with a political movement that will achieve economic democracy. This is what the CFDT wants to do through the indispensable autonomy of trade unionism. We think that we shall find many others around, with and ahead of us intent on pursuing the same path.

Chapter 5

Yugoslavia

MILAN RUKAVINA
President, Central Board, Industry and Mining Workers' Union of Yugoslavia

Since workers' self-management represents a part of the overall social self-government in Yugoslavia, it is quite difficult to deal with the relevant problems within a limited space. This paper will be dealing, therefore, with workers' management in industry only.

Distinctions should be indicated also between the workers' self-management in Yugoslavia and a whole range of forms of workers' participation in decision making in other countries. Particularly so because in different capitalist, socialist and developing countries there are diverse forms of workers' involvement in decision making, particularly in industry. In the capitalist countries there are various forms of workers' participation, workers' control and industrial democracy among the conditions of hired labour relations. In the socialist countries there are also certain forms of workers' participation in decision making, which for the most part are accomplished through the work of trade unions, whose role in this area is regulated by legislative acts. In some developing countries, along with the programmes for construction of a socialist society, certain forms of workers' participation in decision making are being introduced.

The fundamental difference between workers' self-management in Yugoslavia and workers' participation in decision making practised in other countries is that in Yugoslavia the social conditions are being created in which self-management is possible and in which the workers decide on their own destiny, while in other countries, workers' participation in decision making is of limited extent, or simply of an advisory nature.

Workers' self-management in Yugoslavia in the full sense of the term has been made possible by the following basic factors:

- power is in the hands of the working class;
- social ownership over the means of production plays a dominating part in the economic and social life of the country, particularly in industry;
- the political system and legal order are subject to continued changes depending on the stage of development of the workers' and social self-government;
- the economic system, economic policies and planning system are becoming increasingly subordinated to self-management; the power of the state apparatus is increasingly being curbed, and progressively transforming it into an instrument of workers' and social self-government. Alongside this the power of the working people is growing through advancing workers' and social self-government;
- a broadening of political and economic decentralization is being accomplished, together with a transfer of basic power in management from the wider Federation or Republic level, to the narrower socio-political communes and enterprises;
- under progressive Yugoslav legislation, the enterprises are the basic cornerstones of the plan and the planning process, and of other central features;
- the self-managers are gradually achieving an agreement between the enterprises, the enterprise councils and socio-political committees on various matters of individual and common interests.

It should also be borne in mind that in Yugoslavia workers' self-management is an integral part of social self-government, that is, of its socialist democracy. A socialist democracy implies for us the participation of citizens in decisions on all questions in which workers' self-management has a dominant part. Consequently, it is only natural that workers' self-management was first introduced in industry as a basic area of the economy. Workers' self-management is not to us a mere economic democracy, as interpreted by some theoreticians in the world – it is a political democracy as well. In the system of workers' self-management, the workers decide not only on the division of the income of their work organization and the distribution of their individual incomes, they also decide on whom they will elect to the parliaments of the socio-political communities, from the commune to the federation, to the particular workers' councils which make each enterprise equal in rights in the parliaments through which the workers' interests should come to a most direct expression in the formation of the general social and economic policies. Likewise, the workers take a direct part in the elections to other bodies of the self-governing interest committees and organizations, such as social insurance, education committees, and the like.

It must be stressed that, with its existence, results and experience which is enriched daily, the workers' self-management system in Yugoslavia is not an experiment, but the twenty-year-old reality of a socio-political and economic system which has fully justified its own existence. Within a system of this kind the worker is increasingly becoming a person who decides, and less and less an object of decisions made elsewhere. Through the system of workers' self-management the well-known idea of Marx–Engels–Lenin is realized in which power exercised on behalf of the workers is transformed into power exercised *by the workers themselves*. Given conditions of ever-greater emancipation of the human individual and increasingly rapid technological advance, this transfer of power becomes one of the basic prerequisites of social development.

WHY WORKERS' SELF-MANAGEMENT WAS INTRODUCED IN YUGOSLAVIA

In order to understand the basic reasons for introducing workers' self-management in Yugoslavia, it is necessary to know that in the post-war period Yugoslavia was an undeveloped, agrarian country wherein 75 per cent of the population lived on agriculture just as it had been in the pre-war period. The industrial potential had for the most part been destroyed during the war, which aggravated the otherwise grave economic situation of the country and was coupled with a tremendous shortage of skilled personnel. The bureaucratic apparatus was growing in power and influence, whilst the socialist countries imposed an economic blockade on Yugoslavia, and the capitalist countries exerted different economic and political pressures on her. In such a situation, any further development of socialism had to follow one of two paths only. One was to strengthen and develop state centralism which had produced numerous harmful effects but had already been established in practice in other socialist countries; the other was to introduce workers' self-management, of which there was very little practice and experience, but which enabled the worker in his role as manager to express his whole being through his activity. The League of Communists of Yugoslavia, the Confederation of Trade Unions, and other socio-political organizations decided on the latter path, aware of the great responsibility they had undertaken in the historic development of the country and in the development of the international labour movement. In this way the working class of Yugoslavia has made a significant contribution to workers' participation in decision making on a world scale.

The basic reasons for the introduction of workers' self-management in Yugoslavia were:

1. Only through workers' self-management was it possible to preserve the economic and political independence of the country and to facilitate the development of our society and the increasing emancipation of the human individual.
2. In this way the management of the enterprises by the workers themselves could be realized and their interest in and sense of responsibility for the results and successes of their work increased.
3. Through the operation of workers' management the power of the state apparatus could be restricted, socialist democracy developed, and the initiative of the working class fostered as completely as possible.
4. This corresponded with the teachings of the socialist theoreticians ranging from Thomas Moore and Robert Owen, Prudhon and Bernstein, to Marx and Engels, and was based on various experiences yielded by the history of the international labour movement, particularly from the Paris Commune period and the early days of the USSR during Lenin's lifetime.
5. In discharging its role of ideological guidance in the Yugoslav society, the League of Communists of Yugoslavia, freed from dogma, focussed its creative powers on the application of scientific socialist thought to the Yugoslav conditions.

DEVELOPMENT OF WORKERS' SELF-MANAGEMENT IN YUGOSLAVIA

Some forms of workers' self-management, while of limited range, were found already in various revolutionary actions of the working class in the period after World War I and in the course of the Peoples' Liberation War 1941–5. On the initiative of the League of Communists, experimental workers' councils with advisory powers were introduced in 1949, while workers' self-management in Yugoslavia can be spoken of in more definite terms since 1950.

The development of the workers' self-management and of the socio-political and economic system has passed through several stages over the last twenty years.

The first period – from 1950, the year of the passing of the Basic Law on management of the state economic enterprises and higher economic associations by their work collectives, which was adopted by the then Federal Assembly – till 1954, when under the influence of workers' self-management some changes were brought about in the economic system. During that period the work collectives did not dispose of the means of production; the state controlled distribution so that workers' management was limited in scope. The work collectives were not entitled to buy or sell capital assets for more rational business operation; nor were they stimulated to use the means of production as efficiently as possible.

The second period lasted from 1954, when the changes in the economic system took place, till 1957, when the 1st Congress of the workers' councils was held. In the course of 1954 the means of production were handed over to the work collectives for their own disposal. The enterprises were free to buy and sell the means of production in keeping with the needs of their own production, which all made the economic life more dynamic and rational. The state imposed royalties to be paid by the enterprises on the total value of the means of production, which in fact created a unique ownership relation of the state to the means of production. In the course of that period, the communal system was introduced which implied further development of the self-management principle in Yugoslavia, and *ipso facto* further development of political democracy and decentralization in the socio-political system. This also had direct influence on the development of workers' self-management, the enterprises having become even more independent in their own development. At that stage relations with the USSR and other socialist countries came to be normalized, which also helped create more favourable international political and economic conditions for the development of the self-management system. So in 1955–6

Yugoslavia had normal and friendly relations with nearly every country in the world, having attained the renown of a champion for equal relations among nations and states. That brought about the powerful economic expansion of the country. Thus, for instance, in 1956 alone, the industrial production rose by 62 per cent in comparison with 1952. The situation required an even more autonomous position of the enterprises and, consequently, further changes in the economic system, for which demands were voiced particularly at the 1st Congress of the workers' councils.

The third period covers the time from the 1st Congress of workers' councils in 1957 until the introduction of the economic and social reforms of 1965. Following the demands of Congress, which analysed the development in the preceding period, and due to the inevitability of the development of workers' self-management, the enterprises were given the right to regulate autonomously the division of their net income and fix the personal income or wage levels for themselves. The state still disposed of the predominantly major portion of the surplus labour, investment funds and funds for various economic interventions. During that period work groups or economic units were introduced into those parts of the enterprise in which the gross output and net income could be established. This was a further step in the development and extension of workers' self-management. The enterprises also became more independent and acquired wider rights of passing their own plans of development, operational programmes and various sets of rules. At the same time, the enterprises were enabled, in the statutes which they passed autonomously, to express their specific features more completely. During that period the material foundation of workers' self-management was still not satisfactory because the role of the state was still predominant in this respect. The restricted material basis of workers' self-management was one of the obstacles to a more rapid and intensive economic activity, to more rational business operation, and higher living standards for workers, which all began to develop more strongly only with the introduction of economic reforms.

The fourth period has been unfolding from the beginning of the implementation of the economic reform measures in June 1965, and is still going on at the present moment. The economic reform is of particular significance to the economic development of Yugoslavia, because it was not an economic reform in its literal sense only, but an overall socio-economic reform – which essentially distinguishes it from the classical economic reforms usually implying or signifying changes in foreign currency exchange rates, changes in prices, and the like relatively minor modifications. The 1965 reform indicated essential changes in the further development of those socialist social relations on which workers' and social self-government were founded. We initiated the process of gradually shifting the surplus value of work towards *necessary* work; that is, the process of struggle for a dominating control of producers over the surplus of work. We then entered a new period – the period in which the immediate producer, the one who creates, through associated work in the socially owned means of production, is to master the entire social production cycle.

It was not possible to achieve the above objectives without substantial changes in the political system as well, including changes in the Constitution.

The most important targets of the economic reform were:

– shift from the extensive to a more intensive economic activity;
– better organization of work, better utilization of capacities, and an increase in work productivity;
– higher quality as a result of involvement in the world market.

One of the specific objectives of the reform was also to strengthen the material basis of workers' self-management by enabling the enterprises to become the organs for extending participation in production, taking the living standard of workers as a primary objective. Self-management becomes increasingly focussed on various forms of direct management by workers, thus enabling the workers to decide directly on more and more questions which affect them. That period is also characterized by the further development of autonomy in the enterprises which become increasingly independent in decisions affecting their own development; in the course of this development they become ever more dependent on the working of the market laws, and less on the state and its apparatus. That autonomy is not reflected in the operation of the business policies only, but even more in the organization of self-management in the enterprises.

The trade unions have played a significant part in preparing drafts and in implementing the objectives of the economic and social reforms.

CONTENTS OF SELF-MANAGEMENT

The fundamental socio-economic relation in Yugoslavia is self-management in the enterprise. That is an inalienable basis of the position and role of the individual in Yugoslav society, who is increasingly coming to shape his own destiny. Through self-management in the process of associated work, the working man is, as we have said, coming to the fore in decision making, instead of being an object on whose behalf somebody else is deciding. The state with its administrative organs, regardless of what it may be called, is otherwise liable to usurp the workers' decision-making right. In this system, the man associated in work is also becoming a basic sharer in power who, through continued social change, is implementing and improving workers' self-management.

Social, as opposed to state-ownership over the means of production, is one of the cornerstones of workers' self-management. The essence of social ownership over the means of production is reflected in the fact that capital assets are entrusted for direct management to the workers who operate them in their own interest and in the interest of the social community, being answerable to each other and to their social community. Bearing in mind that nobody, except society as a whole, has the right of ownership over the socially owned means of production – neither the socio-political community, nor the enterprise, nor the individual worker is allowed on any legal ownership basis to appropriate the product of socially organized work, or to manage and dispose of the socially owned means of production, or independently to determine the conditions of income distribution. Consequently, *it is the work of the individual alone* on which is based the appropriation of social production, and management of the socially owned resources.

Therefore, the right to workers' self-management is acquired only on the grounds of one's entering into associated work, that is, on the basis of one's employment, together with fellow-workers, in an enterprise.

Self-management in the enterprise includes the following rights and responsibilities of the working people:

– to run their own enterprise directly and indirectly, through the management organs elected by the entire body of workers;
– to lay down the forms, rights and responsibilities of direct and

indirect management bodies and other executive organs by the statute of the work organization;
– to decide on the use of the socially owned means of production in such a manner as will result in the greatest possible benefit for the enterprise and for the social community;
– to regulate the socio-economic relations between the sections of the enterprise and among workers themselves by statute and the various sets of rules;
– to organize production or other activity;
– to take care of the development of their enterprise and adopt suitable plans for its work and development;
– to decide on shifts in production, and other questions related to the business operation of their enterprise;
– to divide the income of their enterprise into personal incomes and other funds such as business operation funds, social welfare funds, reserve funds, etc.;
– to distribute personal incomes on the basis of the principle of remuneration according to work results;
– to decide on their own employment relations;
– to organize and improve safety at work and leisure time schemes;
– to take care of their own education;
– to promote all conditions for improvement of their personal and social standards;
– to secure public inspection of their work, and internal supervision;
– to decide on the separation or merger of sections of their enterprise, etc.

The concern of the self-management system should not be confined to the enterprise only. Some broader forms and shapes are also emerging in Yugoslav practice, in which the interests of individual enterprises find their expression in combination as, for instance, economic associations, economic chambers, chambers of work communities in the parliaments at all levels, and other self-government common-interest communities.

It should be pointed out that any act violating the self-management rights of the working people is anti-constitutional, while any act of a workers' management organ, irrespective of the way in which it has been passed, is likewise illegal if it does not observe the constitutional and legal provisions. Therefore, both the workers in the enterprises and the assemblies of the

F

socio-political communities are entitled to legal protection in their work and to self-management.

ORGANIZATION OF SELF-MANAGEMENT

Before explaining the way in which self-management is organized, it is necessary to note that under the positive provisions of the Yugoslav economy there are two categories of enterprise in respect of the self-management organization: enterprises employing up to thirty workers, and those employing over thirty workers. In the former, all the employed represent the workers' council; therefore, they decide directly on every question, electing the management board as their executive organ only. In enterprises employing over thirty workers, the self-management system is organized in accordance with the specific features of the enterprise.

Until December 1968 the legislation provided for a uniform organizational arrangement of workers' management in all enterprises. The practice has proved, however, that there are many specificities in the development of workers' self-management in different enterprises, and that the organization of self-management should be adjusted accordingly. Hence the constitutional Amendment No. 15 of December 1968, under which the enterprises, by their own internal acts and statutes, independently determine their self-management structure and regulate other relevant questions. Still, the above Amendment lays down the following obligatory self-management organs:

- workers' council, entrusted with certain management functions;
- collective organs and individual organ, entrusted with certain executive functions, these organs are answerable for their work to the workers' council which elects them.

In this way the enterprises, starting from the general constitutional principles of workers' self-management and the principles laid down in Amendment 15, fix autonomously their own organization of management by workers. Although every enterprise determines the structure of its own self-management by its statute in keeping with its specific features, there are still forms which are characteristic to all of them.

Workers' self-management is carried out in both a direct and indirect way. The legislation and orientation of trade unions underline direct decision-making by workers as a basic task in the development of self-management, although owing to the size of the enterprise and other objective reasons, this cannot be realized always and everywhere. That is why the work collectives transfer to their executive organs certain rights of decision making, on those questions where members of the work collective are not able to decide directly.

Direct management by the workers takes the following forms:

– meetings of workers of a work unit, section of the enterprise or of the whole enterprise;
– election and recall of the indirect organs of workers' management;
– referendum; and
– initiative.

The *indirect forms of management* are:
– the council of the work unit, or section;
– the workers' council of the enterprise.

The indirect management organs have their executive bodies: starting with the management, or business board, the director (general manager) of the enterprise, and section heads.

The example of the chemical combine, Zagreb, will serve to illustrate the rights and responsibilities of the above self-management organs. The enterprise employs 2,617 workers, and consists of eighteen work units of production, two units of auxiliary service, and nine units of common service. The basic activity of the combine is as follows:

– production of paints and varnish;
– production of pigments and organic paints;
– production of paints for ships;
– production of printing paints;
– production of pesticides;
– production of bituminous-tar and grinding products;
– production of perfumes;
– production of additives for textiles, leather, rubber;
– production of detergents;
– production of plastic mass materials.

The average personal income per month in 1969 was 1,438 Dinars.

The new statute of the enterprise which was adopted on 12 May 1970 envisages the organization of workers' self-management in the following way:

DIRECT MANAGEMENT

(a) Meeting of Workers

1. When it is necessary to take a decision on any particular question in the work unit in which the meeting of workers is the only management organ.
2. For drawing up nominations for representative bodies.
3. For nomination of candidates to management organs.
4. When draft statute and other general acts of the combine are to be considered.
5. When the plan of the combine and plans of work units are to be considered and adopted.
6. Before taking any decision on the introduction of interim management in the work units.
7. Prior to the workers' council decision on foundation, merger, annexation, or separation of work units or sections of the combine.
8. In all cases in which the statute or some general Act provides that the decision be taken by the meeting of workers.
9. In cases laid down in the general provisions, or when so stipulated by the workers' council.

According to the type of problems to be dealt with by the meeting, meetings are held at the level of the combine, or in individual work units. Because of the size and location of individual sections of the combine, a meeting of the entire combine can be held by individual work units and locations separately. In that case, the meetings at all locations must be held within forty-eight hours.

The meeting can take a fully valid decision if a majority (more than a half) of the members of the relevant work community are present, the decision being taken by a majority of votes of the workers present. When the meeting is held for the entire combine and is carried out by work units or locations, the decision is considered adopted if more than a half of the meetings voted for it.

When it is necessary to have the prior voiced opinion of the meeting of workers for a decision of the workers' council, the workers' council cannot take the decision without this opinion. The conclusion of the meeting of workers is not binding on the workers' council, that is, the council of the work unit. However, if the workers' council or the council of a work unit takes a decision which is at variance with the conclusion of the meeting of workers, an explanation must be given for this divergence.

The meeting of workers is called by: the chairman of the workers' council, the chairman of the council of the work unit, and the elected chairman of the meeting. Voting is public by a show of hands, unless a secret vote is provided for by the regulations.

(b) Election and Recall of Organs of Indirect Management

Every worker in the combine has the right to elect and to be elected to the management organs of the combine and of the work units. The election of management organs of the combine and of the work units is by direct and secret ballot. The decision to call an election is taken by the workers' council of the combine. The management organs are elected towards the expiry of their term of office, which is two years.

There are ordinary and extraordinary elections. The ordinary elections are held when an enterprise or a work unit is founded, or on expiry of the term of the existent organs. An extraordinary election is held:

1. If in the course of the term of office the number of members of the management organ is reduced by over $\frac{1}{8}$.
2. When a new election is to be held because the interim management has ceased acting.
3. When in the course of the term of office a new independent work unit is founded.
4. When the workers' council in the combine is dissolved or recalled, and a new election is called for the new organ of management.

The workers' council numbers fifty-one members at least, while the total number of members in the workers' management organs is determined according to the formula that one member of the workers' council is elected for every sixty members of the work community, provided that there should not be less than fifty-one members in total.

A proposal to start the procedure for recalling members of the workers' council (i.e. members of the council of the work units) can be submitted by:

– the meeting of the working people of the unit which elected the relevant member of the workers' council and the meeting

of workers of the work unit which elected the relevant member of the council of the work unit;
– one-fifth of the workers – who must be voters at least in the relevant work unit, provided that this is not less than 10 voters, while in electo-rates of over 500 voters this number should not be under 100.

In a large number of enterprises the trade union local also has this statutory right. The trade unions are calling for the obligatory introduction of this right into all statutes.

(c) Referendum

By referendum the working people of the combine may decide directly on particular questions which are of essential importance to their own economic position, or voice their opinion about important matters on which the management organ is to decide.

It is obligatory to call and carry out a referendum in the following cases:

1. Merger, annexation or division of the combine, as well as seperation of some parts from the combine.
2. A decision on changing the location of the combine (i.e. individual work units) given the prior agreement of the competent communal authorities, which is compulsory.
3. When the combine ceases its work, if the natural conditions for its economic operation cease to exist.
4. When the majority of the work units in the combine demand that a referendum be called.
5. When 10 per cent or more of the workers demand that a referendum be called.
6. When the competent management organ finds it suitable to carry out the referendum on other important issues.

In the work units of the combine a referendum is obligatory:

1. On all questions quoted above.
2. When the demand for calling of the referendum is put by:

– the council of the work unit;
– 10 per cent or more workers in the work unit.

The initiative to call a referendum for the combine can be advanced by:
1. A meeting of workers of the combine or a majority of the management organs in the work units.

2. The trade union local of the combine.
3. At least 100 workers of the combine.
4. The business board or executive organ of the workers' council of the combine.

The term for carrying out of a referendum cannot be less than fifteen nor more than sixty days from the day it is called. The decision taken by a referendum is binding on the management organs.

(d) The Right to Initiative

All the workers employed in the combine have the right to initiative, which implies in particular:

1. Proposals concerning the passing of particular decisions of the management organs.
2. Proposing measures for implementing the decisions of the management organs.
3. Proposals to call a meeting of the working people and carry out a referendum.
4. Proposals for improving the conditions of work and safety at work.
5. Proposals for the betterment of mutual human relations in the combine.
6. Proposals for promotion of the self-management of the working people, promotion of the system of distribution of income, and promotion of economic operation in general.

The proposals must receive a response from:

– the business board, within twenty days;
– the council of the work unit, within thirty days;
– the workers' council, within forty days.

The right to initiative is exercised by making proposals orally to the meeting of workers, or in writing to the secretariat of the management organs which is obliged to hand the proposal over to the competent management organ.

INDIRECT MANAGEMENT

Since the combine is composed of a rather large number of work units, indirect management is carried out through the councils of the work units and the workers' council of the combine.

Council of the Work Unit

The work units employing between thirty and fifty workers can decide to elect their own management organ – the council of the work unit. Work units with over fifty workers are obliged to elect their own council. The chief of the work unit is not allowed to be on the council of the unit.

The area of competence of the council of the work unit includes in particular:

1. Passing of plans for the development of the work unit, investment plans, personnel plans and programmes of education.
2. Deciding on the establishment, division of income and the personal incomes of workers, and passing general acts for these purposes, as well as passing other general acts within the powers laid down in the general acts of the combine (e.g. on mutual relations, awards for technological improvements and rationalization, on the procedure for solving housing problems, etc.).
3. Decisions on the use of social welfare funds and on the order of workers' annual holidays.
4. Decisions on the establishment of jobs, opening new, and closing existing jobs in the manner laid down in the general acts.
5. Ensuring that the advice of a good economist is sought in regard to economic operation, and that the socially owned resources are used for designated purposes only.
6. Decisions on purchase, sale, lending, or lease of capital assets, as well as on discarding capital assets and working capital.
7. Discussion of the draft statute and other general acts, and of alterations and amendments of these, and passing of their own general acts as provided in the statute (i.e. in the general acts of the combine).
8. Decisions on terminating the employment of a worker against his will, except in case of senior job positions.
9. Decisions on the appointment and release of its own commissions and their individual members.
10. Decisions on carrying out a referendum within the work unit.
11. Approval, in the manner provided for in the general acts, of:

(a) the foundation of common funds at the level of the combine, and for the common needs of all work units;

(b) the recognition of the standing of an autonomous work unit without legal status and recognition of the standing of other work units;

(c) the undertaking of responsibility for the recovery of the work unit.

Workers' Council of the Combine

The workers' council of the combine is the supreme organ of workers' management in the enterprise. The relation between the workers' council of the combine and the workers' councils of the work units is not in any way one of subordination, but rather of a division of competence between these organs. Within the framework of its basic tasks the workers' council of the combine has to:

– fix the plans and programmes of work and development for the combine, and on this basis divide the production programme between the autonomous work units;

– decide on the division of income at the level of the combine, and establish the principles of distribution in relation to the work units;

– regulate the relations in the combine by passing statutes and other general acts;

– decide on certain questions regarding the legal situation of the enterprise, in relation to status; attend to the election of the executive organs, and other affairs which are laid down by the general provisions as the exclusive responsibility of the workers' council of the combine.

Within the framework of the above basic tasks it is incumbent upon the workers' council in particular:

1. To decide on:
   – questions related to status, which are not decided on by a referendum, or on which a referendum only takes a position;
   – the business policy of the combine;
   – any change of objective concerning business operation;
   – the programme and plan of the work and development of the combine;
   – the division of income at the level of the combine together

with principles for the formation of the total income and distribution of income of the work units;

- investments at the level of the combine (i.e. investments financed by the combined resources of the work units);
- credits at the level of the combine;
- use and disposal of the common funds;
- principles of organization of the combine;
- business–technical co-operation and association;
- approval of proposals for writing off and discarding capital assets;
- complaints of foreign customers and suppliers;
- joint investments with other enterprises;
- modification of the general acts of the work units to conform with the general acts of the combine;
- transfer and taking over capital assets without compensation, purchase and sale of real estate;
- organization and carrying out national defence schemes in the combine;
- combining resources with those of socio-political communities and other enterprises to discharge the tasks of national defence.

2. To pass:
   - the statute and other general acts of the combine, and to conclude contracts on the basis of the statute;
   - periodical statements of account and an annual balance sheet;
   - principles of personnel policy for the combine;
   - a personnel policy plan, and a programme of vocational education;
   - a plan and programme of development for the combine;
   - criteria for the formation and use of combined resources;
   - a plan of national defence in the combine, and a programme for financing it.

3. To elect:
   - the chairman of the workers' council and deputy chairmen, and to appoint its own commissions;
   - the business operation board as the executive organ of the workers' council;
   - representatives of the combine in the organizations of social management such as business associations, economic chambers, and the like.

4. To appoint:

- the general manager, assistant general manager, heads of the work units and technical sections of the combine;
- members of an arbitration committee and their deputies;
- members of the commission for national defence.
5. To settle:
- grievances in the second instance.
6. To interpret:
- general acts of the combine.
7. To consider:
- recommendations of representative bodies, and take attitudes towards these recommendations;
- reports of the collective and individual executive organs and heads of the work units and technical sections of the combine, assess their work and make conclusions on these.
8. To carry out:
- all other tasks which may be placed in its competence by the general provisions and other general acts of the combine.

On the basis of the above provisions and responsibilities the workers' council passes the following normative acts:

1. Set of rules on organization of work in the combine.
2. Standing Orders on election, recall, and functioning of the management organs and business operations board.
3. Set of rules on establishment and division of income of the combine, and distribution of personal incomes.
4. Set of rules on combining the resources in the combine.
5. Set of rules on planning.
6. Set of rules on safety at work.
7. Set of rules on mutual labour relations.
8. Set of rules on vocational education of the workers.
9. Set of rules on insurance of the property of the combine.
10. Set of rules on national defence.
11. Set of rules on confidential business.
12. Set of rules on inventions and technological improvements.
13. Set of rules on use of cars for business purposes.
14. Set of rules on the formation of financial resources for the construction and allocation of flats.
15. Set of rules on waste and weight loss in raw materials and semi-finished products.
16. Set of rules on payments in cash from the social welfare fund, for the organization and expenses of annual holidays.

17. Set of rules on organization of financial operation and book-keeping of the combine.
18. Set of rules on material expenditures of business operations.
19. Set of rules on the employment of young graduates and school leavers and their preparatory term of service.
20. Set of rules on the way of fixing the prices and conditions of the sale of goods and rendering of services by the combine.
21. Set of rules on the operation of the workers' canteen.
22. Set of rules on organization and operation of the workers' rest home.

COMMISSIONS OF THE MANAGEMENT ORGANS

Commissions are auxiliary bodies of the management organs. Their task is to get more closely and thoroughly acquainted with the problems which are to be dealt with at the sessions of the management organs, and to prepare appropriate proposals in this connection. There are commissions attached to the councils of the work units and to the workers' council of the combine:

Standing commissions of the council of the work unit are:

1. Commission for the programme of development and plan of work of the work unit.
2. Commission for distribution within the unit.
3. Commission for pronouncing measures against any violation of work duty.
4. Commission for admission to employment and terminating employment.
5. Commission for implementing a measure excluding a worker from the work community of the combine.
6. Commissions for general acts of the work unit, which it passes in keeping with the provisions of the statute.
7. Commission for writing off and discarding capital assets and working capital.
8. Commission for requests and grievances.
9. Commission for social welfare standards and recreation.
10. Commission for deciding on duration of annual holidays.
11. Commission for safety at work.

The following commissions of the council of the work unit also function with the right of decision making:

– for admission to employment and ceasing employment;
– for pronouncing measures against the violation of work duty;
– for implementing a measure excluding a worker from the combine;
– for determining the duration of annual holidays.

At the level of the combine the workers' council forms and appoints members to the following standing commissions:

1. Commission for planning and production.
2. Commission for research and development.
3. Commission for internal distribution.
4. Commission for preparing normative acts of the combine and assessing the legality of the normative acts of the work units.
5. Commission for investments and capital assets.
6. Commission for writing off and discarding capital assets.
7. Commission for writing off and discarding working capital and other material values.
8. Commission for admission to employment and ceasing employment.
9. Commission for financial and commercial affairs.
10. Commission for inventions and technological improvements.
11. Commission for safety at work.
12. Commission for social welfare standards and recreation.
13. Commission for pronouncing measures against violations of work duty.
14. Commission for implementing a measure excluding a worker from the combine.
15. Commission for requests and grievances.
16. Commission for social supervision.
17. Commission for national defence.

Of the above, the following have a right of decision making:

– Commission for admission to employment and ceasing employment;
– Commission for pronouncing measures against violation of work duty;
– Commission for implementing a measure excluding a worker from the combine.

In addition to the standing commissions the workers' management organs set up ad hoc commissions as necessary.

EXECUTIVE ORGANS OF THE WORKERS' COUNCIL

As the executive organs of the Workers' Council of the combine there are:

– the business board;
– the general manager.

The *business board* is elected as a collective technical and executive organ of the workers' council, which prepares, takes and carries out its decisions on the basis of the business policy laid down in the normative acts of the combine and in the general decisions of the workers' council. The business board numbers nine members, and is elected from the ranks of the members of the collective who have become outstanding for their professional abilities and conscientious attitude in discharging various tasks, for their organizational capability and good results scored in their work. The term of office of business board members is two years.

Particular responsibilities of the business board are:

– to lay down drafts of the forward plan and programme for development, and of the annual plan for the combine, and set up the basic plan in working out plans for the work units;
– to consider the implementation of the business policies of the combine which are laid down in the plans of the combine, and to undertake the necessary measures for the realization of the above policies;

– to discuss the draft of the annual balance sheets, and make appropriate suggestions to the workers' council concerning their adoption;
– to undertake measures and pass binding instructions for carrying out of the provisions on national defence, in case, of war, threat of war, or natural disasters;
– to attend to other affairs which are placed in its competence by the general provisions, general acts of the combine, and decisions of the workers' council.

The *general manager* as an individual executive organ of the combine manages the business operation of the combine, and within the framework of the general business policy laid down in the normative acts of the combine and general decisions of the workers' council and the business board, represents the combine and ensures legality in the work of the combine. The general manager is appointed by the workers' council of the combine, following the publicly performed contest procedure, on the proposal of the commission for considering applications, under the conditions and according to the procedure laid down in the statute. The term of office of the general manager is four years, and it is possible to appoint one and the same person as general manager a number of times.

INTERRELATIONS OF THE WORK UNITS

For a clearer picture of the organization of self-management in this combine, and in the Yugoslav industrial enterprises in general, it is necessary to explain the way in which mutual relations between the work units in the combine are regulated. Those relations are regulated by the statute and other general acts of the combine, plans of the work units and the combine, decisions of the workers' council, mutual agreements of a business–technical nature, and by decisions of arbitration.

Mutual relations between the work units are based on the autonomy of each unit and on agreements and contracts on co-operation within the framework of the general business policy of the combine. The work units establish gross and net income independently, divide the income into a personal incomes fund and other funds, and meet their obligations towards the other work units, the combine, and to third parties.

I shall deal briefly here with the system of income division in the combine. The workers' council of the combine passes a set of rules on the formation and division of incomes, which contains principles only for the formation of gross income, establishment of income and its distribution in the work units. On the basis of these general principles the councils of the work units pass their own sets of rules on establishment and distribution of the units and personal incomes, which contain criteria for the division of income into a part for personal incomes, a part for the reserve fund, a part for business operation fund and a part for the social welfare fund. In concrete terms, the work units decide autonomously on distribution of the realized income. The realized income depends, first of all, on the work results expressed in the market prices for that part of production which is sold outside the combine, and on the market-agreed prices, which are mutually fixed by the ordering and delivering work units for that part of production which is handled within the combine. Consequently, there is a difference in levels of realized income from unit to unit, which is reflected in the difference in personal incomes of workers. So, for example, in 1969, the personal incomes in the Zagreb enterprise averaged from 1·627 Dinar in the pesticide production unit to 1·117 Dinar in the unit producing paints for ships. The distribution of the personal incomes fund to individuals is the sole responsibility of the council of the work unit and is carried out on the basis of its normative acts, which are passed on the basis of the general principles laid down by the workers' council of the combine.

The resources of the *business operation* fund are used by the work unit as basic and working capital in accordance with the fixed plan and the anticipated needs. The work units combine their available resources in the above fund at the level of the combine, provided that these remain in the ownership of the work unit, and that the manner in which the resources are to be used is fixed by agreement. The organ which decides on their precise use must also meet with the approval of the work unit which has contributed its resources. The work unit also gets interest on the combined resources, the rate being fixed uniformally for all the work units by the workers' council of the combine. Consequently, the work units are not deprived of the resources of their business operation fund, although a part of these are consolidated at the level of the combine. From these pooled funds, credits are most frequently allocated to the work units which have insufficient resources of their own for modernization, but this is done, as indicated above, only on the basis of the plan and agreement of the work units which have pooled their resources.

The resources of the social welfare fund are used by the work unit for the following:

- investments in apartment buildings, premises for recreation, household help services, and investments in community standard schemes in the area of the commune responsible;
- current and investment maintenance of social welfare facilities;
- allocation of scholarships to students and pupils, and vocational education of workers;
- meeting the cultural needs of workers;
- organized spending on annual holidays;
- assistance to those afflicted by natural disasters;

- covering expenditure of the health centre of the combine;
- assistance to sick workers, burial costs for any worker who loses his life due to an accident at work, and assistance to his family;
- subsidizing the trade union local of the combine;
- organizing excursions within the country and abroad, grants to sports or other organizations for recreational schemes for the workers.

The work units can agree to pool the above resources for concrete joint actions.

The resources allocated by the work unit to the *reserve fund* are used when the results of business operation have not been satisfactory for various reasons. One part of these resources is left to the work unit, and the other part is compulsorily pooled in the reserve fund of the combine. The council of the work unit by its decisions handles resources at the level of the work unit, while resources at the level of the combine in the form of a solidarity fund are handled by the workers' council of the combine.

Disputes in the field of business relations between the work units are settled by internal arbitration bodies. The internal arbitration board in the combine consists of six members and a chairman. Two members of the arbitration body are appointed by the workers' council, while the councils of the work units involved in the dispute appoint two members each. The chairman of the arbitration board is appointed by unanimous agreement of the members or, if the agreement cannot be reached, by the chairman of the district economic court. Disputes between the combine as a whole and its individual work units on questions involving status, separation, dissolution or amalgamation of units, recognition of the work unit as a legal entity, etc., are settled by the decision of the workers' council of the combine. Under the general provisions, the dissatisfied party can demand mediation by a mixed arbitration board, which is formed by the chairman of the district economic court. This arbitration does not pass a decision on the settlement of the dispute, but only suggests the way in which the dispute should be settled. If the arbitration board makes a proposal which is at variance with the firm attitude of the workers' council, the workers' council is obliged to submit the case – together with the proposal of the arbitration board – to a referendum, which passes the final decision.

RELATIONS BETWEEN ENTERPRISES

In the Yugoslav socio-economic system the enterprise is not only a basis for workers' self-management but also the basis of planning, production, development and, indeed, of the entire economic system. That is why the enterprises are mutually organized into business associations and economic chambers, and relate to each other on a self-government basis. The workers' councils of the enterprises delegate their representatives to the business associations and economic chambers.

The enterprises establish business associations for joint ventures in domestic and foreign markets, joint study of the market, co-ordinated work on studying and solving common business problems, joint development of production, etc. Enrolment of the enterprises in these business associations is voluntary.

Enrolment in the economic chambers, however, is compulsory for the enterprises. Economic chambers are found by and large at all levels, from the communes to the federation, and their task is primarily to pursue the economic policies of the enterprises, branches and groups of kindred enterprises, to seek improvement of production, to co-ordinate economic policy in relation to other countries, and so on.

To help reconcile specific individual interests, and to further their common interests the enterprises employ a system of compacts and agreements. There are three sorts of self-management compacts and agreements:

– self-management compacts and agreements between the enterprises;
– social compacts and agreements;
– social direction.

The self-management compacts and agreements between the enterprises are aimed at securing congruence in terms of pricing policy, development of the enterprises, establishing criteria in distributing income and personal incomes, etc. This is done directly between the enterprises within the branches and within groups of kindred enterprises, as well as within the framework of the enterprises in the area of the commune or the wider socio-political community.

The social compacts and agreements establish the conditions in which the enterprises will be enabled efficiently to realize the agreed objectives of self-management. The principles engaged in drawing up the social agreements are the enterprises, the trade unions, the economic chambers, and the authorized organs of the socio-political community. These compacts and agreements are compulsory for all enterprises and their associations, and for all socio-political communities. They can be introduced at every level, from the commune to the federation. The trade unions play a significant part in initiating these social agreements in practice.

Social direction really implies the intervention of society where self-management and social conciliation have not been effective. This in effect provides social guidance for the enterprises towards seeking common solutions by all means.

A significant part in conciliation between the enterprises as well as in the Yugoslav socio-political system in general, is played by the assemblies or parliaments of the communes, the autonomous provinces, republics and federation. The enterprises and the socio-political communities co-ordinate their economic development policies, and this process is particularly reflected in the planning system. In the Yugoslav economic system the enterprise is the basis of planning, and it is obliged to bring its own plan into conformity with the plans of other enterprises and socio-political communities. To this end the 'meeting' system of planning has been introduced. This is a system in which every participant prepares his own plans, co-ordinating them with those of other participants in the planning process. In this way every participant in planning has a recognized responsibility for carrying out such policies as will secure fulfilment of the basic targets of the plan. The enterprise plans are of a practical business nature, while the plans of the socio-political communities are for the most part concerned with basic economic factors.

The powerful influence of the enterprises is exerted in the socio-political communities through the work community chambers in the parliaments. The enterprises have elected representatives in the above chambers, and thus also able to influence directly the policy of the parliaments in the socio-political communities.

SOME RESULTS OF WORKERS' SELF-MANAGEMENT

Owing to the initiative of the working class, which in the new socio-political and economic conditions was able to develop freely and without hindrance, some results have been achieved which at one time were inconceivable. Here are only some of the successes which have been scored.

The national income, which before World War II amounted to about $125 per capita, has grown to about $600 in 1969, and at this level Yugoslavia is rapidly nearing the level of the medium developed industrial countries. During the period between 1950 and 1970 the annual growth rate of the social product has been 7 per cent while in the advanced countries it was 4·3 per cent (1950–67). This growth rate of the social product resulted both from the increasing involvement of workers in management and from heavy investment at the expense of the standard of living up to 1964. Some figures on the standard of living prove, however, that even in this field significant changes have taken place. Only some of them are quoted in the table below.

	1956	1969
Real growth in personal consumption per head, in fixed prices (in thousands of Dinars)	134·7	302·1
Annual consumption per head:		
Textiles	9·61	21·82
Footwear, pair	0·7	1·47
Electrical energy in households-kWh	36·36	255·52
Television sets per million	—*	16·21
Radio sets per million	7·07	21·13
Refrigerators per million	0·56	18·67
Cars per million	0·02	6·39
Annual construction of flats per million	2·1	6·4
Death rate among infants per million	98·3	55·3
Completion of schooling grades (in %):		
Elementary (eight years)	77·6	90·0
Secondary	16·7	35·5
University	2·2	6·8
Percentage of employed in relation to active population	27·6	40·6

* Yugoslavia only started an experimental television programme in 1956.

The vitality of workers' self-management was strongly proved after the economic reform measures were introduced. In 1967 alone, of the total number of industrial products 84·5 per cent remained in production without any changes, in 1968 (in 38,246 cases out of a total of 205,000 products) changes were made, or new products were introduced.

All the above quantitative data are neither singular nor decisive ones, for we consider that far more important are the qualitative changes as regards the individual. The general level of consciousness of the working class has been enhanced and significant experience has been gained for the further development of workers' self-management and for the country's economic and political advance in general. Workers' self-management represents a great training ground for the working class of Yugoslavia, wherein the trade unions have played a substantial part, particularly in the education of self-managers. The statistical census made after elections for the self-management organs in 1968 shows that in the whole of industry and mining in Yugoslavia there are 2,192 enterprises which employ a total of 1,268,971 workers. In the enterprises employing over 31 workers, 54,405 workers' council members were elected, of whom 34,218 are workers in immediate production, 61,604 are workers in general services, 2,419 are workers in managerial jobs, and 173 are in the scientific-research sector. 16,605 members of business or management boards were also elected. However, this is not the whole of it. In a large number of enterprises there are also management organs at the level of the sections and work units, while a good number of workers are also involved in various commissions of the workers' councils, so that the number of members on the management organs totals far more. In fact, nearly every tenth worker is on one or another organ of workers' management. Considering also the fact that in some enterprises the entire body of employees constitutes the organ of direct management, the mass of workers involved in the management process is enormous. In addition, it is not to be forgotten that all other workers in industry are involved in management through their meetings.

This vast number of participants in self-management and its broad organization when looked at superficially, could make the system appear unnecessarily extensive and inefficient – even irrational. However, if one bears in mind that each of the management organs has its own clearly defined tasks, rights and responsibilities the situation looks different. So, for example, in the case of the chemical combine whose self-management organization we explained earlier in the text, thirteen sessions of the workers' council of the combine (dealing with seventy-five agenda items) were held, and twenty-two sessions of the business board of the combine, while the other organs of management held their sessions in the same proportion. A similar situation is found in other enterprises in Yugoslav industry.

SOME PROBLEMS AND PERSPECTIVES OF WORKERS' SELF-MANAGEMENT

At the present stage of development of workers' self-management there are certain problems which require the co-operation of all social factors in creating further conditions for the advance of self-management, socialist democracy, and more direct influence of workers and enterprises in governing the country.

One of the most important problems certainly lies in the fact that there is not a developed workers' self-management system anywhere in the world, so that there is no body of experience in this respect which can be referred to. That is why our country has to trace its own way to the self-governing socialist society, which inevitably entails incessant analysing of the direction which has been pursued and the employment of substantial effort in grasping and resolving difficulties as they emerge.

A more rapid advance towards workers' self-management in Yugoslavia is also hindered by the fact that it has been developing in the context of a comparatively economically backward country, whose working class does not have a strongly expressed industrial tradition; and, in some circumstances differences exist in the levels of economic, cultural, social and political development of individual republics, where even a number of distinct nations and nationalities exist, etc. The continual development and build-up of the political and economic system help solve the above problems.

Workers' self-management in Yugoslavia has been unfolding in conditions of the expressed centralist function of the community, and so the development of the self-management represented at the same time weakening of bureaucracy, that is, an incessant revolutionary struggle between the forces which were for self-management and those against it, those for the power of the workers and those for power 'on behalf of' the workers. The development of self-management has also implied organization of society, and the development of new forms of socialist democracy in society. This process has not yet been terminated, and for achieving the best possible results it is necessary to have active engagement of workers in the enterprises and in all the socio-political organizations, especially in the trade unions. This is a struggle at the same time for the strengthening of the material foundation of workers' self-management and for a greater influence of workers' self-management over expenditure of the resources handled by the socio-political communities and other self-governing communities and funds.

A particular problem at the present moment in the development of workers' self-management lies in the concentration of resources in the banks and foreign trade enterprises. Lacking their own resources, the enterprises have to apply for credits to the banks and foreign trade enterprises, which set comparatively severe conditions upon the allocation of credits. This tendency is aggravating for the economic enterprises so that the banks and foreign trade enterprises are increasingly becoming centres of financial power beyond production and more and more alienated from it. In this way the income flows from the enterprises over to the banks and foreign trade enterprises so that the economy is being continually impoverished. Under these conditions the enterprises are unable to act properly as the basis for the extension of production since factors outside the production process appear to hold sway. Aware of the fact that the one who controls the extension of production also controls the entire society, the socio-political organizations, and the trade unions in particular, are seeking by systematic means to incorporate the banks to the fullest possible extent in the system of the self-governing construction of the economy, so as to prevent them from becoming a force outside the economy.

Workers' self-management is unfolding today under the increasing effect of market laws, which bring the different industries, groups and enterprises to different positions in the market. Since this is not due to their work results alone, but also to other coincidences, such as monopolist position, extra profits, rents, etc., the position of workers in individual enterprises, industries and groups differs very widely. Substantial differences ensue in the personal incomes of workers doing the same job, with equal work productivity. This problem has also been comprehended and assessed, and the solutions will be provided by systematic measures now in hand, along with the significant activity of

trade unions in relation to self-management and social conciliation on distribution of income and personal incomes. To this
end some basic criteria-indicators are already being prepared to
enable the enterprises to carry out their distribution in the most
realistic manner.

Workers' self-management has been developing not only in
conditions of struggle against state bureaucracy, but also in
conditions of struggle against particularist and localist tendencies,
against autarchic attitudes of the enterprises. These tendencies
also give rise to conflicts very frequently; however, through the
system of self-management and social conciliation, a significant,
although only initial, step has been made towards solution of
these problems. The restriction of the functions of the state
apparatus, and transfer of its functions to the enterprise through
their associations, was not supported by adequate organization
of the latter in taking over these functions. Still more comprehensive development of self-management and social conciliation
is necessary to contribute to a firmer interlinking of the enterprises so as to enable them to assume the corresponding functions
of the state.

At its beginning workers' self-management was based on the
traditional structure of the enterprise, and so the role of the
indirect organs of management, particularly at the level of
the enterprise, was given more emphasis. In the course of later
development, workers' self-management came to be decentralized
and work units were founded as basic units of workers' self-
management. For further democratization and improvement of
workers' self-management it is indispensable for workers in their
work units to have even more comprehensive rights, namely, to
be the starting point for entrusting agreed rights and functions
to the organs of direct management. It is only in this way that
the new structure of the self-governing enterprise can be worked
out.

In the development of workers' self-management some negative
phenomena have also cropped up in the enterprises such as the
bureaucratization not only of the apparatus of operations management, but of some workers' management organs as well, their
separation from the workers, the appearance of a managerial
outlook, and tendencies towards transplanting the capitalist
enterprise type of organization. These phenomena have also been
causing internal conflicts, because the workers felt themselves
separated from management. It is precisely the task of the socio-

political organizations within the enterprises to work on further democratization of the social relations in the collective, and so to prevent anybody from managing on behalf of the workers.

In May 1971 the 2nd Congress of self-managers of Yugoslavia was held. The congress was initiated by the trade unions, which took the main responsibility for its convening. Delegates attending the congress were elected in the enterprises and in all the social activities in which self-management is applied, including the delegates of the socio-political communities. The 2nd Congress of self-managers has served principally to summarize experience to date in the development of self-management, taking into consideration at the same time all essential problems, phenomena and tendencies of present self-managing developments. The above problems were dealt with within the framework of four main themes, as follows:

- the further build-up, development, and improvement of efficiency of self-management in the enterprise;
- the extension of production and integration of the self-management foundations;
- the material development of the self-governing society as a basis for raising the living standard of the working people; and
- the strengthening of the associated producers' role as a basis for further development of the self-governing socio-political system.

About eighty communications from the enterprises and twenty-seven communications from the communes were prepared for this congress, and were handed to every delegate. In this way, it was possible on the basis of actual self-management practices to consider the achievements in the development of self-management, as well as the problems which have arisen in that practice. By this kind of approach in preparing its material the congress was essentially different from other kindred socio-political conferences.

Having considered all positive results as well as the negative phenomena, from the wealth of practice so far and having identified the tendencies and problems which required solution, the congress laid down further directions for self-management development under the present scientific-technological advance and towards the further development of socialist democracy.

The 2nd Congress of self-managers has, therefore, determined the direction of further development in self-management, and pointed towards solutions in the socio-economic and political system, thus marking a further step in the construction of a self-governing socialist society in Yugoslavia.

Chapter 6

Israel

ITZHAK BEN AARON

Secretary General, General Federation of Jewish Labour in Eretz-Israel

HISTADRUT BUILDS A NATION

The Histadrut – the General Federation of Labour in Israel – celebrated its Golden Jubilee in 1970. Its most outstanding achievement to date, perhaps, has been the survival of the validity and viability in the present of those very principles that provided the guiding lines for the founding generation of fifty years ago. The unique nature of the Histadrut reflects its development within the particular reality of Israel, which – to say the least – is a very special kind of society. The most accurate description of the Histadrut is that it is first and foremost a movement devoted to the construction of a nation.

The Histadrut today has well over one million members and its health insurance scheme serves nearly 2 million out of Israel's 2·7 million inhabitants. It is acknowledged by most laws enacted in the Knesset (parliament) as the representative organization of labour. However it in no way or measure enjoys any privileged position under the law.

When the eighty-seven delegates to the foundation assembly of the Histadrut gathered in Haifa in 1920 they chose to blaze new trails. There were then, as there are now, a number of schools of thought in the free labour movement. The British TUC, as the model of classical trade unionism, put stress on class identification, with the trade unions seeking to redress the working class lot through the Labour Party. Another school of opinion as exemplified by the American trade unions held to the premise of job identification without any special political party.

In both instances the movements came into being in order to reform the social evils of early capitalism and to obtain a bigger share for the workers. With the Histadrut, it was not just a question of extracting a bigger share of the national cake, the cake itself had to be brought into being. Unlike the situation found in established countries, the problem facing the early Jewish labour leaders was not a clear-cut need to organize working people in defence of their rights against an entrenched employer class. For neither a capitalist nor a working class in the normal sense existed in the country. On the one hand, private capital was not taking any initiative, and on the other hand, there was no working population with an established tradition of labour and skills.

The immigrants who came to drain the swamps and make the desert flourish belonged to the middle and professional classes of Eastern Europe. Although imbued with the ideal of building up their ancient homeland with their own hands, they were not physically well-equipped for this task. Each of these immigrants had to undergo his or her personal revolution to become a worker. They chose to do this together by pooling their knowledge and resources, so that all of their personal revolutions added up to the national revolution. Thus there emerged a Jewish working class in Israel. The framework and institutions for this profound revolutionary process was provided by the Histadrut. Thus the Histadrut became the spearhead of far-reaching economic and social changes in a long-neglected and abandoned region of the world. Moreover, the harsh realities of those early years forced the labour movement to act by its own driving force, lacking a developed economy or capital of its own to draw upon.

There are two points which must be kept in mind concerning the development of the Histadrut. It began to evolve as a labour movement before its trade unions consolidated into a highly organized unit; and it took over such facilities as the voluntary workers' health insurance scheme created by a union of farm workers in Galilee back in 1911 – decades before the welfare state was thought of. The men who pioneered the labour movement were primarily pragmatists; the theory and ideological dressing accompanied rather than preceded the deed. Every discussion ended with a decision to find concrete expression for new ideas.

The founding convention of the Histadrut set as its aim the

creation of a workers' commonwealth for a working Jewish people in its own land. They fashioned special instruments to achieve this aim. In order to create such a working class they put a premium on education – whether in learning trades or in educating their children to a life of productive labour, or in the dissemination of the new Hebrew culture. This provided the foundation and the purposefulness which have made the Histadrut, and with it Israel, what they are today.

These pioneers also realized early on that it was up to them to strive for the kind of advanced economy that could provide workers with decent living standards. Thus the labour movement launched economic enterprises on a co-operative basis. The enterprises were designed to provide work for members, to help develop the national economy and also to lay the basis for further production.

CREATING A WORKERS' ECONOMY

A self-contained workers' economy based on co-operative principles was considered the best and speediest means to attain adequate living standards and a prime instrument in constructing the national homeland. At the same time, trade unions began to develop as a buttress against the exploitation of new immigrant labour and to exercise control over the labour market. Its structure evolved differently from other countries if only because of the need to fashion an entirely new working community. At the same time, the Histadrut looked after social security. The British colonial administration, to put it charitably, had not been interested in such facilities. A framework of mutual aid began to emerge, providing health and hospital insurance as well as a comprehensive range of social institutions.

Thus from the very start, Israeli Labour combined three distinct but related streams of activities: trade unions, economic operations and social welfare. By keeping them under one Histadrut roof, it ensured the cohesion of purpose and unity of action of the working community, providing it with a power that it might otherwise have lacked. It is only against this background that the complex organizational set-up of the Histadrut today can properly be grasped.

One aspect of Israel Labour worthy of attention is the close alliance between farmers and urban wage-earners within the Histadrut. In many countries farmers tend to be the more conservative element. In Israel the basic pattern of labour organization was laid by farm workers back in 1907. It was among these idealistic pioneers that the unique forms of co-operation – the kibbutz and the moshav – originated. It was this combination of rural and urban sectors that provided the core of Histadrut strength and the manpower to run its institutions and co-operative enterprises.

The move from colonialism to national independence was accompanied by an all-out war against the fledgling state by its neighbours (which regrettably still continues) and by mass immigration. The Histadrut played a key role in the smooth transition to sovereignty which was due to a marked extent to the fact that the labour parties (drawing allegiance from the overwhelming majority of Histadrut members) have always occupied the dominant position in all government coalitions since national independence was won in 1948. The continuity of policy was ensured by the fact that many pre-independence Histadrut leaders were elected by their parties to serve in the government. This identity of political purpose with the parties controlling the government and parliament has meant that legislation and social welfare policies have been moulded along socialist lines. It has also meant that Israeli society has largely held to those egalitarian values that imbued the pioneering generation. Right from the very start public initiative has led the way. Ineed, when the waves of mass immigration swept the land in the early days of independence, it was due to the labour sector that these newcomers had jobs and housing. The present-day reality of Israel is that more than 35 per cent of the economy is in public hands, 40 per cent in private hands, with the Histadrut controlling 25 per cent of the GNP. Israel has a pluralistic economy – state-owned, co-operative and private enterprise. Indeed Israel may be seen as an arena for confrontation of these different economic philosophies, particularly between co-operatives and private business.

At the same time, because Israel is a developing country that is also required to devote a heavy proportion of its resources to defence, it is also deeply interested in attracting foreign investment. Israel's labour movement has always followed a line of seeking to demonstrate by its own successes that it can compete against private business on its own ground without enjoying special privileges. Indeed the Histadrut has promoted partnerships with enlightened private concerns in know-how agreements and in setting up new enterprises aimed at creating new job opportunities.

HEVRAT OVDIM

For the purposes of its economic activities the Histadrut is constituted as the General Co-operative Association of Labour in Israel, known as 'Hevrat Ovdim'. The labour economy falls into two categories – co-operative societies run by their own members, and enterprises initiated by Hevrat Ovdim, which are collectively controlled by the entire working community. The labour economy has developed around two basic industries – agriculture and construction. It produces two-thirds of Israel's farm produce and is responsible for 40 per cent of its building activity. Hevrat Ovdim industrial affiliates produce more than 25 per cent of total national industrial output. The housing programmes have provided homes for 350,000 Israelis, built by Histadrut's Solel Boneh, Israel's largest building company.

The consumer co-operative network started as small units supplying rural co-operatives and urban workers and now caters to one-third of the nation. Today the co-ops are at the forefront in modernizing Israel's retail trade, with 'Hamashbir comerkazi', the Co-operative Wholesale Society, a large-scale importer and manufacturer of consumer goods. It has a turnover today of nearly 400 million Israeli pounds.

Israeli agriculture is predominantly co-operative. There are 545 such villages all belonging to Hevrat Ovdim with their 182,500 members personally affiliated to the Histadrut. There are two types of co-operative. The *kibbutz* is a collective economy where private property does not exist. It is worked as a single economic unit, no wages being paid since members' needs are met by the community. There are 82,500 persons living in 225 kibbutz villages. The *moshav* is based on a group of family farmsteads with each unit belonging to the co-operative. Some 100,000 persons live in 320 such villages. More than two-thirds of the nation's farm produce is provided by these co-operative villages which market their produce through 'Tnuva', the central co-operative marketing agency. Likewise passenger transport and road haulage are dominated by co-operatives.

Every Histadrut member is automatically a member of Hevrat Ovdim which, regarded from this point of view, can be considered a basic co-operative society, whose membership today is composed of the 1,100,000 members of Histadrut. At the same time HO became the co-ordinating organization for all co-operative and non-co-operative enterprises within the framework of Histadrut, and can therefore be considered also as a composite co-operative society – of the third or even fourth degree. To assure the organic link between HO and Histadrut, a full identification of governing bodies was established: Histadrut's quadrennial congress acts as the general assembly of HO, the Histadrut council acts as the council of HO, the Histadrut executive committee equates to HO's supervisory board and the secretary-general of Histadrut is ex-officio chairman of HO. Today, Hevrat Ovdim's co-ops and enterprises (usually called 'the labour economy') account for an output of 2,800 million Israeli pounds per year.

The economic sector controlled by HO is very varied, embracing 1,400 co-operative societies and more than 500 'administered' or non-co-operative enterprises. Co-operatives affiliated to the labour economy make up the bulk of the co-operative movement in Israel. They follow normal co-operative law and practice, being owned and run exclusively by the members. Yet at the same time they are organized by sectors in co-ordinating organizations (such as the Agricultural Centre, the Union of Consumers' Co-ops, the Centre of Producers, Transport and Services Co-ops, the Union of Housing Co-ops, etc. Each has its own audit union, recognized by the Registrar of Co-operatives, and is responsible for auditing accounts, training personnel and giving technical assistance to the affiliated societies). HO has veto powers when basic principles or the interest of the whole labour movement are at stake.

The agricultural sector has long been prominent with 776 societies (233 kibbutzim, 324 moshavim, 219 central co-operatives). Alongside these there are 189 producers, transport and service co-ops, 40 consumers' co-ops (with 210 branches), 103 housing co-operatives and 162 provident and pension funds. 141 co-operative societies of different kinds have developed in areas populated mainly by Arab members of Histadrut.

The non-co-operative enterprises have been set up by HO and are run by managers designated by and responsible to the governing bodies of HO. The most important are: the Building Co. Solel Boneh (which in 1970 carried out projects worth 400 million I£ in Israel and projects worth $60 million in twelve countries); the industrial corporation KOOR (36 enterprises in foundries, steel, glass, cement, rubber, plastics, paint, pipes, plywood, ceremics, electronics; 1970 sales 15 million I£); the housing company SHIKUN OVDIM (5,000 units per year); the workers' bank BANK HAPOALIM (balance sheet 1,700 million I£); the INDUSTRIAL DEVELOPMENT BANK (balance sheet 140 million I£); the insurance company HASSNEH (balance sheet 102 million I£), etc. These are normally joint stock companies and the kind of control HO exercises varies from passive participation in investment, or partial control through a subsidiary, to full ownership and control. In most cases the rights of HO will be anchored in 'founder shares', which enables it to nominate managers, chairmen of boards and decide in matters such as the creation of new undertakings, mergers, associations, winding-up of enterprises, investment in other enterprises and transfer of shares. Budgets and balance sheets are subject to approval by HO.

FINANCING

One of the key problems has been: how to mobilize the necessary capital. It should be noted that members' dues paid to Histadrut cannot be used for the labour economy. Where, then, could financial resources be found? For quite a long time financing was rather precarious, being based on voluntary contributions and loans. In due time, however, undertakings developed, and capital assets grew. Today, HO depends upon four main sources of capital:

1. Own resources and accumulated profits of co-ops and non-co-operative enterprises. HO has been guided by an iron rule of re-investment of all profits – in the enterprises where they were produced or in other HO enterprises.
2. Workers' savings, concentrated mainly in BANK HAPOALIM (and its thirteen subsidiary companies) and in the Provident and Pension Funds. Current savings of workers in these funds reached some 400 million I£ last year.
3. Assets of the Pension Funds. The seven Central Pension Funds created by the unions through collective bargaining (on the basis of contributions by workers and employers, but run exclusively by workers' representatives) have an accumulated capital of 1,500 million I£. According to law, 80 per cent may be invested, half of it in government securities, the other half in 'authorized investments'. The funds have channelled a

G

good part of the second half into the labour economy, to the tune of some 150 million I£ per annum during the last few years.

4. Government loans and foreign capital. HO enterprises may benefit from general incentives and credits given by the Treasury to 'approved investments' and development projects. They have also been able to attract foreign capital.

Since 1963 the central tool of HO's financial programme has been the Investment Fund, established as a public company, limited by shares, and with the aim of centralizing capital for investment in the Histadrut network of enterprises. HO's financial situation provides for the mobilization of 4,000 million I£ over the next five years. To achieve this it will be necessary to tap more of its own resources, obtain more government credits and attract more private capital, whether local or foreign.

THE WORKER AS OWNER AND CLAIMANT

211,000 people are employed in the labour economy – one-third of all wage earners affiliated to Histadrut work for Histadrut, which is therefore the biggest employer of the country. This raises the question of whether there is not a basic contradiction between trade union and economic interests in such an arrangement. The answer would seem to be – not necessarily. (Incidentally, on this issue we are not far removed from the problematics of nationalized enterprises in any political regime where labour parties dominate or predominate.)

First, there is a clear separation of functions: workers in HO enterprises have built up a normal trade union structure; they organize, bargain and, when necessary, strike – although this may seem rather strange from a purely theoretical point of view (and is anyhow not very frequent). Second, if grievances have not been settled by agreed procedure at the different levels, it is left to the governing bodies of Histadrut to arbitrate the conflict, and they will do so in the light of the overall interests of Histadrut membership. Third, at national level, at least, there does not always arise the need to bargain with oneself. National wage agreements are first hammered out with private employers; government and HO then adopt the agreed wage scales if they have enterprises in the branch or area covered by the agreement. Thorough knowledge of industry strengthens Histadrut's position in negotiations with employers and the government, and direct economic power increases the possibility of influencing the shaping of national policies. Furthermore, private employers and the government have come to accept the leading role played by HO as pattern-setter concerning working conditions and social benefits. Fourth, a solid network of economic services increases the real value of wages.

In fact, experience has shown that integration of trade union activities and collective ownership of means of production, when carried out by organized labour, is not only possible but desirable.

BEYOND BARGAINING

Yet, in day-to-day life workers and employees in HO enterprises may perfectly well feel alienated from what they see as 'just another management', controlled by a remote bureaucracy – remote, even if the bureaucrats are fellow trade unionists. Thus, after having mastered some of the greater problems in the field of economic democracy, Histadrut faces now the problem of industrial democracy in its own non-co-operative enterprises.

A first step in the right direction was made, as much as twenty years ago, by creating joint productivity councils. Further progress has been made since the 10th Congress of 1966, which decided to set up a Department for Workers' Participation in Management. Since then workers' representatives have been elected to nearly all central managements within HO (Solel Boneh, Koor, Shikun Ovdim, etc.) and joint management boards have been set up in fifteen plants. These boards are not advisory bodies; they deal with all main problems of the enterprise, without impairing management's executive ability in day-to-day running.

Discussions are also under way on the introduction of profit sharing by workers in HO enterprises. A special committee is to report shortly to Histadrut's executive on concrete proposals for such a scheme, which would mean an important departure from the hallowed principle of re-investing all profits.

STRUCTURE OF HISTADRUT

In the traditional trade union sphere the special nature of organized labour in Israel is that membership of the Histadrut is personal and direct. Collective and group membership does not exist. It is most definitely not a federation of trade unions. The Histadrut encompasses whole ranges of trades and professions, from unskilled labourers to scientists. Members' wives who are only engaged as housewives may also be members. A worker joins the Histadrut and then becomes a member of one of its thirty-five national unions. Dues are paid centrally and funds then allocated to the trade unions. Each member pays according to his salary, and it does not influence the services received. Thus unemployed members, though released from paying dues, still enjoy all services and benefits.

The Histadrut defines centrally the framework of a unified wage and social benefit policy for all members, leaving the unions to negotiate with employers. The resultant balance of national needs and what is the workers' due has brought social and economic stability over the years. One noteworthy aspect is the measure of authority enjoyed by works' committees under collective labour agreements. Managements must consult with them particularly on hiring and dismissals. Likewise, joint productivity councils are the rule.

By law and under collective agreements, employers must contribute regular monthly payments to workers' provident and insurance funds to the equivalent of 20 to 35 per cent of direct wages. These monies enable trade unions to provide their members with decent pensions on retirement. Indeed these and other mutual aid benefits developed by organized labour in Israel meant that Jewish refugees arriving in their new homeland were duly protected and their integration facilitated as productive elements in society.

As public economic sectors develop the world over we find that labour relations become increasingly involved. We are confronted with the situation whereby public utilities are beginning to provide rising tension in labour relations. We must accord top priority to this matter of winning peace in this key area of labour relations. This can be won by a deeper involvement of workers in management and thereby advance us towards the target of greater democracy in public administration. Otherwise public administration will be reduced to the imagery of a giant soul-less octopus with tentacles grasping to control areas far and near. What we have to fight for is to humanize public administration by involving workers in its policy-making and managerial processes.

MAN IN CONTROL OF HIS OWN DESTINY

The wider picture of society seems to offer a gloomy vista of a world suffering from alienation. There is a need for the kind of motivation that will enable people to confront the all-encompassing bureaucracies. We have to help workers acquire the self-image of a man in control of his own destiny.

What we are also witnessing today is the increase in questioning of established notions in international labour movements. The narrow outlook of classical trade unionism has been rendered unviable. The old notion that trade unions can only concern themselves with bread-and-butter issues and leave the government to look after housing and pensions is outdated. It is now generally recognized that trade unions can no longer evade their responsibility to consider the community as a total unit. On the political level it may be said that even if a labour movement wishes to achieve political hegemony in a country it cannot achieve that by means of trade union action alone. On the other hand, even trade unions can no longer rely only on a political party in order to achieve their aims. Rather they must acquire political power through their own resources. This must lead trade unions to produce their own programmes for dealing with social problems and also to be ready to campaign for them as a fighting movement.

Here in Israel as the new decade advances we in the Histadrut have to face up to serious problems. This is especially the case with our labour economy. We must involve the workers in management and extend profit-sharing schemes with the aim of deepening worker identification with their places of work. How well we succeed in this task will affect the future of labour enterprises in Israeli society. The heat has gone out of the old arguments against the very existence of a labour economic sector. After all, if the state is such a big enterpreneur as is local government and if more and more companies are owned by share capital, why should not the workers be owners too? It is becoming widely accepted that the old claims of private capital are disproven – as if they are the only ones who can get things done. Indeed, even in the USA – the capitalist society par excellence – the public sector has expanded mightily. We have already seen new processes at work there with a growing differentiation between ownership and management and the ensuing trend known as the managerial revolution.

New ideas must be included throughout trade unions as well and that applies both inside Israel and elsewhere. Today the trade unionist cannot remain lacking in a sense of responsibility for the wider interests of his society and the economy of his country. Trade union leadership right down to shop steward level must become partners in economic development. Trade unions must have a say in the formulation of national income policies and in overseeing the fair distribution of the national income. This must as a matter of course imply trade union partnership in overall economic planning. Indeed, economic and technological developments have provided considerable impetus in this direction. It is sometimes said that these interests are compatible, but from observation this seems quite unfounded. For the trade unionist interested in obtaining the maximum return for workers for their labour, there can be no question of the worker not becoming a partner in overall economic responsibility.

This notion must be properly considered by trade unions especially in view of the expanding role played everywhere by the public sector. Yet above and beyond all this there remains the human element – of educating man to achieve harmony between his own self-image and the kind of work he must do. This is where education must be involved. We of the Histadrut have always considered ours as an educational movement and devoted many of our resources to this end. Therein, I believe, lies a real challenge to which the international labour movement can rise when it comes to confront the accelerating developments of contemporary society.

Chapter 7

USA

LEONARD WOODCOCK
President, United Automobile Workers

Any consideration of industrial democracy in the United States must begin with an appreciation of the historic and continuing vitality of the American labour movement and of collective bargaining as practised by American unions and management throughout the past thirty-six years.

The industrial union movement of the 1930s, born out of the collapse of laissez-faire capitalism in the Great Depression, was the most dynamic element in the new release of American social energies under the 'New Deal' presidency of Franklin Roosevelt. The successful struggle of wage earners in mass production industries for recognition of their unions by employers must be considered, on several counts, the single most important democratic advance of the present century in the United States.

The implantation and gradual development of an ingenious and intensely job-related system of worker representation and negotiation in major American industries lifted, directly and indirectly, a whole class of abused and deprived Americans into a new status of active economic and political citizenship. Thenceforth, a formerly autocratic management was obliged to recognize and deal with the body of workers and their union as contractual partners in the workplace; and local, state and national power-brokers had to give more respectful attention to organized labour as a continuing party-at-interest in the political and legislative process.

It is instructive, at a time when in the United States it has been fashionable among some university-trained liberals to caricature white wage-earners as racists, to recall that the victories of industrial unionism in the urban centres of the

North in the 1930s and 1940s also constituted the first major civil rights breakthrough in this century for black workers and the black community. Traditional black leaders in the years before the advent of industrial unionism had sponsored a style of humility and excessive gratitude for the relatively small favours blacks received from white paternalism. The black elite's typical response to the colour bar was a plea to black people to improve themselves rather than a demand that the white community square its own behaviour with its democratic credo.

The coming of industrial unionism breached the wall of racial exclusion and gave black workers a practical alternative both to white paternalism in industry and to the passivity and forbearance preached in the black ghetto.

Thus, many years before America as a whole had to examine its conscience and begin to correct its undemocratic behaviour, white and black wage-earners had to begin to learn to live and work together and American industrial unions had to come to grips with the problems of discrimination both in the union and on the job. In the process of facing the problem, they obliged industrial management to face it as well, instead of exploiting racial antagonism as in the past. When the 1943 race riot exploded in Detroit, investigation by the Federal government found that in those plants where the United Automobile Workers had established itself, work continued in calm.

The growth of industrial unionism had another pervasive educational and political effect. The daily necessity of representing workers in the shops, interpreting national contracts, negotiating local agreements and dealing with foremen and other management spokesmen on behalf of workers with grievances led to the training, through direct experience and union instruction, of scores of thousands of rank-and-file leaders, who became representatives and advisers of workers in the plants and active spokesmen of the union in the community.

Nationally, the rise of industrial unionism, its challenge to corporate management, and management's stubborn resistance to unions and collective bargaining had another important effect from the standpoint of industrial democracy.

During the interval between the First World War and the stock market crash of 1929 that ushered in the depression, 'the business of America', as President Calvin Coolidge correctly defined it in exemplary conservative terms, 'was business'. No strong union movement existed to rock the ship of state and siphon off corporate profits to augment the purchasing power of wage earners. Under Harding, Coolidge and Hoover, the pure conservative orthodoxy of political power in Washington would have delighted Karl Marx, so perfectly did it conform to the Marxian definition of capitalist government as the administrative committee of the bourgeoisie.

When business orthodoxy both in Washington and the industrial heartland failed so spectactularly beginning in 1929, the place of the corporation and the narrow economic ethic of the corporate manager in American society were called into serious question. Industrial labour's struggle to organize and and industry's fierce resistance held what today is called the issue of corporate responsibility in the forefront of the national consciousness throughout the pre-war era of the New Deal. A flurry of social legislation in the middle 1930s, including the National Labour Relations Act obliging employers to bargain in good faith with labour, gave a measure of economic security to the average American, but an ambitious inquiry into the concentration of industry and financial institutions (the hearings and reports of the Temporary National Economic Committee) was brought to an abrupt halt as the closing circle of war absorbed the attention of Roosevelt and the nation.

For the next twenty-five years the United States was pre-occupied with hot and cold war, preparation for wars, and such major consequences of war as the reconstruction of Europe and, lately, with the problem of withdrawing from the disastrous intervention in Indochina. A re-discovery of the poverty, inequities and contradictions in American life occurred during the Kennedy years, but the impulse to cope with them was overwhelmed by an increasing commitment of resources to feed a growing obsession with Vietnam.

As we release ourselves from that obsession, a new opportunity opens to confront the realities of the American situation. And again, as in the 1930s, the social and economic role of the corporation is under scrutiny. The worker in the plant, the worker outside the plant as citizen and consumer, and Americans generally in recent years have increasingly perceived that the corporation, with massive assistance from government in contracts and tax advantages, exploits the newest technologies carelessly and selfishly, both in the process of production and with regard to the broad effect of technological change on the society and the environment. Massive social and environmental costs stemming from runaway technology – devastation of the land, pollution of air and water, displacement and unemployment of workers, destruction of regional economies, threats to health and life at work and throughout the community stemming from reckless use of toxic substances – have never been taken into account when crucial decisions have been made with respect to the introduction of new technologies. Corporate executives, frequently in alliance with government technocrats, have consulted only their own immediate economic interests. As a result, these, massive social costs ignored in private corporate decision-making are borne sooner or later by the worker and average citizen. If those who made the decisions were obliged to take such social costs into account, our national use of technology would become more responsible and humane.

If we are to expand the frontiers of industrial democracy, the labour movement and the whole society will have to demand a new approach to technological assessment. The whole process of decision making leading to the introduction of new technologies must be opened up to all persons and groups whose lives will be affected and who therefore have a direct interest in shaping the decisions. Working people and most other Americans have always been obliged to react to the impact of technology after the fact. Workers and their unions have also been in the position of reacting to the impact of management decisions after the fact in the workplace, although their jobs and lives are affected by all such decisions.

A panel of the National Academy of Sciences, in a study on technological assessment prepared for a Congressional committee, stated: 'Decisions concerning the development and application of new technologies must not be allowed to rest solely on their immediate utility to their sponsors and users. Timely consideration must be given to the long-term sacrifices entailed by their use and proliferation, and to potentially injurious effects upon sectors of society and the environment often quite remote from the places of production and application.'

The panel addressed itself to the broad question of technological assessment, but there is a similar need for prior decision-making within industry, in the work environment, where industrial workers have to scramble constantly to hold their own against the hazards and insecurities resulting from managerial decisions based on management's view of its own interest, in the absence of the affected worker and his union representative.

Prior consultation and shared decision-making between labour and management in every area of the industrial process that bears upon the jobs and lives of working people is the necessary counterpart of the democratization of decision making with respect to the introduction of new technologies if American society, or for that matter any industrial society, is to master and manage applied science for humane and civilized ends, rather than, as now, continuing to be pushed and shoved and knocked about by it.

In this imperative movement toward an opening up of decision making, collective bargaining will be, in the United States at least, an essential instrument.

A RECORD OF ACHIEVEMENT

The general malaise in America, and in varying degree in all industrial nations, has left no institutions untouched by public mistrust. It would be cause for wonder if the institution of collective bargaining were an exception. The United States is a society where the myths of the competitive market and free enterprise are particularly strong and hence where there is a predisposition to swallow the employer fiction that wage increases are the prime and perhaps sole engine of inflation. The process of collective bargaining through which wages are set, moreover, lends itself to such distortions. Bargaining for wages and other worker benefits has normally taken place in the glare of publicity and has often been attended by the drama of impending strikes. The raising of prices, on the other hand, before the advent of the Nixon charade of price stabilization, took place in the privacy of executive offices and was often timed to follow the negotiation of new agreements with labour, in order to drive home the implication or outright claim that the wage increase forced the price increase.

Collective bargaining has also to a considerable degree become the victim of its own success in enabling a generation of American workers to gain a more or less precarious foothold on the bank of the economic mainstream, frequently by dint of too much overtime and the presence of wives as well as husbands in the labour force.

Americans, moreover, as Tocqueville found as early as the

1830s, have characteristically thought of themselves as members or potential members of the middle class; and with good reason, because the expanding physical frontier made America a land of upward mobility, as generations of immigrants found and demonstrated. Nothing could be more natural than that American workers would aspire to a higher status in life. The American labour movement and collective bargaining over their share of a rising national product helped them to satisfy that ambition. But this phenomenon is not peculiar to the United States. It can be observed, perhaps to a lesser extent, in the societies of Western Europe where, although working class consciousness has prevailed for generations, the life style of a new generation of workers is changing under the influence of a mass consumption economy.

The irony in this situation, to speak only of the United States, although experience in other industrial nations appears to follow similar lines, is that what the labour–management bargain gives is significantly reduced in value by what is lost through the inequities and other inadequacies of the public bargains that are struck through the current political process.

Before considering that matter, it is important to examine the very great achievements of collective bargaining in the perspective of that generation of American workers whose lives were considerably bettered by it during the past three-and-a-half decades.

Although the divine right of kings had been demolished by the political revolutions of the seventeenth and eighteenth centuries, the industrial revolution in its place enshrined the divine right of property and created the wage earner, who was virtually the property of the employing class and the governments that served employer interests.

This new non-person had to struggle for well over a century to create himself as a human being entitled to basic political and economic rights. In post-revolutionary America, efforts of working men to organize in order to improve their lot were held by the courts to be criminal conspiracies. Throughout most of the nineteenth century and well into the twentieth, labour organizations were reluctantly tolerated as long as they were content merely to exist. When they sought to gain recognition or improve wages and conditions, employer resistance was fierce. If workers resorted to the strike to bring employers to the bargaining table, the courts could be counted on to enjoin union activity as a threat to the tangible or intangible rights of property and/or the smooth flow of interstate commerce.

Workers in skilled crafts succeeded during the 1880s in laying the foundations of viable unions. But employers in most basic industries blocked the organization of industrial workers or rode roughshod over their unions for decades more, until the divine right of corporate management lost its credibility in the 1930 depression.

This lack of credibility, however, did not communicate itself to employers with any abiding force. As soon as the initial shock wave passed, employers reasserted their natural right to determine the economic and social fate of workers and their families, and to resist unions with the aid of elaborate espionage and strike-breaking services. It took a Congressional inquiry into such tactics and a series of strikes in basic industries to compel employers to recognize industrial unions and bargain with them under the terms of the National Labour Relations Act.

As a result of several generations of government bound to the notion that 'that government governs best that governs least', the new unions also confronted a very thin and frail infrastructure of social policy and programme, almost all of it the first fruits of Franklin Roosevelt's 'New Deal' reforms in the 1930s.

A Federal social security programme and a Federal–state unemployment compensation programme had been enacted. But the social security programme was limited to retirement pensions for the elderly. There were no provisions for hospital-medical care or sick pay. Federal laws were enacted providing for minimum wage standards under government contracts and in interstate commerce. But the several states, under the tutelage of industry lobbyists, determined levels and duration of benefits for unemployed workers and those disabled by industrial illness or accident. And despite efforts under the Roosevelt administrations before the Second World War to stimulate the economy and provide jobs through public works projects, the rate of unemployment remained high throughout the pre-war period.

Collective bargaining, therefore, beginning as it did in that unpromising social and economic climate, had not only to move toward industrial democracy in the places of work. In addition, through negotiated supplements or equivalents, it had to overcome gradually the insufficiency or total lack of public, social and economic security programmes.

The record of achievement under these circumstances has

been substantial. Millions of workers throughout the basic industries, as a result of negotiations between their unions and management, are now regularly protected by such benefits as the following, although coverage varies from industry to industry:

- wage increases are related both to annual increases in productivity and to rising living costs, thus assuring a continuing improvement in living standards even when public policy fails to contain inflationary pressures in the economy;
- health care programmes financed by the employer, compensating for the lack of national health insurance. Coverage in UAW programmes includes hospital, surgical, medical and mental health care and payment for prescription drugs;
- retirement benefits to supplement low public pensions, including early retirement benefits enabling workers to retire on a decent income before age 62, when public social security payments become available. Under contracts negotiated by the UAW in 1970-1, workers with thirty years of service on or after 1 October 1972 will be able to retire at age 56 on a pension of $500 a month;
- weekly sickness and accident benefits for workers absent from work because of illness or temporary disability. Benefits negotiated by the UAW provide about 65 per cent of pay for as long as fifty-two weeks;
- life insurance coverage for workers (under the UAW contracts) who die while in the employ of the company, scaled to wage rates and providing in addition a monthly benefit of $175 for the surviving spouse for at least two years and for as long as twelve years depending on the survivor's age;
- severance pay when a plant closed or a job is discontinued and the worker is permanently dismissed; a form of transitional security for workers between jobs, to compensate in part for the inadequacy of public manpower and employment policies;
- a negotiated supplement to state unemployment benefits when a worker is temporarily laid off for lack of work. In UAW contracts this combination of negotiated and public benefits for most workers can amount to 95 per cent of pay after taxes for as long as fifty-two weeks;
- negotiated vacation pay, holiday pay, three days of paid leave when there is a death in the family, paid rest periods during the work day, a pay supplement for workers called to serve on juries in public trials;

– a negotiated paid holiday period from Christmas through New
Year's Day.

In addition to such economic benefits, there are many non-
economic benefits which workers enjoy as a result of collective
bargaining; benefits, that is, which derive from joint decision-
making in matters formerly the exclusive domain of management.
Such benefits include:

– full-time union presence in places of work, with representatives
  elected by workers or, in some cases, appointed by their union;
– shift preference by seniority;
– seniority rules relating to lay-off and recall;
– grievance procedure in the place of work which frequently
  includes, as the last step, binding arbitration by impartial
  umpires selected jointly by union and employer, enabling
  workers to lodge complaints and receive satisfaction, if the
  complaint is justified, against management's violation of the
  contract;
– rights of transfer to other jobs in the plant;
– promotion rights;
– protection against management abuse of disciplinary measures
  and discharge;
– right to share in overtime work; and in some cases to refuse
  it (mainly in smaller plants);
– right to strike during the life of the contract against unfair
  production standards or unsafe working conditions.

A JOB-CENTERED UNIONISM

American unionism has obtained such benefits because it is
firmly rooted in the places where its members work. As noted,
under law the American union is the exclusive representative of
all workers in the bargaining unit, and must bargain for all the
workers in the unit, whether or not they are members. And the
union is organized and administered to perform that function.

The 'union' to almost all American trade union members is
the local union, rather than the national or international union
or some intermediate body. Local unions have a direct relation
to the place of work; the shop itself in the case of industrial
unions, the local community or small labour market area in the
case of craft unions.

Collective agreements between national industrial unions and management are normally negotiated not at the industry level but with each company, and in addition local agreements covering individual plants are negotiated between each local union and the corresponding plant management. The master agreement and the local agreements become the body of law at the place of work during the life of the contract, which may vary from one to three or more years, and disputes under the agreements are adjusted under the grievance system.

DIRECT REPRESENTATION IN THE WORKPLACE

With the concentration of industry and the importance in negotiations of such complex matters as pensions, insurance and supplementary unemployment benefits, there has been a strong trend toward the centralization of the bargaining process at the levels of the national unions and the firm. Under such circumstances the continuing and increasing vitality of the shop-level grievance procedures assumes greater importance. For it is through the handling of grievances, the access of all workers in the shop to the grievance procedure, and the effectiveness of the procedure in protecting the worker's rights under the contract that the union creates and maintains a substantial measure of industrial democracy and in the process proves its worth to the worker every working day. Effectiveness in the handling of grievances creates and sustains loyalty to the union. This loyalty is converted into bargaining strength, which in turn results in further progress in negotiations.

Almost all of the roughly 150,000 collective agreements in the country provide for a grievance system. Generally speaking, a grievance procedure will have a number of steps, beginning with a worker's complaint to his foreman, on his own or in the presence of his steward. If not settled at that point, the grievance would probably be set forth in writing, signed by the aggrieved worker and taken up by the steward with a higher management representative in the plant. Failing agreement at that stage, the written grievance would be submitted by the steward to the union's shop committee. At this level, grievances are subject to review by committee members not only to verify facts and clarify issues but also to consider the possible effects of processing or withdrawing the grievance within the broader perspective of diverse and often conflicting interests in the whole work community of the plant. The union bargains on behalf of all the workers in the unit, and the local union must take due account of the interests of all the workers in the processing of grievances, because virtually every grievance launched into the procedure will have the ripple effect of a smaller or larger stone thrown into a pool. Disputes over job classification, work assignments and seniority can have wide impact within and among work groups and hence cannot be regarded as merely individual complaints. These complaints, moreover, must be adjusted within the framework of the collective bargain made with management. Before the union established itself in the workplace, management's authority was virtually uncontested. That authority is yielded and shared in many areas once the union is established, but it is not wholly surrendered, either in negotiating the bargain or in carrying it out under the daily stress and strain of work relationships. It cannot be expected, therefore, outside of ideological daydreams, that the grievance system will somehow transcend the limitations of the union–management compromise. That compromise, that mixture of conflict and accommodation, is bound to be reflected in the overall performance of the grievance machinery. All grievances cannot be won. Hence, speaking generally, grievances must be screened through the several stages of the process in order to concentrate local union energies on those grievances that can be won and whose winning will redound to the greatest good of the greatest number of workers.

A number of grievances therefore will be screened out by the shop committee. A number will be won as a result of meetings between the shop committee and top local management. Others may be withdrawn by mutual agreement without prejudice to either party. The shop committee will move others to the next step of an appeal, where the grievances will be reconsidered in meetings at which members of the shop committee and representatives of local management will be joined by representatives of the national union and top corporate management. Grievances not disposed of one way or another at that step will be submitted to the final judgement of an arbitrator.

Under major contracts in the automobile industry, disputes over health and safety and production standards cannot be resolved through arbitration. If these issues cannot be settled through bargaining, the local union, following procedure outlined in the UAW Constitution, can seek authorization to strike from the International Executive Board.

No simple model of grievance machinery can begin to suggest the variety and complexity of the means by which workers organized in local unions defend themselves and what they regard as their job rights, against the rigours and hazards of mass production and the natural tendency of management to reduce working men and women to an economic role as factors in the production process. The presence of union power in the workplace has strengthened the worker's position vis à vis supervision far beyond his access to the formal grievance procedure. A high proportion of workers' complaints may have little or no standing under a strict construction of contract language. Before there was a union in the shop the foreman was under little or no pressure to consult more than his own and management's interest in responding to complaints; and since there was little doubt where the preponderance of power lay, fewer complaints found verbal expression. With a union representative at his side or available in the work group, the worker is more apt to give vent to his discontents, and the foreman is more apt to find it in his interest (and/or the firm's interest) to deal with the worker's complaint whether or not it has standing under the contract.

Reduction of such informal bargaining has been a main objective in the professionalization of industrial relations in larger firms. University-trained industrial relations experts have sought to reduce the costs of grievance handling by pressing for more precise and detailed contract language, for the training of foremen in the letter of the contract as viewed by management, for closer co-ordination between higher management and line supervision in grievance matters, for a more careful preparation of management's case in the processing of grievances, for confining management's response to worker complaints to the formal grievance procedure, and for the limitation of union representation in the plant, although the need for such representation has grown with the physical expansion of plant areas and the complexity of such programmes as insurance, pensions and supplemental unemployment benefits.

An arm's-length, strict-constructionist view of management's relations with the union, however, can be self-defeating. A coldly administrative approach to grievance handling that discourages foremen from informal efforts to deal with worker's complaints that do not fit neatly into the formal procedure is a short-sighted evasion of the human realities of the work community. Foremen are closer to these realities than higher supervision. A majority of them were promoted from the rank-and-file, and they work on the shop floor, where it is more obvious than in the offices of higher management that the human and mechanical problems of production cannot be disentangled. Many foremen therefore instinctively appreciate the practical wisdom of making a human response to a human problem, even if the problem has to be solved without recourse to the formal grievance system.

When this instinctive wisdom is not forthcoming, which is often, and when the formal grievance system becomes a frustrating obstacle course rather than a channel of communication and mutual accommodation, the human problems don't disappear; they fester. And the troubles stemming from management's insensitivity and remoteness have lately been compounded by the influx of a new generation of young workers, many of whom have not yet acquired the self-interest in industrial discipline (or union solidarity) derived from senority and other work-related benefits and from long memories of economic insecurity. It should not be surprising that managements which never tried very hard to understand an older generation of workers have failed to come to human terms with the nature and expectations of the new. Over the years progress has been made in the 'humanization' of working conditions through union pressures in organized shops and through management initiatives to forestall unionism; yet the 'science' of management all too often remains a dismal science, denying or downgrading the human element in production.

WORK AND THE MACHINE

A member of the 1929 Committee on Recent Economic Changes wrote: 'The true significance of the Industrial Revolution was that it carried the transfer of skill to such a degree as to make the worker an adjunct to the tool whereas, formerly the tool was an adjunct to the skill of the worker.'[1]

It would be a gross understatement to say that this transformation of the worker and of his relationship to his work has had the most pervasive and radical effects on human life and society during the past two hundred years. We have hardly

[1] Quoted in *The Employment Impact of Technological Change*, Appendix volume II of the report of the National Commission on Technology, Automation, and Economic Progress, February 1966.

scratched the surface in coping with those human effects, yet the transformation in recent years has continued at an accelerating pace. The 1966 report states: 'An important shift occurred in the American economy in the early 1950s, when it changed from one which for 30 years had emphasized mass-production technologies and the jobs appropriate to them, to an economy which is emphasizing automatic techniques and the jobs appropriate to such innovations. . . .'

Whereas the pre-industrial artisan had command of his skill and could practice it with relative autonomy, the 1966 report of the Automation Commission makes it clear that elaborate efforts must be made by engineers and managers from initial research to trial production runs if today's American wage-earners are to find satisfaction in their labour, over and above the basic satisfaction derived from having a job at all in an economy marked with high unemployment. Furthermore, managers frequently do not care to make such elaborate efforts: '. . . the designer of new technologies and the work structures into which they will be fitted has a certain latitude. He can make the work structure thoroughly unsatisfactory or even dangerous for the man who must live in it every day, or he can model it with more satisfactory dimensions. In short . . . the nature of human work as it develops over the next decade is, in a considerable degree, within the control of the engineers and managers who will design the occupational structure.

'However, many elements in the new hardware or organizational structure are frequently frozen too early, leading to the inclusion at the manning stage of many technical innovations with features undesirable both from the standpoint of operating management and the worker. These might have been eliminated had consideration been given to them at the stage of blueprinting, etc. . . . or of designing jigs and fixtures. . . .'

The 'findings and the recommendations' of this part of Appendix II of the 1966 Automation Commission report nicely suggest the degree to which the intrinsic human satisfactions of jobs in our society have been destroyed, aside from their economic value and their importance in consuming time:

1. Because of the enormous growth of scientific and engineering research over the past decade, the technological component in human work has become decisive in defining job dimensions in the modern world.

2. The rapidity, depth, and extent of changes offers managers and engineers a twofold opportunity: To redesign human work in the interest of maximizing the quality and the quantity of the product and to redesign it in the interest of the basic human needs of men and women at work. Limits exist in both areas, but the degree of flexibility is greater than currently realized. In many cases the two are not in serious conflict, and where they are, a compromise should be fully explored, considering the interest of both parties.

3. Old work environments should be analyzed as well as the new from a broad dimensional approach, using the kind of analysis illustrated in this report or another of equal scope.

4. Success in changing either the hardware or the surrounding organizational structure within new work environments depends upon a major factor – *timing*. In the genesis of new products and new technologies, the point of maximum flexibility should be seized by managers, engineers, and behavioural scientists. An outstanding example of advance planning and interdisciplinary co-operation between the physical and the life sciences may be found in certain areas of the aerospace industry.

5. With intelligent planning, an enormous reservoir of skills, both technical and psychological, can be conserved and made productive in the transition from old to new technological work environments. Two examples, cited in this report, are automatic and semi-automatic steel mills, and most of the industries installing numerical control systems.

6. If managers and engineers, as architects of the future, are to meet the fundamental needs of their clients, they must study the individual and group personalities of those who will occupy the industrial world they have been called upon to design. Universities and engineering schools probably hold the key to that broadened understanding.

7. It is as important to appraise the differences as it is the similarities between one work environment and another. Some new technologies bring features favourable to workers; others introduce new types of stultification, danger, or instability. *There is no substitute for an objective examination of each work environment by responsible managements and unions that makes full use of the analytic tools of behavioural science.*

8. The quality of civilization cannot be divorced from the work

men do and the tools they use within the society which gives that civilization its form and content. Not machines themselves but the ways they are *designed, used, or abused* determine the quality of industrial society.' [italics added]

The obvious implication of such findings and recommendations is that intrinsic job satisfaction is at the point of death in much of American industry and already needs intensive care if it is to survive. The wholesome bread of meaningful work, which used to be the staff of life, is hard to come by; and the commercial mass-produced product must be injected with nutrients because it has little value in itself. It is mostly a way of making money.

All this is not an indictment of technology itself, as the last sentence of the findings makes clear; rather that the quality of industrial society is determined by the ways machines 'are designed, used, or abused'. There is little need for 'the analytical tools of behavioural science' in improving the quality of the work environment. The same old challenge remains: to treat the worker not as an adjunct of the productive process but as an adjunct of the productive process but as an autonomous human being. The Automation Commission's report stated:

'. . . Today it is possible to view jobs as broad entities in which the human personality may be considered just as vital a component as the non-human mechanism.

'The task of introducing this new approach requires extensive preparation. It cannot be accomplished by men accustomed to dealing with these problems in traditional ways. . . .'

JOINT DECISION-MAKING

What the new ways shall be cannot be left to corporate management. The new technologies that have transformed the American economy during the past twenty years or more were introduced with an eye to their profitability from the standpoint of corporate managements, but without regard to their effects either on working people or on the environment. As the American environmental scientist Barry Commoner has pointed out in his book *The Closing Circle*, it is substantially more profitable to produce polluting detergents than to produce harmless soap, to cite only one example. And because corporate managers found it profitable, they deluged work environments with an unceasing flood of toxic substances and processes, without taking precautions such as those recommended in the Automation Commission study in order to create work environments in which the risks of occupational illness, injury and death would be minimized. As a result, the mounting toll of work-related trauma and disease became a national scandal. The demands of workers and their unions for relief obliged the Congress to pass, and a business-oriented administration to sign, a Federal occupational safety and health law setting uniform standards for health and safety covering more than 57 million workers and more than 4 million employers. This set penalties for employer violations and authorized full participation of workers and their unions in the law's enforcement.

Participation of unions in the policing of in-plant health and safety under the 1970 Act offers a crucial opportunity for joint union–management action. Such action can have its optimum effect only if managements are wise enough to encourage it as an exercise in joint, *preventive* decision-making having to do with worker participation in the creation of wholesome work environments and better methods of performing tasks.

The development of labour law in the United States in recent years has had the effect of restricting the scope of bargainable issues, by making fine distinctions with respect to which employers must bargain and those concerning which the employer may refuse to bargain. This trend is anachronistic and counterproductive in a period when mounting problems of work and a new social awareness among workers, mainly but not exclusively of the new generation, require full use of bargaining's great potential not only to solve problems but to foresee and prevent them.

In the coming years, workers of the new generation will inevitably seek a participatory role in all areas of decision making, not out of some ideological compulsion to destroy the 'system', but out of a pragmatic interest in protecting themselves and their families from the multiple insecurities and inequities the current governance of the system breeds.

The younger workers, as the us Labour Department has acknowledged in a profile of the American labour force in the 1970s, will be more insistent than their elders on having a continuing voice in matters that affect their jobs, their income and their environment.

In other words, management can look forward to a further

erosion of its self-arrogated, arbitrary and non-negotiable rights throughout a whole range of decision making hitherto beyond the reach of collective bargaining. Not only will collective bargaining be pressed in new areas; it will be pressed not to give workers relief from the consequences of management's unilateral decisions, but rather to share in the decisions for the purpose of preventing the adverse consequences.

Such joint decision-making will not be limited to the job and what might be called its management. It will extend to such matters, all of consequence to working people, as the removal of work from bargaining units, the closing and location of plants, and at least the right of consultation in such matters affecting workers as price, production and investment decisions.

It would serve no purpose to attempt to prescribe or predict what precises institutional forms such joint decision-making will assume; but the presumption would have to be that whatever new approaches are attempted would be made within the general framework of collective bargaining, which has demonstrated its capacity to accommodate both the adversary and co-operative modes of the union–management relationship.

CORPORATE RESPONSIBILITY

The focus of these next moves toward industrial democracy will inevitably be within the large corporations which, along with the Federal government, are the dominant decision-makers and planning entities in the American economy. The question of corporate responsibility has become a matter of public concern in recent years. There is a widespread and growing awareness that the larger corporations are in practice industrial governments and pace-setting social institutions, although they go about their business legally camouflaged as private persons. Thus camouflaged, they have all too often been bad citizens, operating on the basis of a very narrow economic calculus and letting the frequently heavy adverse social fall-out from their actions do its damage where it may.

Harvard sociologist Daniel Bell, writing (*Public Interest*, Summer 1971) of 'The Corporation and Society in the 1970's', had this to say: 'The modern business corporation has lost many of the historic features of traditional capitalism, yet it has, for lack of a new rationale, retained the old ideology – and finds itself trapped by it.

'*The point is that today ownership is simply a legal fiction.*
'A stockholder is an owner because, in theory, he has put up equity capital and taken a risk. But only a minor proportion of corporate capital today is raised through the sale of equity capital. . . .

'Given the pattern of stock ownership today – particularly with the growth of mutual funds, pension funds and trust funds – the stockholder is often an "in-and-out" person with little continuing interest in the enterprise. Such an in-and-out procedure may be a useful discipline for management and a measure of economic performance – but then it becomes a form of countervailing power, not ownership. True owners are involved directly and psychologically in the fate of an enterprise; and this description better fits the employees of the corporation, not its stockholders. For these employees, the corporation is a social institution which they inhabit. It is politically and morally unthinkable that their lives should be at the mercy of a financial speculator.'

'As a business institution, the "corporation" is the management and the board of directors, operating as trustees for members of the enterprise as a whole – not just as stockholders, but workers and consumers too – and with due regard to the interests of society as a whole. But if this view is accepted, there is a significant logical corollary – that the constituencies which make up the corporation themselves have to be represented within the board of corporate power. Without that, there is no effective countervailing power to that of executive management. More important, without such representation, there would be a serious question about the "legitimacy" of managerial power.'

PLANNING FOR PUBLIC GOALS

The legitimacy of corporate power, however, will be determined not alone by the readiness of managers to proceed with the further democratization of decision making in the private sector. American society is moving rapidly into an era whose problems will demand a drastic democratization of the decision-making process by which public goals and priorities are defined and resources are allocated.

The Automation Commission in its 1966 report stated:
'. . . The social map of the United States in recent years has been reworked more by government decisions in regard to

spending in science, research defence, and social needs than by any other combination of factors.

'In this second kind of change we are able, in the felicitous phrase of Dennis Gabor, to "invent the future". Since social change is increasingly a matter of conscious decisions and social choices, and given the huge resources we possess, we can decide what kind of future we want and work for it. In effect, we can spell out national goals, and seek to meet them within the framework of our capacities.'

The clear implication of that proposition is that we need some form of national planning to meet our national goals. Daniel Bell, who was a member of the Commission, states further in his *Public Interest* article that we are moving toward a society: '. . . in which the most important economic decisions will be made at the political level, in terms of consciously-defined "goals" and "priorities" . . . there is a visible change from market to non-market political decision-making. . . .'

The degree of political centralization required to set and meet goals under a democratic system will depend very largely on how far corporate managers are willing to go in resorting to collective bargaining and other forms of industrial democracy in order to render more socially responsible the governance of the private sector.

In any event, the United States needs a framework of democratic planning that will assure both that the private and public sectors are not working at cross-purposes, and that the process of setting goals and achieving them, instead of being monopolized by private managers and public bureaucrats, will be at every stage the real expression of the whole nation's views and interests.

COMMON GROUND

In this larger arena of decision making, the bargains will of necessity be a product of coalition politics. The future of industrial (or post-industrial) democracy will depend upon how successfully the forces of movement – labour, farmers, the working poor, blacks and other deprived minorities, and the more enlightened members of Galbraith's Educational and Scientific Estate – can find common ground.

Chapter 8

Norway

TOR ASPENGREN
President, Norwegian Trade Union Federation

WHAT DO WE MEAN BY DEMOCRACY IN INDUSTRY?

In the discussion in recent years of the more long-term tasks of the international labour movement we have often come across the terms industrial democracy, co-influence, co-determination, and democracy at work. To begin with it may therefore be appropriate to say a few words about what we usually mean by these terms.

In conformity with its fundamental views the labour movement supports the creation of a society that to the greatest possible extent is characterized by freedom, safety, human equality and brotherhood. During the last decades we have experienced a gradual development that has incorporated these values in an ever more living and marked reality. They have become increasingly a fundamental part of our whole way of life and our general view of humanity and society. Democracy has become something which is far more than rules on free and secret elections and legal equality. The labour movement has been the most important social motive power behind this process of democratization in our countries. Democracy at work, or industrial democracy, means that the fundamental demands which have been realized today in the political field also are gaining a foothold and are becoming realized in industry. Workers and employees should feel that in their work, they will be evaluated and respected, irrespective of occupation, placement and function, as free persons of equal value within the framework of the rules, order and discipline that will always be needed in a well-regulated industry. They should feel that through their daily work they are engaged in a common task in which everyone counts. In an atmosphere of co-operation, mutual respect and tolerance, they should have the natural right to influence conditions and measures that affect themselves directly and also the whole community inside the undertaking.

But obligations are also demanded of everybody in industry, because democracy is a demanding form of government which requires that our freedom and liberties are always administered with responsibility, understanding and knowledge.

Democracy in industry is dependent upon a broad co-influence by workers. What we usually conceive by the term 'co-influence' is that employees in different ways have a real possibility of influencing the various conditions at their workplace. In a number of fields in industry the various problems and differences have to be solved by daily negotiations, talks and discussions in advisory bodies and by more informal exchanges of opinions at all levels. What is decisive in the first place, however, is the general climate for human contact and the existence of mutual understanding and respect. In a democratic industrial setting the views of the employees will influence the life of the undertaking even if they do not have the formal right of co-determination.

But in order that the democratic rules may have full validity, the employees should also have the formal right of co-determination on the leading bodies in industry. When talking about co-determination in this connection we have in mind in the first place the legal right of the workers to adequate representation on the leading and governing bodies concerned with drawing up the main directions for the undertaking. Through such a system the workers will obtain the formal right to participate in the management of their own workplaces.

OUR AIMS

In the Norwegian labour movement there is no fundamental disagreement on the long-term goals for our work in this field. We are aiming at creating a society in which democratic conventions, rules and principles are implemented within industry. We hold fundamental democratic views and we shall never accept that the place where people spend one-third or one-fourth of their time should be dominated by a technocracy or by authoritarian leadership. We should also create within industry the basis for free and independent people to regard themselves as active members of a co-operating community.

The further development of democracy in industry is one of the greatest tasks of the labour movement in the years to come. In it we face the reality of a challenge that will put to a new and great test all our willingness to contribute, our constructive abilities and our sense of reality.

AN EVEN AND GRADUAL PROCESS

During recent decades the democratic development which has characterized our whole society has made itself felt also in our labour and industrial life. The intervention of popularly elected bodies in the private disposition of capital has given us increased guarantees against the abuse of national values in contravention to social interests.

In industry certain changes have taken place. A few decades ago the owner was the complete master in all questions concerning the undertaking and his employees. It was generally accepted that he, morally as well as legally, had the full and unabridged right to decide on all questions concerning wages and working conditions, and his employees were left without support for their demands.

Through the work and struggle of the trade union movement this picture has changed gradually. The supremacy of the employer over wages and working conditions has been partly replaced by co-operation and mutual recognition, and partly by a balance of power and interests at the collective bargaining table. New agreements now need to be established in order to give workers co-influence over wider questions, and co-operation between the political and trade union wings of the labour movement should be strengthened in order to lead to the regulation by clear legislation of conditions in important fields. All this would contribute towards giving workers a more upright back and making them more conscious of their own human dignity.

Society should make its own form of co-determination felt in parallel with the influence of the workers through their trade unions. This co-determination should be expressed by laws and regulations limiting the freedom of management action and protecting the interests of society as well as of employees. Today the management of an undertaking dares not act without any sense of responsibility towards society. The press and public opinion take an increasing interest in the disposition of the individual undertaking, so that management, whether on a large or small scale, is becoming gradually a more public affair – and no longer a private matter which does not concern the public at large.

It is our conviction that strong trade unions and vigilant public control will form the real basis for a continued development of workers' co-determination and industrial democracy. We may draw the conclusion from this that industrial democracy should not be organized in such a way that it would weaken the real co-determination represented by strong and dynamic trade unions. Workers' representatives on management boards should not become 'hostages' whose presence commits the trade unions when they should be safeguarding the interests of the workers. Nor should they become another set of shop stewards, thereby creating confusion in trade union matters. We may also draw the conclusion that systems of workers' co-determination should not be allowed to replace or to weaken the more general control over management which takes place through legislation and public debate.

It is also necessary to keep in mind that the development of co-determination should run parallel with the development of co-responsibility through new efforts for democracy in industry.

THE UNSOLVED TASKS

Although this even and gradual evolution has led to increased democracy in industry, there is still a lot to be done before the ideas of human equality, freedom and fellowship may be considered as fully implemented. Old ideas and evaluations often tend to remain, even though new views and ideas are gradually emerging. We may still come across many proponents of the old autocratic style which presumed that the labour force should be managed and regulated like a living car park. In addition there is another factor which tends to be paramount: it is the most vital and important task of the undertakings to yield surplus and ever-increasing production. This can cause one to lose sight of the fact that the factory and workshop should be places where living people can display their natural urge for activity and creation, and where sensitive and conscious individuals can have a sense of welfare and community in their daily work. In the years to come it should be the task of the labour movement to bring these human and social elements into the evaluation of industrial life.

The old system still retains too much influence over the functions and tasks of supervisors and foremen. Our educational institutions provide technical, economic and clerical experts with a good education in the traditional sense of the term. Graduates are trained to become skilled at handling production plans, economic calculations and modern machinery. But much too little emphasis is placed on the fact that when they start active employment they will not only manage dead and passive objects but will also manage and co-operate with a living labour force. They should also have an appreciation of trade union agreements and social and labour legislation and should be able to interact with human beings who are all individuals and each of whom is more than just a unit of manpower. In recent years much has been done in this field at our technical colleges and universities.

Nevertheless, there is still a lot left to be done in the years to come. Futhermore the old division into social classes, which is incompatible with the idea of human equality, still has a strong hold on our labour and industrial life. The individual function and job are still taken to represent different levels of social and human prestige. It should be borne in mind that a good many people still deem it to be natural and correct that manual workers should have longer working hours than non-manual workers, even though the loads and burdens of work often seem to justify the opposite view. Lines of demarcation are still being drawn – not for practical reasons, but simply out of tradition – between the different 'co-workers' in a factory, and these lines are in effect rooted in old and undemocratic traditions and circumstances. The quality of the various social measures introduced into the undertakings are often affected by the tendency to such social divisions.

Today workers have no formal rights of co-determination (there are exceptions to this rule), other than that concerning the central question of wages policy in the undertaking. The workers have no representatives on the governing bodies that have the formal responsibility for production plan and invest-ment policies in an undertaking, and by whom the most im-portant work appointments are made. In all these matters the daily management is legally responsible only to the capital owners. In this connection we may underline what we have already mentioned that close contacts and continuous co-operation between the representatives of workers and management may often mean as much as formal rights and policies. Labour and capital are two necessary and mutually dependent factors in the production process. Those who place the work of their hands at the disposal of others should therefore have the right as a principle to decide on the results and values achieved such joint efforts.

THE TASKS ARE MANIFOLD

When in the years to come we strengthen our drive towards the development of democracy in industry we shall still be facing a great many tasks which may not always be solved overnight. If we are going to solve such problems in a realistic way, one thing should perhaps be emphasized which we should not forget: namely, that we can never create a living democracy in industry by adopting legislation alone nor merely by including new provisions in an agreement. Industrial democracy in the deepest sense of the term is something which may only gradually grow out of a positive social setting in the undertakings and will almost deposit itself, so to speak, as the natural way of life. That is why, in the long run, such measures as information, training and industrial policy will be most important for our work.

SOCIAL AND HUMAN EQUALITY

In order to create such a suitable social setting in the undertakings in the future, it will be important to work consciously and intensively to remove all tendencies that divide workers into social groupings associated with their placing, title and function, and used as a social label. This effort should take place through practical measures in a number of fields: by the reasonable and natural equalization of working conditions, by the achievement of legal equality with regard to fringe benefits, and by other concrete measures which can eradicate the existing lines of demarcation which seek to place certain groups in a social position. All this would contribute to the realization that everyone who fulfils a useful and necessary function in industry, is entitled to equal social and human evaluation as of right.

ATTITUDE

We believe that new efforts for democracy in industry should take place on two parallel lines.

In the first place the development of joint consultation agreements should be followed by conscious training in order that the right of co-determination may become real. Our educational institutions will play a decisive role in the introduction of industrial democracy as well as in democracy as a whole. A well-developed educational system benefiting everybody is the cornerstone of industrial democracy. It is also of special importance to this democracy that elementary training at school is supplemented by modern adult education making a smooth passage into continued training for adults after they have started employment. Such a system will contribute towards breaking down social divisions and irrational barriers in industry. It will facilitate conditions for each individual person, irrespective of the level at which he commences employment in an undertaking, to be promoted according to his abilities to higher positions and more responsibility. This is an important aspect of industrial democracy. It should also give workers a better chance of exercising their right of co-determination and of bearing their co-responsibility in the management of the undertaking.

Workers acquire experience and knowledge in their jobs which they should be able to put into practice through co-determination both as a democratic right and for the benefit of the undertaking. In our times co-determination also requires of the workers, and especially of those who represent them at a higher level in the undertakings, that they have a knowledge of complicated economic and technical questions which they would otherwise have to obtain in different ways. Decisions on technical and economic questions of this kind although difficult to penetrate may frequently have the most far-reaching consequences for the workers concerned. For these reasons, knowledge is an important contributory factor towards obtaining real co-determination.

The training needed to enable workers to participate in industrial democracy in an effective way may take different forms. The trade unions have their own responsibility in this. We would underline, however, that society and management should also be conscious of their responsibilities in the matter.

In the second place, the organization of the undertaking

H

should be changed. From a democratic point of view the present organization of the undertaking has outlived its day and should give place to democratic bodies inside the undertaking.

The existing organization is based on the principle that the needs of capital alone should influence governing bodies in the undertaking. We would maintain that this form of organization in the undertaking is obsolete and does not correspond to our modern conception of democracy and the importance of labour. We are therefore proposing that the organization of the undertaking, the shareholding company, should be shaped by legislation in the first place, so that the employees may also have a forum where they may discuss and decide on matters, concerning the firm together with the capital owners and managers. We would underline that these measures should be taken in parallel and simultaneously. Each of them is only a part of the total reform.

We are proposing further that the present stockholders' committee should be replaced by a democratic plant assembly. This plant assembly should be something different from the original committee and more than a passive controlling body. Its importance should be reflected in the fact that the plant assembly alone should elect the board and that the plant assembly should be the body to which the board should be responsible.

We also believe that the board have the positive support of the plant assembly on matters concerning investments of any considerable extent, and concerning changes in the operation that would lead to extensive adjustments of the labour force. Moreover, the assembly should have the right and duty to to comment on the accounts and profit-sharing arrangements before these matters are considered by the general assembly. We are proposing that the employees should have one-third of the members of the plant assembly. The employees' representatives should be elected directly by all who are employed in the undertaking.

The workers' members on the plant assembly should have the right of nominating candidates for the board on an equal footing with other members of the plant assembly. They should be entitled to nominate candidates both inside and outside the undertaking. There should be a free right to debate the appointment of any of the proposed candidates regardless of their nomination in the plant assembly. In this way the elections of the board of directors would be taken out of the twilight world in which they take place at present. The election of board members should be one of the matters giving life and colour to the plant assembly.

TOWARDS INDUSTRIAL DEMOCRACY IN NORWAY

The latest step taken in that direction is a draft bill submitted to the Norwegian parliament calling for a revision of the present law on stock companies. In that draft bill the Ministry of Labour proposes an extension of co-determination for all employees (blue collar and white collar workers).

The draft is based on recommendations made last year by a public committee (called the Eckhoff Committee) that the government had appointed early in 1968. This Committee was headed by Mr Eckhoff, a judge of the Supreme Court, and comprised two other neutral experts, two representatives from the Norwegian national centre, LO (Tor Aspengren and Harry O. Hansen), and two representatives from the Norwegian Employers' Federation. The terms of reference agreed upon in advance between the LO and the Employers' Federation were an analysis of various questions that are usually summarized under the heading of industrial democracy. The committee would evaluate existing arrangements in Norway and propose unbiassed fundamental directives and other measures that would be of help in promoting the further development of industrial democracy in Norway. It was understood that the Committee would restrict its findings in the first place to industrial companies.

In its recommendations the Committee split into three sections. Aspengren and his colleague Hansen recommended the establishment of a company assembly (apart from the stockholders assembly) in all stock companies employing more than two hundred people. One-third of the members of this company assembly should be elected by and from among the employees of the company. The remaining members should be appointed by the stockholders' assembly. The board of directors (like the German Aufsichtsrat) should be elected by the company assembly. Important investment issues, projects involving rationalization or readjustment or major changes in the work-force would require a decision by both the board and the company assembly.

The chairman of the Committee and his two expert colleagues suggested the introduction of workers' representation at the board of directors provided the majority of the workers employed by the company in question agreed to such an arrangement. Two of them felt that this kind of workers' representation should be established only tentatively to begin with. The third expert was of the opinion that the law on stock companies should be revised at once so that workers employed by industrial enterprises with more than two hundred employees would be able to elect two representatives to the board. On the other hand all three experts rejected the establishment of a company assembly as proposed by the union representatives.

The two employers' members of the Committee followed the three experts in the rejection of the company assembly. In principle they suggested that any further development of industrial democracy would best be served by voluntary co-operation between the parties on the basis of provisions laid down in the Main Agreement of 1969 (a national agreement concluded by the LO and the Employers' Federation, comprising rules on workers' representatives at shop level, their rights and obligations, etc.) They also thought that workers' representation on the board should be introduced tentatively, as proposed by the three expert members. They felt that a special agreement to this end could be concluded at company level with the assistance of both the LO and the Employers' Federation. Aspengren and Hansen suggested alternatively – in case their proposal on the company assembly was turned down by parliament – that workers in industrial enterprises should have the right to elect among themselves two members to represent them on the board of directors.

As is the usual practice in Norway the proposals were submitted to various organizations, institutions and ministries to get their view on them. Detailed information on these views is available as well as on the general remarks made by the Ministry of Labour.

MAIN POINTS IN THE PROPOSAL SUBMITTED BY THE MINISTRY OF LABOUR

Essentially, the proposals made by the Ministry are based on the views put forward by Aspengren and Hansen. The Ministry suggests the establishment of a company assembly for all stock companies with more than two hundred employees, consisting of at least twelve members, of whom one-third should be elected by and from among the employees and the remaining two-thirds by the stockholders' assembly.

Furthermore, the Ministry points out that the introduction of such a company assembly has been discussed in public for many years already and any indefinite delay of the whole issue might have an adverse effect. The ideological basis of the government's endeavours is a favourable omen for the draft bill. The socialist government in Norway has sought to build a society where everybody can influence decisions affecting his or her own interests to the fullest extent practicable. Otherwise, it would be contrary to the idea of what democracy really should be, that important decisions determining to a large extent the situation of an individual, of the company and of the surrounding society as a whole, should be made by bodies where only owners' interests are represented. The Ministry believes that the proposed establishment of company assemblies in the best way would increase the employees' influence and open up new roads. In such a situation, industrial activities would be based increasingly on workers' participation in decision making and in responsibility.

The Ministry also stresses the fact that workers' representation, in decision making at the company level, according to the draft bill, will by no means render superfluous trade union activities and the trade union position at the factory level, or in industry in general. Trade union strength as a whole within each industrial plant at the company assembly and within the board will in future decide any real influence the workers may have within their factory and over their own conditions. According to the draft bill, the company assembly would elect the board of directors and the chairman of the board. The company assembly would be the highest authority in deciding matters relative to comprehensive investments compared with the resources of the company. or concerning rationalization or adjustments involving major changes or replacement of labour.

No provision is made in the draft bill for workers' representation on the board. But it is assumed that workers will have their candidates elected if the arguments in favour of their nomination are well-founded. Special emphasis is laid on the further development of these company assemblies, so that they may become an active platform for lively discussion and co-operation on matters relating, among other things, to the election of board members.

In the first place a solution must be found for bigger industrial enterprises. But at the same time, the Ministry says, it would be just and reasonable that workers employed by minor companies should be entitled to representation at the management level. Therefore, it is suggested that in companies with more than fifty employees, these employees may ask for one-third of the members of the board, or at least two board members, to be elected by and among the employees.

Certain problems are also dealt with which may arise in connection with workers' representation on decision-making bodies of a company. According to the present Act on stock companies, persons becoming members of decision-making bodies are expected to look after the company's interests. Therefore, workers' representatives in these bodies may face serious personal conflicts if the interests of the company on one side and the workers' interests on the other side are at stake. Questions relating to disqualification and duties not to divulge confidential matters are also dealt with at length. In this respect the Ministry believes that the question whether workers' representatives should resign because of disqualification should be decided according to the same rules that apply to any other member of the board or the company assembly. Provision is made explicitly for that in the present law.

The Ministry also is of the opinion that the question of workers' influence in decision making should not principally be restricted to stock companies. Therefore steps should be taken to work out similar arrangements for other types of enterprise as well. As a matter of course, co-operative enterprises should have similar types of workers' representation. If satisfying arrangements cannot be arrived at voluntarily, special legal provisions will have to be made to this end.

Furthermore, it has been emphasized that proper representation should not only be achieved within a single stock company, but also at the level of the leading firms. Similar provisions will be drafted for private firms that are not stock companies.

Chapter 9

UK

HUGH SCANLON
*President, Amalgamated Engineering and Foundry Workers'
Union*

For differing and often conflicting reasons, all kinds of organizations and individuals are concerning themselves with an
examination of the potential of organized workers to demand
and achieve a voice in, or eventual control over, their work
environment and their industrial destinies. With the rise in social
and economic expectations over much of industry, 'Work group
sanctions against management have gradually become effective
and "management by consent" generally necessary.'[1]

Of course, this tendency can be grossly exaggerated. Even
in well-organized factories with a strong shop stewards' organization, the power of workers is strictly limited and circumscribed. This fact has been exposed with brutal clarity by the
wave of giant mergers and takeovers, which have affected so
many important sections of the British economy over the past
few years. These moves have entailed drastic changes in the
country's industrial structure, often with grave repercussions
for the labour force concerned.

The power of private employers to circumvent even the most
developed form of workers' organization which aspires to an
effective voice in decision making, is graphically illustrated by
those examples where management can unilaterally close down
plants and threaten the livelihoods of thousands of workers.
These instances give an indication of the capacity of private
ownership, despite modifications introduced in the post-war
period, to impose strict boundaries to the development of democracy in industry.

[1] Arthur Marsh, *Managers and Shop Stewards*, London, 1963.

Yet, even if it is misleading to state simplistically that 'power lies on the shop floor', as a Minister in the late Labour government did, it is also obvious that there have been tremendous changes in the position and attitudes of shop floor workers, which are already having great repercussions in industry. If we look for a parallel one can only take the years before the First World War, when expansion of industry coupled with inflation provided the basis for militant union action and the growth of ideas connected with industrial democracy and workers' control. Significantly, it was during these years that the shop stewards' movement first developed to assume an important role in the big industrial struggles of the war years – particularly on Clydeside. Despite the revolutionary enthusiasm of some sections of workers after the First World War, the movement was effectively defused by the failure of the 1926 General Strike and, even more important, by the adverse economic conditions. In the dark years of the inter-war period, particularly during the depression and the resultant high unemployment, a largely defensive struggle had to be waged by the trade union movement. The prime task was to defend minimum national rates of pay, which was no easy task.

Despite this difficult situation, demands for industrial democracy were still raised, although the position in industry at that time was hardly conducive towards a strong struggle on the issue.

The effect of twenty-five years of economic upswing since 1945 was to recreate pre-1914 conditions at a potentially higher level, and to place the whole question of industrial democracy on a new plane of importance for the labour movement today. In a sense, the knot of history is being unravelled. The pre-1914 period was one of expansion of the trade union movement; it was a period not only of 'wage militancy', but of the forging of far-reaching ideas concerning industry and the working class.

There are many similarities with today's situation – although on a far wider scale. The labour movement has become infinitely better organized and more confident since the depression years of mass unemployment and hunger marches. An entire generation of workers has grown up who have not known a serious defeat. Trade union membership has more than doubled over this period, encompassing previously unorganized workers, such as white collar workers and technicians, who are being drawn into the ranks of the labour movement.

Added to this organizational strength, there is a feeling of confidence which has, in the recent period, communicated itself even to the worst paid and most oppressed sections of workers such as dustmen, roadsweepers and sewermen, who have already contributed to the so-called 'wages explosion' in Britain at the present time. While sections of workers such as these rise to their feet, strong trade union organizations have been built inside the modern and expanding industries, such as engineering, chemicals and the motor car industry.

It is, above all, in industries such as these, that shop stewards today 'tend to believe that any subject which affects their members is a fit and proper matter for negotiations and agreements' (W. S. McCarthy).

The shop stewards' movement, which was practically extinguished between the wars, has taken on new scope and new importance. In engineering, for example, the shop stewards' movement had been broken by the 1922 lockout; today, there are some 32,000 shop stewards in the engineering section of the AUEW alone.

These men are acknowledged to have taken a crucial role in industrial relations, particularly as the trend in negotiations over much of British industry is towards shop floor bargaining.

Despite this fact, the structure of bargaining does not recognize, in many cases, the realities of the new situation. The engineering industry is a prime example. The procedure established in this industry – based on the York Memorandum – was imposed on engineering workers in the aftermath of defeat. Not only is it weighted in the interests of the employers, but it also totally fails to adapt to a situation where shop stewards and workers are demanding more control over procedure at local level. Such demands are the stuff of industrial reality, and call attention to aspirations for genuine industrial democracy.

This example is just one symptom of the changed relationship at shop floor level in much of industry. Workers today are not necessarily bound by the limits of the largely defensive struggles of the past. Every serious work of research on the subject has brought out the fact that conflict in industry today is not just motivated by wage issues, but is evident in other matters which were popularly supposed in the past to be the sole realm of the hallowed 'managerial prerogative'. Issues concerning the hiring and firing of labour, the allocation of overtime, the introduction of new machinery, and safety measures are considered by many shop stewards, very properly, to be at least questions for joint negotiation. Significantly, disputes arising from such issues, as distinct from wages questions, are becoming a high proportion of the total. This change in emphasis is a direct expression of the desire of shop floor workers to achieve a measure of democratic control over their own conditions of work ... and it is simultaneously a reflection of the hostiltiy of management to so many of their demands.

The new aspirations of workers have to be taken into account increasingly by politicians and industrialists. As a prominent Labour politician, Anthony Wedgwood Benn, stated earlier this year: 'The new worker simply will not accept the old idea of authority, if by authority is meant the maintenance of the sort of blind discipline imposed from above that we associate with the past. ... Moreover, as manufacture becomes more specialized and the inter-dependence of all production grows still tighter, the worker will have the power to dislocate the whole system by withdrawing his labour. This is real power, indeed, and we must take account of it in exactly the same way as we have taken account of the development of the power of the international company.'

It is an indication of the pressure building up behind this demand within the British labour movement, that the Labour Party's National Executive Committee has issued a document on 'Industrial Democracy' which specifically argued that it was time for 'a serious attempt to widen the area of common decision-making and acceptance of responsibility to replace managerial prerogatives'. The question is posed in a more radical form inside the movement from other spokesmen but, in whatever form it is posed and whatever the end in view, it is not a standpoint held only by minorities cut off from the direction of the movement; rather it expresses a very real response to a changed situation so far as the British working class is concerned.

The employers have also been forced to make an assessment and to take positions in relation to this movement. No exposition of the workers' movement for industrial democracy in Britain would be complete without an analysis of employers' responses, since so much of the tactics and strategy to be employed by trade unionists in this campaign will be conditioned by them.

ALL THINGS TO ALL MEN

Basically, the employers' response is either one of conciliation or of the heavy hand so far as industrial democracy is concerned. Both attitudes, in different ways, pose pitfalls and dangers for trade unionists. The former response can present dangers for the viability of the movement, albeit in an insidious manner. It is a notable fact that approval for some form of industrial democracy is being voiced from all sections of society. Employers have grown to realize that the simple exercise of unrestrained authority, while it may have worked in the past, can no longer be maintained under modern conditions now that unionism is strong. Concessions to workers' aspirations have to be made and, all too often, a facade of 'democracy' is presented to conceal the realities of power and to 'involve' the workers' representatives in the implementation of unpopular managerial decisions. This form of 'industrial democracy' is expressly designed to head off the movement; it represents 'participation' in industry on the terms set by capital. It is this kind of managerial response that provoked one left-wing socialist to remark caustically that 'Just as Lenin could remark in 1915 that "Absolutely everybody is in favour of peace in general, including Kitchener, Joffre, Hindenberg and Nicholas the Bloody" – so it is true today that "absolutely everybody is in favour of industrial democracy".'[1] 'Industrial democracy' is even taken by some managements to involve nothing more than a new opportunity for administrative convenience, in that technological change can mean small groups working on a specific job. This attitude is typified by a comment in the management journal *Industrial Society* that: 'Everybody in an organization makes decisions about his work and managements are increasingly acknowledging the value of delegating as much decision-making as they can to the lowest possible level.' Whatever their motives, many managements have had to recognize from experience that, as the Edwards Report on Civil Aviation stated: 'a sense of worker participation is important and becoming more so – and that experiments are essential'.

Although what 'participation' means in practice often depends upon what workers want it to mean, or can use the available machinery to force it to mean, yet it is true to say that, as one commentator remarked: 'There are types of industrial democracy that are little more than window dressing and others that

[1] Royden Harrison, 'Retreat from Industrial Democracy',

require a radical change in the whole social structure to succeed.'[1]

Even at a minimal level of 'industrial democracy', however, workers will see it as a method of extending the power, organization and scope for negotiation of their trade unions. As the Labour Party NEC document on 'Industrial Democracy' stated: 'There is no worthwhile future for forms of organization of industrial democracy which seek to abstract participation from trade union membership and organization, or which go even further and seek to separate workers' participation from trade union structure and procedures.'

Many managements, however, see such participation as a method for bypassing the negotiating function of a trade union. One industrial relations expert, Mr Sawtell, puts this position precisely: 'In firms with a high level of participation . . . negotiating of such functions in such companies may be superseded by a form of trusteeship on behalf of union members, together with a growing importance attached to educational facilities.' This seems a dangerous strategy from the point of view of workers' interests. Such attempts to make unions innocuous can only be of to the long-term disadvantage of workers, despite any appearance of progress in the short term. The aim is often to give workers managerial 'responsibility' without managerial power.

Perhaps this is most clearly seen in the present structure of our nationalized industries. It has been suggested, indeed, that trade union members in these industries are getting the worst of both worlds. Nationally, they have no control over management policy yet are expected to act responsibly in 'their own' industry. The management boards of nationalized industries, as established in the first few years after the Second World War, were composed of state appointees – largely from the old top managerial strata, together with top businessmen from other industries and academics. The trade unionists appointed, a small minority, were not drawn from the industry and, in practice, had to sever all connections with trade unionism upon taking up their posts. Certainly, joint consultative committees were set up with the purpose of enabling boards to consult workers on matters relating to safety, health and welfare, the efficient operation of the industry concerned and all matters of common interest to boards and employees. In theory, but in theory only, the com-

[1] Jeremy Bugler, *Observer*, 5 April 1960.

mittees give the workers a say as to what is done in the industry and in how the industry is run. However, since they are only advisory bodies they have no power to compel management to do anything. They are quite inadequate for the purpose of curtailing management power – quite apart from the process of initiating changes on behalf of the workers and their representatives.

Despite the wishes of trade unions and despite the concrete proposals that were put forward, the nationalization of the steel industry during the term of the last Labour government did not produce radical changes from this kind of structure. The only concession to trade union feeling was that 'workers' directors' were appointed (not elected) to the regional boards of the industry. These regional boards account for only 20 per cent of the management bodies and have purely an advisory function. Even such a newspaper as *The Times* (2 December 1969) commented on the question of workers' directors that 'This method did not transfer genuine participation to shop floor workers. You cannot start this kind of thing at Board level.'

Participation on purely management terms has thus meant either involving workers in 'responsibility' without real power or else transmitting managerial opinions and attitudes more effectively in the name of 'good consultation'. This inevitably presupposes, at some stage, a clash with effective, militant, shop floor organizations. The strategy is consciously used to circumvent a 'balance of power' situation in industry. This position can be put politely, of course. Michael Shanks (*The Times*, 12 August 1968) stated that: 'To involve people as much as possible in decisions about the work that they themselves have to do is not only democratic, it is good management.' However, the point is more bluntly, or more correctly, made in another survey of the issue: 'A cynic, or perhaps a realist, would say this management style isn't democracy, but giving orders in such a way that they are most likely to be obeyed' (*Observer*, 5 April 1970).

Any serious analysis of the few, very few, private companies in Britain that presume to have initiated an advanced form of 'industrial democracy' would swiftly reveal their innate deficiencies. As one worker was reported to have said concerning the Scott Bader Commonwealth (a prominent example of this type of enterprise): 'In this Company, you can say what you want – but you do what you're bloody told.' In fact, the Commonwealth principle does little more than clip the wings of the managers. On basic issues, the power resides with the management and the board. Similar, reservations can be expressed concerning other participative establishments. Considering the John Lewis Partnership, Alan Flanders argued that: 'The emphasis is decidely on government for the people rather than government by the people. As a result, perhaps, the staff look on John Lewis as a good employer, but not much different from any other enlightened Company.' This does not mean that trade unionists should not, and cannot, avail themselves of every opportunity to take advantage of a management-inspired and initiated attempt at 'industrial democracy'. It does signify, however, that trade unionists should be under no illusions and should beware lest such 'experiments' clip the wings of trade unionism rather than of the managerial prerogative. It must be borne in mind that many employers are forced to make concessions to strong shop floor organizations nowadays. The methods used during the Depression years to deal with labour have simply proved impossible to apply under modern conditions. This is the reason for the emergence of this strategy of conciliation. It can serve both as a concession – a desirable concession – to workers' strength, and as a method of outflanking the trade union organization which employers dare not directly oppose in an open confrontation.

THE EMPLOYERS' OFFENSIVE

Many employers have been clamorously demanding measures to combat and deprive workers of the gains and rights they have achieved to date, however. Although they are not prepared to take action themselves to 'sort out' workers' organizations, they are proving more than willing to lean on the government to take legislative action on their behalf. That is the true significance of the legislation on industrial relations introduced in 1971, by the Conservative government in Britain. It is necessary to examine this legislation against trade unions and trade unionists if we are to appreciate the full threat of the employers' offensive against pressure for industrial democracy in Britain.

It has been made apparent that the intention is effectively to impede the democratic control of trade unionists over their own organizations and to stifle their basic rights and defences in industry. The bill has posed a basic challenge to even the most minimal gains of democracy in industry, being geared for the edification of managerial autocrats. The establishment of a Registrar of Trade Unions has meant that registered unions would be excluded from exercising full control over the rules of their own organizations. The Registrar, indeed, is empowered to delete rules decided by the membership and may intervene in the day-to-day running of a trade union. Basic trade union democracy has come under attack. It is clear that those powers are being used, not only to give law courts the final say about discipline, but also to supervise the admission of members and to ensure that the officials of registered unions adequately 'police' the membership. Because of this threat, nearly all British unions have remained determinedly unregistered. But as a result they are exposed together with their shop floor organizations and shop stewards, for there is a total absence of protection at law for any action they take, or merely advocate. Although the government has been anxious to avoid such an open confrontation, prison could be the outcome for workers taking continued action in defence of living standards and conditions of work which can change so rapidly, largely through the actions of employers.

It is left to the law courts and the legal profession (never a friend of the labour movement) to decide what constitutes 'unfair' industrial practice and action. This has meant an attack on the right to strike above all else. The right to withdraw labour is probably the most fundamental democratic freedom of all, so far as organized labour is concerned. In attacking this right, therefore, the British Conservative government has set the clock back a hundred years – to before the 1871 Trades Disputes Act, to be precise.

The extensive list of what constitutes an 'unfair' industrial action, even for registered trade unions, is a threat to every trade unionist and to any basic concept of democracy, in or out of industry.

Quite unilaterally, and without the trade unions' consent, legally enforceable procedure agreements may be imposed upon an industry. We have had bitter experience of imposed procedure agreements in the British engineering industry, before the present sanctions were put into operation. The efforts of trade unions in the industry to draw up a voluntary and effective procedure agreement, with disputes speedily settled at local level, have been set at naught. The provision is a calculated blow at free collective bargaining, at shop floor democratic rights, and at the authority of trade unions.

Sacking due to redundancy or 'the employee's conduct or capability' (which can mean anything) is classified as 'fair practice'. Even proven 'unfair' dismissals (with the onus of proof laid on the worker) are not intended to lead to reinstatement, but to a minimum amount of compensation paid by the employer. This measure, hailed in some quarters as a 'concession' to trade union feeling, may be utilized by employers as a blank cheque for weeding out shop stewards who have a responsibility to those that they represent.

The definition of an outlawed 'unfair' industrial action extends to the basic means of applying effective sanctions against an employer. Sympathy strikes and 'blacking' of goods to help workers in dispute with a particular employer are expressly forbidden, and workers acting in solidarity in such a manner are liable for financial penalties. The selectivity of the government in applying its newly acquired armoury of anti-union provisions during the crucial early stages whilst a body of case law is built up has been obvious. The success of the mine-workers' strike action in early 1972 was due in large part to the effectiveness of their picketing to prevent supplies being transported into power stations. Because of their traditional strength and public feeling towards their cause, they were able to carry through this strategy without major intervention from the new bill. In the case of an action by dockers to 'black' lorries of a port employer who sought to destroy work methods and to initiate wide redundancy in the industry quite unilaterally, however, the issues were not so easy for public outsiders to grasp and the matter could thus be clouded by technicalities to the point where the central dispute became confused in the public mind. Taking this opportunity, the full force of the new legislation was brought to bear on the Transport and General Workers' Union, whose members were involved in the action at local, unofficial levels. Sizeable fines were levied under threat of annexation of union property and suspension of union functions, but quashed in the Appeals Court. The onus was then put upon shop stewards in their unofficial capacity to provide a scapegoat.

Even 'fair' industrial action is delayed for a sixty-day cooling-off period and the state may impose a secret ballot. As well as potentially building up bitterness in industry, this is a calculated blow at the authority of trade unions and trade union leaders to have the power of decision making inside their own organizations. Despite this attempt, however, the government received an early indication of the rank-and-file response to this particular piece of effrontery, when a 'cooling-off period' was invoked to delay a threatened action by railway workers. The secret ballot which followed the sixty-day delay showed such a resounding solidarity behind the union leadership that the workers' demands were met virtually in full, from this state-run enterprise.

Independent trade unions, backed by strong shop-floor organizations, are the only effective vehicles for workers' rights and for the extension of industrial democracy. It is precisely these organizations which are subject to a comprehensive two-pronged attack by such measures.

Not only is it intended that the right to bargain effectively with employers should be drastically restricted, but an Industrial Relations Court has the sole power to decide organizing rights.

Unions may, indeed, remain unrecognized as workers' representatives in an establishment without the approval of this court while it is maintained that to be recognized, union representatives shall be vetted by state agencies to decide whether they are sufficiently 'qualified' to undertake their responsibilities.

Linked to this is an open assault on the effectiveness of workers' solidarity and rights on the factory floor. This is connected with the attack on the official national structures of trade unionism; in fact, the two go hand in hand. Not only are any actions of workers on the shop floor now liable to legal scrutiny, but it is sought to undermine the very basis of organization. The closed shop has been outlawed. Employers now have the right to 'employ anyone with the necessary skills' – including professional non-unionists and strikebreakers. 'Agency shops' have been introduced in a hope to appease vigorous trade union rejection of the bill, but even if trade unions get past the legislative impediments to organize, they are made responsible for bargaining on behalf of workers who would not necessarily undertake any responsibility nor contribute towards trade unionism. The 'scab' is fully protected in his activities and employment; many trade unionists stand to be harshly dealt with. Established trade unions are bound by manifold legal chains; breakaway and disruptive minority unions now have a legal structure in which to flourish.

These seeming 'contradictions' fall into a pattern. The obvious intention is to break the effective strength of organized workers and ruthlessly to cut back their rights, not only within industry and in relation to employers, but even inside their own organizations which have been built up and maintained by them. Certainly, it may be true that this assault on trade union rights comes about not from a position of strength on the employer's part but from weakness. After all, this bill has been introduced at a time when workers' organizations are strong and likely to become stronger, not when they are divided, weakened and defeated. But that does not alter the seriousness of the challenge. By inviting an all-out confrontation with organized labour at this time, trade unionists are reminded of the seriousness of their responsibilities to defend what has been struggled for and to overcome the new opposition to the cause of developing and extending democratic rights in industry.

CONTROL AND THE CORPORATION

It is becoming increasingly clear that the struggle for democratic accountability in industry is of immediate practical importance. The development of capital itself has transformed it into a 'bread and butter' issue. In Britain, over the last few years, a concentration of economic power into fewer and fewer hands has occurred at an unparalleled pace. It has reached such a stage that by the end of 1968, the twenty-eight largest companies held at least 40 per cent of the total assets of all companies in manufacturing industry. These top firms have an annual turnover greater than that of the national exchequer.

The degree of democratic control that can be enjoyed under these circumstances by the public at large, or by the workers actually in the industry, is minimal. Suffice it to say that, at present, no public body even has the terms of reference to examine how these combines develop after a merger. Under present legislation, a technical monopoly might exist for decades without any legal requirement even to notify the existence of a monopoly situation. The interests of shareholders are treated with extreme consideration by these merged monopolies or semi-monopolies. Any rights of workers and consumers to an effective voice and to effective safeguards of their interests are almost ignored, however. This applies particularly to monopolistic price rises which have a direct bearing on inflation. It also applies to the elementary question of job security. In present circumstances, the last thing that workers and their unions receive is adequate prior consultation, yet all too frequently these mergers are very much 'hatchet jobs' so far as plant, materials, investment and the labour force are concerned. Unions have demanded, and will continue to demand, effective commitments by large companies to their social responsibilities and social priorities. To date, no such commitments have been forthcoming.

Industrial mergers have become synonymous with large-scale redundancy (often occurring in areas of already above-average unemployment) and provoke a general feeling of insecurity among the workers concerned. While government legislation is attacking the right to strike, economic forces are undermining the right to work. In both cases, the decision-making process is wilful, arbitrary and totally alien to any notions of effective negotiation or genuine democratic accountability. No wonder workers have a clear feeling that they are remote from, and therefore remain indifferent to, the centres of power and decision making! Workers are perfectly prepared for and capable of exercising creative authority over administration. Their 'indifference' is not due to hostility to decision making as such, but to the control of decision making and power by an unrepresentative few, who have so frequently shown themselves to be antagonistic to the workers' interest. The recent spate of mergers followed by mass redundancy exposes the hypocrisy of managers who accuse workers of 'lacking loyalty to the company'.

The rapid rate of technology itself in an industrial structure which is devoid of democratic control intensifies feelings of frustration and insignificance by introducing job insecurity. Surveys have shown that the highest number of unofficial strikes take place in those industries where uncertainty regarding jobs alongside new technology is greatest. These tendencies are only magnified when considered on an international scale. The growth of international combines, straddling and bypassing national frontiers, poses fresh problems and challenges to the trade union movement. *The Times* (19 September 1969) in fact spelled out the position: 'the change in the nature of the corporations that working people must confront into larger combines, sometimes international, able to shift their production to low wage areas or away from countries where trade union opposition – or even Government welfare legislation – have been specially effective.

'The balance of power which Hugh Clegg saw as the guarantee

of industrial democracy, has tilted against unions and even against potentially radical governments.'

Although this may be an overstatement, it poses a question which must increasingly become an important preoccupation of trade unions and trade unionists. Far from devolving more responsibility to its national subsidiaries, the international company is tending, through the combined weight of technology and organization, to centralize decision making more and more. Indeed, as a TUC paper on the question of international companies recently stated, the plant-level trade unionist now needs to know much more clearly where decisions are being made affecting employment in order to fulfil his function properly from day to day. This need is acutely obvious when the fortunes of local subsidiaries are seen to be dependent on the fortunes of the parent corporation on the world market and, in our experience, the fight for elementary collective bargaining rights is particularly intense with foreign-owned subsidiaries of such companies in the UK. Experience in other countries will probably reinforce this viewpoint.

Many of the real powers of decision making in collective bargaining, as far as management is concerned, are moving away from plant or company to conglomerate or holding company level. Unless we develop parallel national and international structures with real authority, organized workers will find themselves increasingly in a position of weakness before such remote, concentrated managements. To develop trade union unity in action on the international plan is an essential step for the whole movement. This is all the more true because the potential power of the working class has never been greater. The possibilities have never been greater to develop such unity and strength. At the same time, the need for such development is urgent. The gains that have been made and that can be made in the near future, are threatened, not only by governmental action (as in Britain), but by the monopolies, on both a national and an international scale, who can use their resources to inhibit and undermine the strength of our movement. Only by building on the basis of our own organizations and our own resources can we advance towards any measure of industrial democracy. As a minimum aim, our power for collective bargaining purposes must be strengthened at both a national and increasingly also at an international level. This entails defending the rights that we have already gained from the state and the law courts.

But obviously the organization of power involves far more than this. Certainly, under the present system of society, 'workers' participation' must be most closely identified with trade union organization and representation of workers'.[1] The significance of the demand for a single channel for the functions of both negotiation and consultation lies precisely in this. Works committees and forms of 'participation' which stand outside these structures are simply managerial tactics to weaken trade unionism by offering what are usually quite illusiory baits to the workers concerned.

Not only must all restrictions on free collective bargaining be removed, but the structure of bargaining must correspond to reality by giving more power and responsibility at shop floor level. This is a basic issue of industrial democracy. Obviously, we are faced at present with an attack on fundamental shop floor rights but, even without this, employers have utilized every other method to exclude shop stewards from effective power in negotiations – except on management's own terms.

The efforts of this union to obtain a new procedure agreement in our engineering industry are viewed as an issue of democracy in industry. The procedure previously imposed upon the industry by the employers was expressly designed to frustrate legitimate shop floor aspirations. Its unwieldy and long-drawn-out processing of shop floor grievances up to a national level, its negotiations that can last for months, while leaving employers full rein in the meantime to introduce whatever changes they desire, are to be condemned and opposed. A speedy procedure settled and finalized at local level which prohibits employers from introducing innovations into an establishment without prior negotiation and agreement has been the essence of trade union demands.

Disputes are increasingly concerned not only with straight wage issues, but with all aspects and conditions of the place of work. This is all to the good. One of the prime evils and scourges of industrial life is the arbitrary power of employers to introduce new machinery, change methods of working and move labour around in an establishment. This 'management prerogative' is a standing incitement to industrial conflict, particularly as it is so often carried out with adverse effects for the workers concerned. In fact, the case for industrial democracy and full consultation is particularly strong and immediately relevant in those

[1] Labour Party NEC, 'Industrial Democracy'.

areas that directly affect labour. This includes such basic and contentious subjects as the flexibility of labour, hiring and firing and industrial training and, indeed, covers the whole spectrum of manpower planning.

Certain concessions have been gained in some areas and it is no accident that the government's Industrial Relations Bill was expressly designed to reassert the employers' authority in these directions. In particular, the legislation has sought to re-establish the employers' prerogative to employ whom he likes, irrespective of the opinions of other workers and their trade unions.

All aspects of manpower policy should become matters for prior negotiation. Trade unions are concerned to have effective negotiations not only about wage rates, but also on questions concerning the introduction of new machinery and its effect on the workers, the level of manpower required in the future and the level of skills of the workers employed. The question of projected redundancies is of overwhelming importance. Over the last few years we have seen from our own experience how vital this issue is. The merger wave, where huge combines come together, putting the security and welfare of hundreds of thousands of workers and their families at stake, highlights the issues involved. These mergers have been carried out with virtually no hint to and certainly no consultation with the workers concerned. Yet all too often they have had an immediate and adverse effect on employment as they have resulted in factory closures, pruning of jobs and mass redundancy. All this is enacted with a minimum of consulation with the trade unions and workers concerned. Any contact entailed management directives rather than consultation.

Our immediate objectives are clear. Prior to any merger there must be full consultation and agreement with the workers and unions concerned on manpower policy, as well as on such issues as changes in working practices. We must insist on effective consultation and not be satisfied with an empty reply that 'your views will be taken into consideration'. Guarantees against redundancy, backed by legislative action, must be given in every case. In fact, we firmly proclaim it as our policy in the AUEW that there must be comprehensive guarantees that workers remain on the firm's books, and are kept at their jobs, until comparable alternative employment is offered. Above all, we demand the right to work.

It is an essential prerequisite of even a minimal form of industrial democracy that people come before profits. We do not accept that industrial efficiency can be improved by drastic cuts in the utilization of plant, labour and equipment. Furthermore, the livelihoods of the workers who have contributed to the wealth of the country are our prime concern. There is no limit to the area of industrial policy-making and activity in which we want an effective voice. Price fixing, the moulding of investment and production policies and the utilization of assets are vital subjects for every worker. We need to break the conspiracy of silence that stops workers from knowing the details of a company's financial situation, prospects and policies. 'Open the books' is an essential demand right down to shop floor level.

Finally, if we are to be realistic, trade unionists must recognize that private ownership of the means of production can be the greatest obstacle to any future advance of this kind, besides posing a threat to the gains that we have already made. In the last analysis, industrial democracy can only flourish under public ownership, subject to popular control. Only then will skills and talents of the working class have full rein to increase the wealth and prosperity of their society in a peaceful, planned and harmonious manner.

Chapter 10

UK

JACK JONES

General Secretary, Transport and General Workers' Union

At its policy-making biennial Delegate Conference in 1970, the Transport and General Workers' Union passed the following resolution:

'That this Conference rejects the inclusion of penalty clauses in wages and conditions agreements, recognises the need for agreements to conform as closely as possible to the wishes of the membership concerned, and directs that the fullest possible consultation should take place between permanent officials and shop stewards before agreements are finalised.'

This straightforward and seemingly undramatic statement marked a milestone in the drive for industrial democracy in Britain. For with the motion went a statement of Union policy which I was privileged to make and which, after being unanimously accepted, has started to have a decisive effect on industrial relations and workplace democracy in Britain.

That statement made it clear that the executive of Britain's largest trade union welcomed the growing mood in the Union that the shop stewards, and through them the workers, should play a full part in determining their wages and the working conditions under which they are employed.

The statement continued:

'Now the principle of lay participation, lay representation in negotiation, is one which this Union has accepted in principle over a long period of time, and indeed we have operated it in many industries. You know we have a lay representative in the port transport industry negotiations, in the bus industry negotiations, and on the road haulage wages council. But there is a growing need and a growing demand for a greater representation of this kind and we subscribe to this outlook, but nevertheless it is not easy in negotiations with an all national coverage to meet the demands completely for maximum lay representation, and this is why the Union has turned or one of the reasons why it has turned increasingly to local agreements, local negotiations, because one of the great advantages of this trend is the possibility of involving a much greater number of shop stewards, elected lay representatives, in the actual negotiations.

'The other value of local agreements is that they cut the frustration of the protracted delays in procedures for negotiations which often go with national agreements. Indeed, in the engineering industry and the motor industry, the major cause of strikes has been these paralysing delays. We take the view that it is quite illogical to accept and extend local agreements and then assume it will be quite acceptable to workers to see their disputes disappear into long-winded disputes procedures from which announcements may emerge weeks and perhaps months later.

'Employers and other unions will have to accept that the disputes procedures must end in the localities, after which there will either be voluntary conciliation or voluntary arbitration or an official strike. The effect of this would be to increase perhaps the number of official strikes but at the same time would decrease the total number of strikes because the employers will be forced by the pressure of local negotiations to agree rather than to delay and pass the buck causing the situation to reach the strike stage.

'In our opinion industrial agreements must be subject to the test of speed and democracy. The old system where a few people negotiated with employers and reached decisions in isolation was never in our view satisfactory. It led often to unions getting less than they should for members, it led to some joint bodies, national joint industrial councils and the like, fixing rates of pay often unrelated to actual earnings and where the national rates were rigidly applied under the principle of national fixation, known certainly to the bus industry. It meant that people were forced on to long hours of overtime to maintain a reasonable standard of living, an intolerable situation at this time of industrial modernisation.

'But today anyway negotiations are no longer confined to just a 1½d. an hour or 2d. an hour increases. Negotiations have increasingly come to deal with new methods of working, operating new types of equipment, flexibility and so on, a whole wide range involving work study, merit rating, the whole damn lot, and in that circumstance it is quite clear that no negotiator has the moral right to start to change a worker's life without asking him.

'When the West Coast dockers in the United States were negotiating their famous agreement on modernisation the concept of "fishbowl negotiations" was applied, that is the negotiations took place with an audience of 200 working dockers who were thus kept in touch all the way with the negotiations. That principle could not be applied in every instance, but the case for the greatest possible participation of shop stewards in negotiations is overwhelming and the case for adequate reporting back and consultation with the membership is overwhelming. Certainly we should seek, where possible, report-back meetings during working hours because it is essential that agreements should be understood. It is no use employers complaining of breaches of agreements if the workers are not aware of the agreement themselves. Even if agreements are circulated or published in the newspapers it isn't quite enough, because you have to have the verbal explanation and the answer to the members' questions which can only be given at report-back meetings.

'These are not just words, it is the policy of the Union that shop stewards should be closely consulted before negotiations commence, during negotiations and certainly before any decision is reached. This conception can be found in the Trades Union Congress's "Programme for Action" as a proposal adopted at the Croydon Conference, and it was put there at our suggestion.

'Our policy is to insert into industrial agreements the provision that there shall be consultation so that democracy is built into the industrial agreement, and employers should bear the cost of this necessary consultation. From now, if this motion is carried we will expect Union Officers to seek to negotiate this principle into all local agreements.

'There is no aspect to which I am more personally committed than this principle. What we are talking about here is practical democracy and that is what the trade union movement should be about. Democracy sometimes causes difficulty, and may be troublesome for some people in authority, but it is never a luxury for trade unionists, it is an essential. We are not dealing with morons or sheep, we are dealing with human beings who are increasingly growing in intelligence and increasingly demanding to take part in any decision that affects them.'

This statement is quoted in full because it illustrates the modern British approach to the extension of industrial democracy, and also demonstrates that this is very much a matter of practical progress, not merely for academic discussion. For, the progress that is being made towards greater mass participation in industrial decision-making in Britain is closely linked with the growing importance and status of the 'shop steward'.

The shop steward is primarily the lay negotiating representative (and may have the title of office representative, site steward, garage representative, etc., according to his industry). He (or she) is fundamentally a union representative still working at the job, still employed by the employer and not the union, and elected by the members whom he or she represents. Calculations vary, but there are up to a quarter of a million shop stewards active in the British trade union movement. One of the distinguishing features of recent industrial relations in Britain is the way in which more and more responsibilities in the negotiating field have been taken over by these lay representatives. In the Transport and General Workers' Union alone, well over a thousand senior stewards (often called 'convenors') are virtually full-time, being paid by their employers but doing full-time union work in the interests of their members. Whether full-time or not, the shop steward is both the symbol of, and the means through which membership control of negotiations is being established – and this is a fact of enormous significance in British industrial relations.

It is useful to illustrate this with two examples of the demand for the extension of industrial democracy – the first (a special report by the Labour Party) was in writing, the second (the Ford dispute) in action.

The Labour Party report on 'Industrial Democracy' is referred to elsewhere in this collection, but its central view is worth repeating: 'Workers' participation must be closely identified with trade union organisation and representation of workers. We see no worthwhile future for the forms of organisation which seek to abstract participation from trade union membership and organisation.' This view represented a substantial change from many of the theories of the past and new thinking has been evident also in the TUC when, for example, it pointed out in its evidence to a recent Royal Commission that there would be a wide welcome for legislation allowing private companies to provide for union representation on boards of directors. This demonstrated a major departure from union views of the 30s and 40s, when it was felt that trade unionists in management would have to sever their links with the movement. Today the TUC says that: 'In future trade unionists should be able to retain their union connections when appointed to serve on a central or regional board of a nationalised industry.'

The Labour Party report did not come down firmly for workers on the boards of private industry, preferring to observe some examples in operation first. But wherever the experiment takes place, in nationalized industry or in a private company, the report felt that the people concerned should represent their fellow workers and should be responsible to them through the medium of trade union organization. Industrial democracy based on a lively, actively functioning trade unionism at the place of work would, the report said, be a major step forward for the whole of industry, the significance of which should not be hidden.

UNION OVERHAUL

1. In the case of the trade unions, real industrial democracy will mean a thorough overhaul of our communications system, our representation arrangements and our methods of debate and discussion.
2. The same process will need to take place inside the firm or undertaking.

Above all, industrial democracy would imply full recognition of union representatives, both for manual and non-manual workers. It would involve extending the collective bargaining field from the normal wages and conditions questions into many areas now regarded as managerial prerogatives or at most reserved for 'consultation or notification'. The representatives in this wider field would still remain responsible within a single channel of the shop steward or his equivalent; the dual system of negotiator or consultant is suspect and outmoded. The Labour Party report was quite positive on the view that there should be experiments in placing representatives of workers directly concerned on the boards of publicly owned firms and industries and that 'workers' representatives should be drawn into decision-making at every level and particularly at the various points of production'. In general it felt that there is a clear need for a new approach in the management of industry and that the infusion of workers' representatives into decision making could provide the impetus towards better management and more efficient industry, as well as providing the prospect of improved material rewards for workpeople.

This was not to suggest 'management by committee'. On the contrary, management is accepted as a specialized job requiring thorough training. Indeed, far more should be done to 'professionalize' management by increased training and by ensuring selection according to ability rather than personal connections. Management should be free to manage on a day-to-day basis, but should be called upon to justify decisions to a joint shop steward/management committee. On main policy questions, consultation and agreement should be required before action is taken. The joint committee would be a single channel, comprising the wide field of consultation, local wage and condition bargaining and executive functions on such questions as safety and overtime. In such a joint committee the manager and his senior staff would sit with an agreed number of elected shop stewards (representative of the recognized trade unions in that workplace).

PRIMARY RESPONSIBILITY

The primary responsibility of the workpeople's representatives would be to those on whose behalf they were appointed. They would not necessarily accept collective responsibility for management decisions. (They would not be expected to serve two masters.) Their main role would be to ensure that the workers' voice was heard and heeded at the formative stage of policy making. This would help to prevent management making the type of mistake which it often made at present due to decision making 'in isolation'. It would also deal with the key issue of making adequate information available to trade union members. At the same time, any problems would be negotiated on as far as possible. This would imply taking collective bargaining into the management area.

POLICIES FOR DEBATE

The policy questions which the workers' representatives would expect to take a special interest in would include:

(a) efficient use of manpower and equipment;
(b) pay and productivity questions other than those decided at national level;
(c) disciplinary matters, i.e. the exercise of joint control over discipline and dismissals procedure;
(d) safety–control of accident prevention measures including the power to stop dangerous processes;
(e) ensuring adequate welfare provisions;
(f) arrangements for the selection of supervisors (including participation in appointment panels);
(g) control of overtime working;
(h) ensuring adequate training for workpeople and shop stewards.

The basis of the approach is that local management and local union men sit down and jointly work out ways to increase the effective use of manpower and equipment and agree on the sharing of savings effected. It means taking collective bargaining into the area of management with all the cards on the table, 'race upwards'!

A great deal of time often has to be spent explaining to advisers and outsiders the systems and methods of work and the organization of the workplace or service. To many workers in the concern all this is known thoroughly; they work in the system; they know its advantages and deficiencies. With this background it would be to the advantage of the undertaking to train workers in the methods of administration and of applying cost accounting techniques, etc., to enable the workers' representatives to play a more effective part on the committees suggested. The necessary precondition is that the results of the more efficient management which would emerge should be fairly shared, with a good allocation in the form of extra bonuses and possibly extra holidays for the employees. This approach could take productivity bargaining to a new height, as a continuous operation with the role of the union representative being firmly embedded in the running of industry, while management would be committed to improving the standards and opportunities of the workers.

DISCLOSURE

The provision of information is a necessity for effective functioning of the joint committees mentioned and should be granted without delay in maximum detail in the public sector. In the private sector we are expecting that the new Companies Act will require companies to disclose information on various aspects to the representatives of the recognized union or unions in the establishment concerned on request. In addition, an annual detailed statement should be made available to employees to include the following range of information:

(a) details of the order book;
(b) manpower changes and remuneration;
(c) production and investment plan;
(d) cost structures;
(e) purchasing and pricing policies.

In this report the British trade union and labour movement had before it an authoritative statement recommending a new approach to industrial democracy, based on practical possibilities rather than remote blueprints. Its influence would not have been felt, however, if it had not been in line with what was, in fact, already happening in industry and the unions; and undoubtedly this thinking was given a massive boost by the events concerning the Ford dispute just over a year later.

This, the second example chosen, was undoubtedly of great international significance. Early in 1969, the massive Ford Company in Britain was engaged in a substantial pay dispute with its workers. An understanding was reached, that included substantial penal clauses against industrial action which, though apparently acceptable to the full-time union negotiators involved, proved completely unacceptable to the membership.

In the resulting stoppage, tens of thousands of Ford workers took part. Both of the major unions, the Transport and General Workers' Union and the Engineers (AEF), made it clear that they officially backed a strike against any agreement that did not receive the sanction of the executives of the union involved, and that it was the decision of the members that counted, not the negotiators' voices alone.

Subsequently not only was a new agreement made, but a new negotiating structure was established. The TGWU insisted that there would be no acceptance of the agreement without a mass vote of the members being in favour. We further insisted that the negotiating committee be reformed to give a larger voice to the majority unions that would enable us to put senior shop stewards on the negotiating committee. Moreover, we instituted a system of involving shop stewards themselves in consultation on negotiations at every stage. This radical departure from the old method of Ford negotiation symbolized a new approach to membership participation in many industries, and was used to the full during the Ford negotiations in 1970. The old system under which a few union officers negotiated to reach an agreement in isolation was ended. Undoubtedly this gave a great boost to the extension of workers' participation.

Just as significant was the development in the London docks. Here, in an industry where the negotiating had been done traditionally by the full-time officers, the major new agreements in 1970 were ratified only after two ballots had been held. Even more important, special 'stop-work' meetings were held so that the agreements could be examined by the mass of membership and questions answered.

In industry after industry local negotiations have replaced national negotiations, or stewards' conferences, frequently paid for by the employers, have been arranged to consider the course of negotiations.

In Imperial Chemical Industries (ICI) the old system of works committees, separate from the unions, is being replaced with one in which the workers' representatives are the stewards themselves. In British Road Services elected shop stewards are now serving the key committees.

In London Transport (buses) the elected, lay members' committee sits with top management for the first time to consider the future working of the undertaking and now takes an active part in policy making.

In trawler fishing, an official report (Holland Martin) accepted the need to experiment with 'safety representatives' on each vessel. This is a radical departure from the old tradition that any representations on the part of the fishermen might constitute mutiny!

While it never proved possible to get working busmen appointed to the governing authorities of the new bodies controlling bus transport in the major provincial conurbations, the Labour government did accept that busmen could serve on authorities other than their own, while still retaining their jobs and union positions. Thus a whole principle that workers' nominees must never retain their union jobs was abandoned.

What backsliding there was came primarily in the industrial legislation field. The Labour government's acceptance of local port committees, with very wide responsibilities, having elected union representatives, failed to materialize with the Conservative victory in the election. New industrial safety laws designed to provide for workers' safety representatives from the unions lapsed for factories and trawlers alike. Undoubtedly, however, this was merely the tip of a quiet revolution. More and more lay workers, usually in a representative capacity, but often through a direct vote, are taking part in industrial decisions.

To sum up, therefore, it is possible that Britain is making more *progress* towards industrial democracy at this time than any other country. Certainly it is moving more rapidly in this direction than at any time in its history, though the new legal barriers of the anti-union Conservative government are clearly aimed at impeding this advance.

It is most encouraging, however, that the movement towards greater democracy in industry is not based on legislation, nor on elaborate 'blueprints' for the future. It is founded on day-to-day reality at the place of work. It is a two-pronged attack. On the one hand there is the move towards the decentralization and 'democratization' of decision making within the union itself, while on the other there is an extension and a widening of the range of subjects being opened up for *joint* agreement, or even joint *control*, instead of remaining a purely unilateral management decision.

This is the most practical contribution that can be made. If we can bring *most* workers into making decisions about many things previously regarded as being the sole prerogative of management, then a major step will have been taken towards industrial democracy. We shall have laid the basis for a more open and democratic industry and society.

THE BRITISH CONTRIBUTION

We in Britain have a unique contribution to make to the advance of industrial democracy which could be applied with great value in other countries. Our system of shop stewards has advantages over much that exists in France, Germany or Sweden. While the United States can provide many examples of vigorous

I

local union activity, their stewards are much more rigidly cir-cumscribed by the law, which produces inflexibility and a rather ponderous approach to industrial matters at times.

There are many criticisms of our system of industrial relations, but it demonstrably has the flexibility to cope with great techno-logical change on the one hand and with a rising level of expectations so far as wages are concerned on the other hand. This rising level of expectations is a world-wide phenomenon. It may have been experienced in Europe first by Britain because of the peculiar problems we faced and the restraints imposed supposedly to cure them. If so, the contrast between the 'bad' industrial relations here and the 'good' industrial relations in, say, Germany or Sweden, may simply have been that they have not yet experienced the stresses and strains that Britain has undergone.

The German co-determination system, for example, seems to me to suffer from two defects. Firstly, it isolates the intervention of workers' representatives to an indirect body, the supervisory board, and can, I feel, raise the danger of workers getting responsibility to some extent without power. Secondly, and much more seriously, the German system provides for a duality of representation because the workers' representatives are elected outside the trade union structure. This can cause both confusion and mistrust, neither of which are objectives of workers' partici-pation.

Centralized negotiations or centralized co-determination may be relevant to a situation of defending wage rates against wage cuts, or seeking to impose decent standards on a new industry, but they are not in our view capable either of providing dynamic wage increases, or of giving the individual an effective 'say' at the place of work. For this reason the emphasis in Britain has been on establishing the trade union as an actively functioning, fully representative body at the place of work – with full reporting back and with workers being responsible for their own agree-ments.

We have thus raised the issue, not of the worker running industry in isolation as an experiment and an example of some-thing unusual, but of workers operating jointly with technical management as a normal thing in industry. This is not a syndicalist conception; it has something in it of the co-determina-tion of Germany's steel and coal industries (with its concept of 50/50 committees) and something of the self-management of

Yugoslavia. In Britain, we do not have the legal structure that either of those countries has, but very often *their* weakness is the lack of a fully effective trade union movement at the place of work. We are aiming at a fully effective example of this – which draws from both the German and Yugoslav system perhaps – but which is primarily something that the ordinary man and woman at work would recognize as being valuable to them because it gives them some sense of control over their own working lives.

Clearly such a step forward is needed, for industry is growing more bureaucratic as it becomes more concentrated and more complicated. It has been calculated that in the near future three-quarters of industrial activity in the non-Communist world will be dominated by about two hundred companies. Latest figures show that already 102 companies control 48 per cent of the assets and 53 per cent of the profits of industry in the USA. This has particularly strong implications for Britain, since American firms account for a tenth of all plant and equipment in Britain, provide £2 out of every £3 invested here and by 1980 will own nearly 25 per cent of all British industry.

Given the rapid growth of complicated technology which interposes a further barrier between the worker and the products of his labour, a situation could soon arise in which control of industry is in the hands of a small management elite (responsible only to itself) while the mass of people in industry may be regarded as sheep or morons so far as their role in running industry is concerned. This is not an inevitable state of affairs; the alternative is to involve the total intelligence of workers by means of representative participation – that is, extended industrial democracy.

As giant combines – both national and international – come to dominate the economy, the value of the trade union as a voice and as a protection for the individual in industry is increasingly obvious. The Transport and General Workers' Union has said clearly that as far as we are concerned trade unionism is a weapon with which to defend human values at the place of work. But this is not a propaganda battle – it is a question of the extension of self-government in industry. Participation is not a new gimmick for the trade union movement – it is the essence of our being. Increasingly the unions are showing this within their own structures and challenging the arbitrary pre-rogatives of management at the same time. For it must never be forgotten that what makes trade unions necessary is that in power terms one worker does not equal one employer. The opportunity for bureaucracy is always there. The chance for an individual worker to be crushed by the size of the management machine is always present. That is why workers in industrial economies, wherever they have been free to do so, have formed trade unions.

Trade unions represent an independent power base that is open to all. Moreover it is a *significant* power base because it has direct access to a key factor in any economy and any society, namely, the level of wages and the conditions under which those wages are earned. Trade unions will always remain effective while they use that direct access and follow a vigorous wages policy. That is why they must never move far from satisfying the attitude typified by an American trade unionist, who told a sociologist, 'For most guys the union is like a slot machine. You put your money in and see what comes out at the bottom. It's good insurance.'

But there has always been a further dimension to trade unionism – a dimension that is idealistic both in the short term and the long term. This perhaps is demonstrated by the rules of the United Society of Cordwainers, founded in 1792, which said: 'Let everyone lay aside his own private interests and study the good of the whole. And let us study friendship and unanimity with one another; this will cement our structure and render it permanent. Make us the joy of the present and the praise of ages yet to come.'

There is, however, no contradiction between having both materialistic and idealistic aims; most individuals combine the two to some degree, and in a situation where materialistic rewards are unequally shared there is nothing unidealistic in seeking to share them more fairly.

Moreover, the wider aspirations of trade unions have a very firm practical basis. For low wages have not merely represented physical poverty, they have usually been associated with personal oppression. The man or woman who gets a low reward for his labour has most often had insecure employment as well. Such workers have been on the receiving end of victimization and managerial bullying and have responded either with great courage or a most understandable surrender. The worst thing about overweening management authority is that it can create a sub-servient character on the part of the worker himself.

All this arose from the very simple equation mentioned already that 'one worker does not equal one employer in power'. And from this well-understood equation has arisen the drive for collective organization. When workers can break free from the vicious circle they will do so to form trade unions – and those trade unions will always concern themselves to an increasing degree not only with wages but with the quality of life at work. Of course, it will not be called a 'struggle to improve the quality of life'. It will take the form of unity against arbitrary dismissals, an insistence upon 'washing time', an imposition of regular rules about the allocation of work and rules that lead to the equalization of earnings. It may go on to achieve control over overtime – both the amount done and who does it. But control over the workshop is both a means to achieving better wages and something in addition to that aim. No fact is more significant today than this to the movement and any outside observer who fails to realize its central importance will make a serious omission.

It is particularly encouraging today that the movement for greater industrial democracy is not founded merely on sentiment, but is growing on the basis of concrete aims and firm progress. It is based on control over the job, popularly controlled local *and* national bargaining, and opposition to arbitrary acts of management both at board and workship level. It has given expression to both the materialistic and idealistic aims of the trade union movement.

I believe that this trend came just in time for the British trade union movement, following a period in which we had moved dangerously away from both these endeavours. But I do not believe that anyone should underestimate the significance of the growth of the British trade union movement at present. Whereas a few years ago it was fashionable to say that the strength of the unions was overrated, that complaint is hardly heard at all today. The unions count more because they have returned to their roots – their relationship with workers at the place of work. Despite the manpower decline in traditional union centres such as mining, railways, docks and buses, the trade union movement is growing rapidly. Informally, this has already meant that wide sectors of industrial decision-making have become subject to the comment workers through their union representatives. I think it is clear that, as time goes on, this process will become more formalized through joint union/

management committees that will have joint control over discipline, safety, communications, overtime and promotion.

This trend is in my view irresistible and it would be wrong in principle to resist anyway. A citizen's working hours are probably more influential upon his or her behaviour than anything else. We cannot expect to achieve a democratic society if industry is bureaucratic or authoritarian.

It is no use ignoring the fact that the pattern of government in Britain has important implications for the extension of industrial democracy here. Over a period of a year or more, the question of greater democracy versus the extension of authoritarian management had been a matter of debate with a Labour government. This was an important, if often quite tough debate, but out of it there arose a general recognition of the fact that progress in industrial relations in this country had to be based on opening up management to greater worker participation, and on decentralizing and symplifying agreements and procedures. I think it is necessary to state again our basic argument.

Relationships between workers and employers have to be based on agreement and consent, not on instructions given from above. The approach to industrial efficiency has to be democratic, not authoritarian. Management is not a mystery, it is a *practical* function. And in that practical operation, the joint contributions of men and women who have gained practical knowledge in the industry itself will often be able to make a much more valuable contribution than the trained brain from more academic spheres. There is no magic key that has only to be turned to open a door on a new world – so let's stop behaving as if management is like that.

But there is a more specific reason for industrial democracy too. The key to modern industry is good labour relations and the participation of workers' representatives in ironing out problems certainly improves labour relations. This is because, above all, the workers know about labour problems and it is therefore foolish to exclude them from the management of industrial relations.

And there is a third good reason for democracy in industry. Namely, that *because* it involves more people, it opens up a whole range of managerial problems that are too often shrouded in secrecy. A survey by a major European bank showed that British management was so secretive that the firm itself frequently did not know what it was supposed to be doing. Democracy opens up issues and that is why we look to a situation where the *total costs* of a firm are laid bare; not just the marginal costs related to labour, but the whole range. We believe that more informative management *is better management*, because in the interplay of argument and negotiation about a wider range of issues, new problems and new solutions become possible.

But if management rely on the 'tell 'em nothing, give 'em nothing' approach, then the result is only bitterness and distrust.

WORKER PARTICIPATION–THE WIDER ISSUE

It is clear also that, while certain legislation would greatly encourage increased worker participation, the extension of industrial democracy is not entirely or even mainly dependent on legislation as such. For, contrary to what has been done in other countries, we are not seeking to graft on to our industrial relations structure a new system of worker participation by law. In fact we are building on the best of what we already have. It follows from this of course that it would be foolish if we did anything to *weaken* the best of what we have.

There are basic requirements which provide a framework within which more detailed progress can and should be made, such as guaranteed rights of organization and protection against arbitrary dismissal. Other basic contributions are needed to give a basis of intention. For example, the government should ensure the provision to workers' representatives of increased information on the firm, its costs, investments, etc.

Management and Union

When we refer to the wider dissemination of information, we are of course moving into the whole range of what managements and unions can do themselves to extend workers' participation. The most practical immediate assistance that management can give is to provide facilities for convenors and shop stewards to do their job. This would involve much more than merely not opposing, or not victimizing, active trade unionists.

It should also involve:

– Time off to do union work, with reimbursement for loss of earnings.
– Office facilities and ready access to union members for conducting ballots, holding meetings and other means of communication with members.

Such matters apply not only to local agreements but to national agreements as well. It is vitally important that management should recognize the value of, and support, the moves that the TGWU and other unions are making to involve stewards and other worker representatives in the formulation of claims and in taking decisions on agreements. Where conferences have to be called to consult on the progress of negotiations, and particularly to obtain rank-and-file views on an agreement before it is signed, management should be ready to allow stewards to take part and should be prepared to meet both loss-of-time and travelling expenses.

In the present atmosphere few agreements are likely to prove acceptable unless this sort of process has been gone through. Yet clearly while such expenses would be too high for unionists to meet to any large extent, they are a small cost to management compared with the costs of a dispute if an agreement is not acceptable.

The prime aims of both unions and management should be *to produce an agreement that is understood by and acceptable to the workers involved and not something that is foisted upon them*. And it is important that this should involve something more than using the latest communication techniques that rely on the written word, important as these are.

Members need first of all to *understand* what is being offered. That is why agreements should not be only *comprehensive*, but simply expressed. But more than understanding is needed. Workers need to feel that they have participated in the making of the agreement – and that means providing *actual* participation, not merely a *charade* of participation. It requires, as I have said, the facilities for stating verbally what the offer is, what the snags are, and having questions answered about those snags.

THE UNIONS

This approach brings with it a responsibility for the unions, too. For I am not arguing that we should replace management bureaucracy with trade union bureaucracy. We cannot reform human relations in industry without continuing to reform participation inside the trade unions. We have got to have increasing devolution of authority in industry which has implications for both sides. If the unions preach participation for others they have to practice it for themselves. They should not merely accept local initiatives and local control – they need to welcome it and provide for it. There has to be a recognition that the shop steward is not a nuisance, but a senior man or woman within the organization – and that the role of the officer is much more to advise, guide and co-ordinate and not to give instructions.

This job is much more difficult than hitherto; in some senses it requires a new approach, but certainly there is no loss of status involved. The local district officer is far more important than he was; he has the key role of contact with the active lay members, and to a large extent the success of the unions and the degree of participation depends upon him.

It means a new role for the trade union leader. Not authoritarian; not dictatorial; not paternalistic. Leadership means leadership in ideas, justifying your arguments, using your experience – above all laying down no barriers of either bureaucracy or pomposity between the worker and the decisions that affect him. It means accepting that we are creating a society of intelligent people – and that means involving them, not pushing them about or 'bribing' them.

Ernest Bevin, the first General Secretary of the Transport and General Workers' Union, and later British Foreign Secretary, one said: 'I have no confidence in the superman; the limitations of supposedly great men are obvious. I have spent my life among ordinary people; I am one of them. I have seen them faced with the most difficult problems; place the truth before them – the facts whether they are good or bad – and they will display an understanding, ability and courage that confound the wisdom of the so-called great.'

I believe that those words represent a serious approach to industrial management – they are not just rhetoric. We should be ready to introduce the active lay members and the local officer much more into national negotiations, training boards, etc., than has been our past practice.

Efficiency in all aspects of union work is clearly required, and that means using the best technical methods available. For the unions, too, there is an enormous responsibility to provide better training for members and shop stewards. In the Transport and General Workers' Union we have always spent a lot on training, but we are finding that we are having to adapt our educational programme to meet new needs. Whereas in the past we devoted a large part of our central educational expenditure to improving communications within the Union, we are now concentrating more on the trade union reaction to management techniques.

FURTHER PROGRESS TOWARDS INDUSTRIAL DEMOCRACY

But whatever is done in the way of training, research, formal communications and the like, the key to the expansion of industrial democracy remains in the process of negotiation itself. This fact is the key to the whole question of localized productivity bargaining. The most significant thing about this is that the work performed by the employee is part of the whole context of production within a firm. Thus the concept of 'total cost' bargaining comes into effect, whereby even reductions in management or marketing costs come within the area of negotiation.

Harry Urwin, Assistant General Secretary of the Transport and General Workers' Union, has pointed out that there is often a sharp contrast between points of view as to the nature of productivity bargaining. 'Active trade unionists regard productivity bargaining as an arrangement whereby workers might supplement their earnings and improve conditions by mutual agreement at the place of work through more efficient work or other factors – "a continuous arrangement, a continuous right to bargain at the place of work for supplementation of income". On the other hand, some managements – stimulated by some academic writers and representatives of the DEP – took the view that what they wanted was not productivity *bargaining*, but *a* productivity *bargain* – a bargain where the employer hopes to obtain sole control in return for one substantial change in the wages structure.'

This is an important distinction. Collective bargaining as a process is itself a recognition of the fact that certain things have to be agreed between employers and workers and not unilaterally imposed by the former. The basic tension between workers and employers is in fact a difference between those who seek to maintain authoritarian management, and the aim of working people to control their working lives. Some of the most bitter disputes have been about the question of 'managerial prerogatives' and the extent to which the employers could impose an absolute 'right to manage', 'hire and fire', etc.

The growth of productivity bargaining in this country has

been too greatly influenced by American examples of 'selling the union rule book' where management were conceded new areas of unilateral action in return for substantial sums. The TGWU has pointed out officially, however, that 'The important thing to remember is that union involvement is not for sale, and bargaining at the place of work should bring increased consultation with the membership and more facilities and involvement for the shop stewards, not less.'

The major ingredients in raising productivity levels are (1) the capital equipment, plant, machinery, etc., provided; and (2) the quality of management and its ability to plan the best use of available resources. The emphasis in productivity bargaining should centre on improving the means and methods of production through negotiation and joint control, with consequent increases in wage levels and welfare provisions through collective bargaining at the place of work. Productivity bargaining should, therefore, never be regarded as 'selling out'. On the contrary, it should result in positive gains for the workers by way of more satisfying and less arduous work, shorter hours, higher wages. So much is obvious. But more than higher earnings is involved. Productivity bargaining should also achieve increased bargaining rights and an extension of the range of mutual agreement. This should be expressed in greater shop floor controls, better shop steward facilities, improved union organization, greater job security on an agreed basis, joint controls on safety, discipline and transfers.

Trade unionists have to take the view, when techniques such as work study, job evaluation, measured day work, etc., are encountered, that they are *management techniques, designed to give management greater control over wages and use of manpower*. But on the other hand, in an age of productivity bargaining, more and more issues of investment, manning, type of machinery and so on, are coming to be regarded as inextricably involved in negotiations themselves and subject in practice to joint control. Much will now depend on the unions. British unions now have to contend with regressive and punitive legislation. But if they stick to the policy that democracy is the best course, that the more people involved in the control of industry the better, then they must win. A victory for them will be a victory for workers and democrats throughout the world.

Chapter 11

Sweden

ARNE GEIJER
President, Swedish Trade Union Federation

During the 70s, as in the decade around World War II, we are faced with the task of renewing our system of collective bargaining and co-operation between workers and employers.

This in itself is no cause for astonishment. The conditions which still govern relations between the two sides in industry were largely drawn up at a transition stage in the development of our society. At the same time, the labour movement, its organizational structure already nearly complete, was able to begin its drive for economic growth, employment and social security for the whole population. The aims and means of the joint wage policy began to take shape.

The Saltsjöbaden talks between LO and the Swedish Employers' Confederation SAF, led in 1938 to the signing of the so-called Basic Agreement, which established at national level a set of negotiation and grievance procedures; rules regulating dismissals and layoffs; limitations on strikes, lockouts and other types of direct action; and a procedure for dealing with conflicts jeopardizing vital interests of the community. Since 1938, the two sides have concluded additional co-operation agreements on specific subjects – industrial safety; training of apprentices; works councils, etc.

Employers and trade unions accepted voluntary restraints on industrial action to forestall public intervention in conflicts which might have hampered the pace of economic advance, such restrictions in this case being acceptable since the general provisions of the Basic Agreement were compatible with the requirements of the joint wage policy.

By gradually centralizing discussions on the most controversial employment problems, the way was smoothed for local co-operation on the mutually important question of increasing productivity. The trade unions accepted the need for rationalization and indeed encouraged it. As a *quid pro quo*, we demanded the right to take part in formulating working methods and conditions, and to have both information and influence on developments inside the undertaking. These co-operation agreements were in effect the first concrete recognition of the legitimacy of the worker's claim for a voice in shaping the conditions under which he works.

The criticism which we now feel justified in making of the broad system in which we operate does not bear on its main principles. The rule that agreements, once made, should be kept and respected, is not questioned. But this means that the agreement must not leave any significant ends untied; important decisions on working conditions must be brought into the orbit of collective bargaining and not be reserved for the sole judgement of the employers.

Further, whilst we do not intend withdrawing from continuing co-operation on the development and rationalization of the firm, this very fact demands that we be recognized as equals and that the wishes of the workers be properly respected.

We are thus not attacking the whole system in order to break it down. We feel that it should be extended and refined if it is to fulfil its tasks in the future.

THE PROBLEM OF STRUCTURAL CHANGES

The root cause of an increasing number of trade union problems is to be found in rationalization and structural change in industry. The insecurity caused by closures or short-time working is an example; information which could dissipate unrest and ease the hardship of redundancy is simply not being made available to the works councils. There is the problem of performance levels in industry which are being pushed beyond reasonable limits, causing grave handicaps for elderly and handicapped workers. As jobs get duller and more repetitive, school leavers reject the idea of working in industry. And alongside the monotony go a deteriorating environment and alarming risks to health.

Industrial co-operation which limits the worker to a consultative role has not been enough to prevent the mushrooming of such problems. They must now be dealt with directly at the workplace through increasing workers' influence in company management and the organization of work.

INCREASED STRAIN ON CO-OPERATION BODIES

The strain on co-operation is increasing. With higher material standards and better social security, new claims on work inevitably follow. Growing numbers of people expect increasingly more of the environment in which they work. They want the physical and mental strains of their work reduced. They want their jobs to be diversified, made interesting, given a meaning. People are demanding greater autonomy, more say in how they carry out their jobs. They want to be able to develop in their work, making jobs secure for the future. It is difficult to see how these rising expectations can be fulfilled if trends in technology and organization follow past patterns.

Many people are wondering whether the time has not come for the trade union movement to take the plunge into the management pool – to take on managing functions and set itself on an equal footing with the capital owner in the direction of the affairs of the undertaking.

We have always taken a cautious line in these matters, believing that to be able to assert ourselves both at work and in society at large, the trade union movement needed not only to be strong, but also free and independent.

We are not yet convinced that co-determination in itself provides sufficient guarantees of a fair hearing every single time the interests of a worker clash with those of the company. It will still be essential to have a trade union organization standing firmly on the side of the individual worker both at work and in the larger community.

Further, we do not believe that co-determination can by itself guarantee a balance between economic and technological demands on the one hand and human considerations on the other. To supplement it, we shall also need a trade union organization which can intervene when adaptation and job satisfaction are threatened by technological change and rationalization.

Nor do we believe that the presence of a number of elected workers' representatives on boards or other management bodies meets the individual's demand for a personal hand in the shaping of his environment and working tasks, as most people seem to think. A trade union organization will still be needed to ensure that the work is organized to give each worker a measure of independence and responsibility in his daily routine.

Nonetheless, even if we feel for all these reasons that the trade union movement should on the whole stick to its role as a free, external and primarily claim-making party, there is still room for much closer management–trade union co-operation on general problems inside the undertaking.

For a start, the works councils must be given a proper picture of their companies' true situation. The most logical development would be for these councils gradually to take on responsibility for questions of long-term planning.

REPRESENTATION ON THE BOARD

The most discussed means of trade union participation in management is representation on a company's board of directors. Although this idea has in the past had a rather lukewarm response from the trade union movement, in the long run it becomes increasingly clear that a practice whereby workpeople and their representatives are excluded from the most important decision-making bodies in the firm is unsatisfactory. We shall probably therefore finally opt for a formal system of workers' representation on the board.

However, discussions on industrial democracy have centred far too long on the single question of co-determination in management: there are other, equally important aspects to the problem as well.

An enterprise is a place where many people work together in a system of organized co-operation. The organizational mould to which they must adapt is not constructed on a democratic basis. On the contrary, our workplace is often the most authoritarian environment in which we find ourselves. In fact, it is frequently so authoritarian that many people lead a kind of double existence – liberty and autonomy at home contrasting with regimentation, constant supervision and control by other people at work.

In a democratic society, each person ought to be treated as an independent and aware individual, willing and able to participate in the shaping of his own life. At work, on the other hand, personal liberty is severely curtailed, people having to adapt themselves to tasks and working speeds decided by others or even by the exigencies of machines.

In a democratic society, everyone is supposed to be equal. In working life there are still great differences between various categories of workers.

In a democracy we insist that the governors are elected by, and thus in the last analysis dependent on, the governed. In the enterprise, leadership is not based on the confidence of the collaborators or on a person whom they and management jointly consider competent to be in charge of directing the staff – on the contrary, its main job is thought of as being to protect the interests of the company against the collaborators, whose activity the head of staff will organize and co-ordinate.

In a democracy, laws are made with the consent of those who have to live by them, and the individual is guaranteed a fair trial if an accusation is made against him. In the enterprise, management decides unilaterally on the rules to be followed and just as arbitrarily on the disciplinary sanctions to be imposed in cases of misdemeanour. And so forth – the list could go on and on. Point by point, the comparisons show us that the pattern of relations in the enterprise is often diametrically opposed to what we are aiming at in society as whole. For the ordinary worker, this fact is quite as important as the degree of technical participation in management.

THE RIGHT TO DIRECT AND ALLOT

We are also up against a legal problem. Our difficulty – and it puts us in an awkward position in the application of agreements at the workplace – is that according to precedents established by the Swedish Labour Court, the employer has the right to direct and allot work, in spite of what any particular collective agreement may say on the subject. Swedish legislation of 1928 defined collective agreements and established a Labour Court. Under this legislation, the parties to a collective agreement must not resort to conflict during its life if a dispute arises over its interpretation and application. Such 'juridical' disputes must be settled by the Labour Court or arbitration. Disputes of interest arising in negotiations over the content of new agreements are settled by the parties themselves, with or without resort to direct action. In practice, this means that the employers can impose their interpretation of an agreement until such time as the trade union can reverse the decision either by arbitration or in the Labour Court. Such a bias in favour of one party in a freely concluded, two-party agreement is unreasonable, and we think it should be corrected.

Other important questions – such as the organization of work, the composition of management bodies, manpower policy and working conditions – are also affected. In effect, they are taken out of the sphere of trade union influence. The right of collective bargaining in such matters is purely illusory, since the obligation to bargain according to law and agreement in no way affects management's unilateral power of decision.

I have already mentioned the new dimensions taken on by discussions of industrial democracy over the last few years. Particular emphasis has been laid on the limited possibilities of the individual to influence his own working conditions. This has sometimes been construed, especially by the employers, as a reaction against the kind of organized co-operation resulting from trade union activity. In a general way, one could perhaps bracket growing demands for personal influence under the same heading as the alleged communication gap between representatives and represented, both in society as a whole and in organizations within society; but when such claims are made in the enterprise, they have a specific and particular purpose.

Desire for influence over people who decide on working methods and organization is often based on criticism of a rationalization which has greatly reduced the scope of personal liberty, independence and responsibility at work. In other words, the influence aimed at would be used to alter the whole working relationship.

What we want to do is to reintegrate the production process with planning, organizational, decision-making and control functions which are at present entirely separate. This would appear to be the only possible way of increasing personal responsibility and adaptation, and with it job satisfaction, within the enterprise.

This does not mean that management becomes altogether superfluous. What it does mean is that management must be composed of both workers and employers, and their powers must be fixed accordingly by both sides.

Staff policy and personnel management have been sadly neglected in most firms. The relevant co-operation agreement does not seem to have brought about much change in this respect. Staff policy determines the security and advancement prospects of every worker, and for this reason we need to strengthen trade union influence over manpower policy in general and the particular areas in which it operates for individuals. To exclude such matters from our discussions would be positively to invite unrest.

In all these fields, long-term experiments currently being tried out in certain companies toll the deathknell of the employers' sole right to manage. It will certainly take time for us to find the right way round all the problems arising from changes in the organization of work, management and decision making in staff questions. But no one should mistake our determination to achieve real co-determination in these areas.

And we took a very important step forward at our congress in the beginning of September, when a programme for further action in this field was unanimously accepted. The content of this programme I can summarize in the following way.

Article 32 of the Plant Committee Agreement stipulates that no member of the Employers' Association (SAF) shall be party to a collective agreement unless this agreement includes clauses to the effect that the employer shall have the sole right to control and distribute work to be performed in an enterprise, and the sole right also to hire and to fire workers whether they are organized or not; in fact, the article embodies and consolidates the employer's supreme right of sovereign control within an undertaking.

Therefore, if improvements are to be made in relationships with the enterprise in the direction of increasing influence of workers and improving their co-determination rights, the principle laid down in this article would need to be changed to prepare for a continuous process of transformation. Over the years this article has been a thorn in the flesh of shop stewards and unionists. Its operation has been limited regarding the free right of dismissal, but in matters of executive control it has not permitted much to be done: it embodies the employer's sole right of management. In the administration of labour law as practised by the courts up to the present time it has been like a red-hot wire apparently impossible to remove. Something else must be substituted for it.

This will leave a wide scope for negotiations. Regulations based on agreements will thus be enforced, the employees and their organizations will be given influence over the enterprise on different lines from hitherto. The employers will have to give way a little more in their rights of managerial control, whilst the employees will have a bigger say and greater democracy at plant level. After this one-sided right of control has been removed, a pattern must be introduced making it possible for the parties to find *joint* solutions of major problems relating to control, organization of work and to personal policy matters, but also to questions regarding work environment and health safeguards. The workers and their organizations must be given a chance of participating in shaping the organization of their own work and of their own jobs, to exert influence over its management and control on a basis of firm agreements. Workers should also have opportunities of training and of developing their capacities at job level.

The opportunities thus opened for the employees to participate in policy and action to establish their own position at job level should be directed towards giving them greater individual satisfaction in their work, rather than giving priority to matters of technology and of organization. Authoritarian rule must be replaced by co-operation and mutual trust. This again will obviously mean that the employee himself must have influence over the demands which are made by giving orders and supervising or controlling the work performed, and thereby also over the selection of those who are to perform functions of supervision and control at production level.

One experiment now under way, under the auspices of the Swedish Development Council, should give us valuable indications on ways and means to be sought for these principles in the Agreement to be given practical application. Personnel policy measures would then be controlled by a committee with certain decision-making prerogatives on important questions. This committee would deal with the hiring of workers and their introduction, future personnel planning, opportunities for personnel training and development, but also with transfers and any changes made in job requirements at plant level.

Safeguards for the employees must be improved at the same time. Wherever necessary transfers must not result in downgrading for the individual worker. Work stoppages because of breakdowns, leave of absence and dismissals must be regulated on lines of better safeguards than present regulations permit. Considerably longer terms of notice must be stipulated in the collective agreements – all of which places the employee in a better position. His relationship to the job will have more substance and involve greater interest, security and safeguards.

And this is what we are striving for. But this can only be accomplished, as stated before, if the principle at present enshrined in article 32 disappears, so that the employer's sovereign right of management is moved into the sphere of participation between the enterprise and its employees. The employer's prerogatives based on statutory provisions should also be changed to a greater extent into a function of the new joint machinery. A primary commitment on the part of employers to negotiate when, or before, new techniques or changes in the work pattern are introduced should give greater satisfaction or well-being for the employees and possibilities for them to participate more than before in shaping the pattern of their own working environment. This can also afford protection to the individual by giving him opportunities to obtain support from the trade unions on a number of questions that may cause disputes and grievances at workshop level.

The technical aspects of these demands have been refined by LO Legal Adviser Sten Edlund, whose special task it is to follow up questions related to the drive for greater influence at enterprise level and who has undertaken research into the removal of this objectionable article 32 from the statutes.

An investigation based on these studies has been proposed in parliament which, it is hoped, will be taken in hand and completed as quickly as possible so that the necessary amendments can be introduced speedily into the relevant legislation. Certainly we can in no way be reluctant to negotiate with the employers on questions relating to the wide range of greater plant-level democracy and more influence for the employees. The amended legislation may provide for negotiated agreements, but the latter can also reduce the necessity of statutory provisions.

The plant committees are to remain as co-operation bodies. They will constitute the point of contact between management and the employees. Their influence must, however, be increased in terms of greater commitment in group projects of any kind that penetrate into or influence the enterprise and its future. The plant committee must not be merely a coffee-drinking gathering, but should actually promote influence as a group. This we feel is the natural entrance-gate to group project work through the information system initiated by proposals made by the Co-operation Committee a few years ago.

Forecasts for the two-year or five-year plans of the company should go before the community bodies, and in the discussions that take place in the plant committees there should be possibilities for group project consultation over more detailed decisions on important problems concerning investments, manpower requirements, etc., arising out of these forecasts. This will indeed mean consultation before decision making on important questions.

To make is possible for the employee to digest or assimilate the economic information that is often processed in such committees and presented there backed by expert knowledge in economics, an auditor should be appointed by the employees themselves as a guide to such expert knowledge. He should work in the same way as the other auditors and always be in a position to obtain any information that may be required, but should also advise and inform the workers' representatives on the plant committee in the enterprise to clarify many important issues for those who represent the employees on the committee. His presence would also ensure better safeguards for the employees.

A step consistent with such greater availability of information and insight would be for representatives of the employees to take their place on the company's managing board. The reserved attitude so far taken by the trade union movement concerning representation on company boards should be abandoned. The influence we claim should reach down to the workshop floor to cover:

- matters of participation over shaping job and workshop patterns;
- matters of personnel policy and internal plant organization;
- the demand for open accountability;
- influence in project groups and co-operation generally whenever significant approaches have to be made;
- the demand for plant committees to discuss and state their views on company forecasts.

All these issues need the support of machinery enabling the employees to gain insight and thereby influence at the level of the top management bodies where direct decisions are made.

This is not a long-term programme, seeking to suggest how the jobs and the enterprise of the future should look from the employees' position. It is a short-term action programme; in fact, an element in the structure we are building to achieve a better, a safer and a more satisfactory work environment for the worker, which we must and will accomplish.

This is a programme that should not be controversial, but probably will become so. There are not so many today who like to choose a manual job in industry. It is difficult to recruit the necessary manpower. The younger people shy away from the dull, dangerous and often trying conditions under tightly controlled, severe regimen industry today offers in many cases. If we are to overcome the recruitment crisis which already prevails and may tomorrow be even more marked for many jobs, there is no alternative but to alter the aspect of the enterprise. The solution must be to establish different and better conditions at job level, successively to improve the environment, psychological as well as physical, to improve the individual worker's possibilities of influencing his own position, to provide for greater security and safeguards, and to even out the gap which today continues to separate different groups of employees. It is said sometimes that influence by the employees along these lines is a danger for productivity and its development in industry. I rather believe the opposite to be the case. Allowing the present situation to persist is a danger for the enterprise and for its development.

Implementation of the programme will have a positive impact on manpower recruiting; there will be less fluctuation and absenteeism – these are factors which influence productivity to a high degree. It should be in the interest of the enterprise itself to co-operate towards rapid practical application of these suggestions.

This programme which we present is not a programme that only makes demands on the other party, and on the community; it also makes great demands on ourselves – of this we must be very conscious. We shall have more to say at job level, and questions that so far have not been covered by collective agreements and therefore been open to negotiation. Thereby we also claim a wider field for our trade union organizations to develop their activities, but this at the same time involves greater responsibility on the part of the unions.

We shall have real influence at enterprise level on matters concerning personnel and on questions touching job organization. This demands that our representatives must have the knowledge required to deal with job and workshop problems in project group work. It makes demands on those who will have to co-operate in plant committee activities and on company boards.

We cannot evade the higher responsibility involved in all this, but to be able adequately to live up to it the provisions in respect of training for union shop stewards must be tightened. There are moreover commitments to be met in this connection by trade unions as well as by the employers and by the community. The local trade union organizations themselves – with their branches, workshop units, groups and sections – must henceforth bear the brunt of union activities. We cannot and never will allow this role to be relaxed. They must be in a position to afford the help and support needed by the individual at his place of work.

Our claim for more influence and greater commitment from the employees at enterprise level also means more influence, more commitment, more work and more responsibility for our local organizations, but this is the necessary prerequisite to be met so that a new shape can be given to workshop conditions and job structure can be redesigned on appropriate lines.

Chapter 12

Austria

WILHELM HRDLITSCHKA
President, Chemical Workers' Federation
President, Austrian Labour Council and Chambers of Labour

It is a source of satisfaction to me that the editor of this book had the idea of asking authors from different countries to contribute chapters on workers' co-determination in their countries. This is a matter affecting the great majority of working people, about which they have put forward demands, and which is of world-wide importance at the present time. It is therefore interesting to have reports from various countries about developments there and the progress that has been achieved. Even where there are differences as to political objectives, all these reports will still be the expression of a common effort: the workers' struggle to improve their situation, to realize their justified aim, to decide their own destiny, and to demonstrate their willingness and readiness to accept their responsibilities in this regard.

A book like this presents a special advantage when it arises out of the tradition of the international labour movement – it is a spur to co-operation, and allows comparison to be made between different national experiences. Thus, useful guides to action can be drawn up.

Inside the European Economic Community, for example, in 1970, the EEC Commission published a draft text on the status of a European limited liability company. This arrived at certain conclusions and made an attempt to establish the basis for an international company law. Such initiatives should be closely watched by workers' representatives and considered in the context of the legal situation in the different countries, even in those that do not belong to the EEC.

EXTENSION OF RIGHTS

Discussion about the problem of co-determination has been going on for a long time and will not be silenced. Depending on the legal situation, on agreements between employers and workers, and the vigour of the trade unions, a number of European countries such as France, Federal Republic of Germany, Holland, Belgium, the Scandinavian countries and Britain already have various degrees and methods of co-determination at the company and higher levels. In all countries discussion is going on about extension of such rights.

It is understandable that national conditions should provide the basis for future improvements. Social, economic and ideological aims, together with the views and attitudes of the various interests, all have their repercussions in a particular situation. Nowhere in the world, and certainly not in Austria, will the workers be satisfied in the long run to depend on the opinions and goodwill of those whose political power is used against the interests of the community, who have arbitrary autocratic control over the means of production, and who take economic decisions in their own individual interest and not in the interest of the economy as a whole.

Co-determination at the national level is one of the most important objectives of our time. Democratization in our societies cannot stand still at the half-way mark. What is the point of having public affairs of a political nature decided by democratic means if the economy – which is certainly the most important of all public affairs – is excepted from this process?

In former times, the economy was a matter reserved for business management only. Today this attitude is an anachronism, particularly now that management functions are frequently carried out by appointees.

The trade unions had first of all to fight for the freedom to join legally recognized organizations and to obtain decent working conditions and wages that at least assured a minimum subsistence.

Only with time were the unions able to obtain not only improvements in social conditions, the adoption of laws for worker protection and social security for their members, but also to obtain increasing influence over economic affairs.

Our demand for co-determination in Austria has as its objective not a change in ownership of the means of production, but a redistribution of authority. It is unjust that property rights can only be guaranteed if the owner has sole uncontrolled authority over his property. Economic activity should not be an end in itself, but should be part of a larger social responsibility. What is involved is not just a matter of producing and distributing goods but also of ensuring that working people have a guaranteed living standard by providing them with employment opportunities.

The Catholic Church itself, from its highest office, has also repeatedly proclaimed that the owners of the means of production have social responsibilities. These find their strongest expression in consideration for the needs of working people. But it cannot be left to the property owners and their agents alone to find such a motivation. Co-determination for workers' representatives will make it certain that these modern ethical principles will be applied in daily life.

So we have in this demand a social policy objective which it is urgent to realize on an increasing scale in democratic communities. It is to be expected that a whole series of unforeseen consequences will arise from the acceptance and practice of this principle, but any kind of democratic progress brings such changes with it. The trade unions accept the responsibilities they will have to bear when industrial democracy and co-determination become a reality. For example, they will have to make greater efforts in the field of training, so that the works' councils are still better equipped to exercise the extended right to co-determination that must in any case be obtained. But the trade unions have dealt with other responsibilities in the past and do not fear what they will have to face in this field in order to attain their objectives. In any event, we, on the trade union side, are aware that this is not something that can be achieved overnight.

Co-determination is of fundamental importance from the standpoint of economic policy. It is a commonplace that in a modern economy the labour force is just as indispensable as machines and other productive equipment. A logical consequence of this realization would be to arrive at an equilibrium between capital and labour and this can only be done by means of co-determination. Furthermore, co-determination in its widest sense must relate to all sectors of economic life and thus reinforce the pluralistic character of our democratic society. Acceptance of democracy and recognition that it can and must evolve entails a necessary and consequential extension of democratic rights and customs from the political to the economic field. As long as the democratic principle remains valid the forces that oppose the trade unions' co-determination demands will find themselves in an increasingly difficult position, all the more so because at the international level developments are moving inexorably in the direction of industrial democracy.

Anyone who tries to postpone democratization of the economy is also willy-nilly doing harm to democracy itself, because it is indivisible. Democracy can be accepted or rejected, but it cannot be half one thing and half another, because this inevitably has undesirable consequences. Economic democracy as the logical complement of political democracy is a principle that cannot be subject to conditions within a democratic society.

The principle of democratic legality also applies here. This is based on recognition of social justice which itself depends on equality of rights and duties of individual citizens. In the long run workers will never finally accept that duties in the economic field should be distributed more or less equally, while rights exist only on one side.

In a democracy, equality of rights is the basis of political freedom. Freedom without the possibility of exercising one's rights is unthinkable. In everyday life in industry, there are still many real features of the master-and-servant relationship remaining for those who work in the plant. This absence of freedom must be eliminated by giving workers the corresponding right to co-determination. This means that new responsibilities must be given to elected workers' representatives, just as such rights are guaranteed to elected representatives in the political field. This does not mean that the individual worker or his elected representative will enjoy unrestricted freedom, because such unrestricted freedom does not exist, not even for management. Only mutual understanding and recognition of the principle of a fair balance of interests guarantees to everyone the maximum of individual liberty. A citizen in the modern state is also entitled to the freedoms of citizenship in having full rights in the economy in his work situation.

This is obviously not achieved merely by co-determination at the plant level. A modern economy is much too complex a structure in which everything is mutually interdependent.

The natural opposition and the resulting conflicts between management and workers' representatives will be resolved in a democratic balance within the framework of co-determination on an institutional basis. This is in the interests of everybody concerned. There is no such balance now, but only unilateral decisions having binding effects so that conflicts are inevitable. Economic development requires harmonious, organic growth of production, and experience has shown that conflicts only damage and hinder it. So far the Austrian trade unions, because of their strength, have been able to avoid major conflicts, and therefore Austria has very few strike situations. The economy has been very little affected by strikes. However, this is not because the unions have been particularly easy-going, in avoiding conflict situations, but rather because of the very forceful attitude of union representatives. The unions therefore cannot be accused of unilateral abuse of power. This example shows that co-determination, when properly understood, can be put into practice on the basis of democratic principles and in the ultimate analysis works to the advantage of the economy and the general welfare. There is no reason why the same cannot happen at the company level. This does not mean, of course, that the unions renounce direct action measures in case of need.

If their demands for co-determination at the company and national levels were realized, the workers and their representatives would not be making a bid for power. Democratic co-determination has existed for decades in the political life of our society, without any unilateral seizure of power by undemocratic means.

Co-determination would not restrict management initiative in a way that would damage the company's economic success, because the workers are just as much involved in a company's prosperity and success as the shareholders or the manager they appoint. On the contrary, it may be expected that ideas and suggestions from many people will give better results than one-sided decisions on the part of management. In any event, social justice requires that the workers alone should not have to bear the brunt of any mistaken decisions in management policy by losing their jobs, as has often been the case in the past.

On the other hand, the question of industrial democracy also raises that of the degree of economic development. This is the reason why so far no single technique of industrial democracy has proved itself to be feasible for the world as a whole. Each country and each national trade union movement must judge for itself how far there has been progress towards industrial democracy. The development of social policy depends on many factors. Nobody is thinking in terms of generalized uniformity on a super-regional basis, though the objectives and the direction, as far as Europe is concerned, are uniform. It is to be expected that a highly industrialized country with a solid democratic structure and other essential pre-conditions will move ahead of other countries in this regard.

To be sure, ideas about industrial democracy differ from one country to another just as much as conditions in those countries differ. While all the European trade unions have the same common goal, and while political forces everywhere are all striving in the same direction, the progress that has so far been made is uneven.

As far as Austria is concerned, we can look back on a very long union tradition and see that we have already made some important first steps in the field of co-determination.

Austria's relatively small-scale economy makes it highly dependent on the world market for its exports, and also open to international corporations. Austria being short of domestic capital, international capitalism has taken over, so that all co-determination problems are much more difficult to resolve than would be the case if we had only to deal with Austrian capitalists. However, even these foreign corporations fall completely under Austrian law, particularly social legislation. Thus, if co-determination is established by law this will be obligatory and binding in this sector also. Nevertheless, it would be useful if there could be co-ordinated trade union action in the field of industrial democracy, at least in the European region. The International Chemical Workers' Federation has already accomplished valuable preparatory work, including the publication of this book which presents an international comparison and is a contribution to the effort to put into practice the unions' aims with regard to industrial democracy and co-determination.

Today, the unions are firm in their purpose to win co-determination; they demand it at the company and at the national level, and they accept all the consequences of their policy. They must gain influence over the economy in order to preserve real wages and jobs, and obtain for workers and employees an optimum share in the product of economic growth.

In Austria, the nationalized sector of industry holds an important position, and this provides a good basis for co-determination, while there are very few large private corporations because the country is so small. Many of the more important companies are subsidiaries either of the major Austrian banks or of foreign corporations. The two biggest banks in Austria, Creditanstalt-Bankverain and Länderbank, have been nationalized since 1947. However, these two banks operate on purely private enterprise principles. At least up to the present, decision-making functions have remained in the hands of groups which show little understanding of industrial democracy. This hinders future development in many important sectors of the Austrian economy. However, we may expect a gradual change in outlook, particularly to the extent that our socialist government, which stands very close to the unions, is able to impose its viewpoint on the nationalized banks.

In most countries, the struggle to win co-determination centres on the medium and larger industrial companies. This is a good starting point. In European countries these are usually limited companies, often belonging to major corporations. This provides an opportunity to obtain seats and votes for workers' representatives in the management bodies established under company law: namely, the board of directors or the supervisory board. The trade unions are usually strongly implemented in such companies. Some of the members of the works' councils have time off from their work so as to be able to devote themselves completely to representing the workers. These representatives are generally in close contact with the responsible trade unions and usually occupy leading positions in them, and they are therefore the channel by which the unions' objectives can be attained.

While success is most likely to be achieved in the above-mentioned companies, other enterprises should not be forgotten. Other types of co-determination are required for different circumstances.

In many countries there are legal provisions that establish participation by worker representatives in company supervisory boards. In Austria, the Works' Council Law provides that in joint stock companies, limited companies and limited liability companies above a certain capital, two members elected from the works' council shall belong to the supervisory board. The works' council representatives have the same rights as the other members of the supervisory board. The labour movement – the unions and the chamber of labour – are demanding a reform in the law to increase worker participation by means of co-determination. Details will be given below.

CHAMBERS OF LABOUR IN AUSTRIA

In Austria, certain legally established institutions give the workers a significant degree of co-determination in matters outside the operation of individual companies. These are the 'Chambers for Workers and Employees', or more briefly 'Chambers of Labour'. They are based on the so-called Law on Chambers of Labour, in its version of 19 May 1954. Each of the nine federal provinces of Austria has its own Chamber of Labour, with a central body called the Austrian Chamber of Labour Conference. The aim and purpose of the Chambers of Labour is defined in the law as follows: 'The Chambers of Labour are called upon to represent and promote the social, economic, occupational and cultural interests of employed persons.' There were already Chambers of Labour in Austria under the First Republic, based on a law of 1920.

The following description will show what a far-reaching and comprehensive field of activity is laid down for the Chambers for Workers and Employees in the relevant legislation.

The Chambers of Labour and the Chamber of Labour Conference are called upon to submit to legislative bodies and authorities reports, proposals and opinions on all matters affecting industry, commerce and transport; finance, credit and insurance questions; energy; radio; education, teaching and training institutions; food; housing; public health; culture; employment relationships; and so on.

These bodies have to express their views on draft legislation, appoint representatives on public bodies and put forward nominations. They are also called upon to co-operate in economic and industrial administration and economic policy-making to the extent that this is provided for in specific laws or regulations.

They are also supposed to co-operate in improving the workers' social and economic conditions, in promoting their technical and cultural education and also in fixing prices of goods and services. In addition, they participate in economic, social and statistical inquiries and maintain their own statistics.

The Chambers of Labour also have the following responsibilities: supervision of the application of provisions in labour law or concerning accident prevention, establishment of bodies for the protection of apprentices or young workers, supervision of apprentice training, participation in examinations for industrial and commercial apprentices, etc. Finally, they advise works' councillors and shop stewards in the execution of their functions and establish institutions to help and support them in their work.

In addition to participation in the legislative process formally by submitting opinions and informally in discussions in government and parliament, the Chambers of Labour are the vehicle for workers' co-determination on innumerable commissions, advisory bodies and similar administrative institutions. These activities range from the tax commission, the advisory committee on foreign trade, the industrial law commission, and the administration of the agricultural fund to the Joint Committee on Wages and Prices with its sub-committees, including that on economic and social questions.

This enumeration is not exhaustive. There are more than sixty bodies in which co-operation by the Chambers for Workers and Employees is foreseen, either on the basis of legal provisions or less frequently under regulations. It is not only important that such above-mentioned rights and responsibilities are prescribed for Chambers of Labour in legislation but also that practical co-operation is effected as implementations of the laws by discussion in the various commissions.

These activities provide an opportunity for highly effective participation in economic, social and cultural affairs – in other words, in everything that affects the people generally. It is true that the Chambers of Labour present proposals and can only ensure that they are accepted under certain conditions. Each case depends on the balance of forces. However, these proposals have usually been well prepared and programmed by experts and have behind them the great majority of industrial workers, employees and transport personnel who are represented in the Chamber of Labour Conference, so that the legislative bodies usually cannot but pay due regard to the proposals.

At the present stage of production technique it is necessary to allow full scope to the decision-making power and personal initiative of working people, and it is therefore not feasible to go on withholding the right to equality in responsibility and decision making. Workers today – and even more in the future – are in almost every case 'creative' in their work, and from now on they can be expected to show readiness to participate in the widest sense of the term.

But such participation is conditional on the right to co-determination. This is why all our efforts are being made to obtain improvements from the legal standpoint. In particular, we should leave no stone unturned in exploring all the practical possibilities that exist on the present state of the law. Both the Chambers of Labour and the trade unions will have much to do in the field of propaganda and education.

The Chambers for Workers and Employees, and particularly the Chamber of Labour Conference, have extensive co-determination rights in the economic field, as we have seen, and they exercise them conscientiously. The Chambers represent all workers, to the extent that their organizational structure and jurisdiction permit. At the company level, however, it is the competent trade unions and works' councils that exercise these functions.

The importance of the role in public life of the Chambers for Workers and Employees, which operate in close contact with the unions, is seen in the fact that in the present Federal government five ministers and two state secretaries previously held office in the Chambers and the unions. This seems to show that a considerable degree of participation in decision making exists even at the highest level.

FUNCTIONS OF WORKS' COUNCILS

The new Austrian Works' Councils Law of 13 July 1971 gives the elected works' councils certain co-determination rights, particularly the right to be informed by the company. It is often more instructive, striking and precise to have the text of the law verbatim rather than in the words of a commentary. For this reason we shall quote below certain important legal provisions which form the basis for co-determination.

The relevant provisions that existed before the revision of the law read, in part, as follows:

'In the exercise of its right to co-operate in the management and administration of the undertaking, the works' council shall have the following functions:

'1. The works' council is called upon to make recommendations and proposals to the company owner, with the aim of promoting the prosperity and increasing the production of the company in the interest of the company and its workers. This shall be particularly the case with respect to the preparation

K

of economic plans (production, investment, sales and other plans).

'2. In commercial undertakings, banks and insurance institutions employing at least 30 persons, in other undertakings permanently employing at least 70 persons, in manufacturing and mining undertakings, the owner shall submit annually to the works' council a copy of the balance sheet for the previous year, together with the profit and loss account, at the latest one month after these have been communicated to the tax authorities, and also give the works' council such additional information and explanations as are required for their understanding of these documents.'

The following additional provisions are new, and not only lay down a right to information but also provide the opportunity to make proposals that would prevent a company's difficulties from having harmful consequences:

'3. The company owner shall give the works' council information about the company's economic position, the nature and volume of production, state of the order-book, volume and value of sales, investments and any proposed measures to increase the company's prosperity. Furthermore, he shall inform the works' council at the earliest possible moment of any proposed changes in the company.

Changes in the company include in particular:

(a) reduction or closure of the whole or part of the company,

(b) removal of the whole or part of the company to another location,

(c) merger with other companies,

(d) modification in the legal status or ownership of the company,

(e) changes in the purpose of the company, its equipment, organization of work and production,

(f) introduction of new work methods.

'4. The works' council is called upon to make proposals to prevent, eliminate or reduce harmful consequences to the workers of measures listed in 3 (a) to (f) above. The company owner shall be obliged to discuss these proposals with the works' council. The latter shall have due regard for the company's economic needs in this connection.'

The Works' Councils Law also provides the opportunity to convene a national economic commission that has been established under the Federal Ministry for Trade and Industry. The relevant provisions read:

'5. Irrespective of the provisions in 1 to 4 above, a works' council in an undertaking employing more than 500 persons may, if its proposals are not taken into account, and if it reaches the conclusion that the company's management is acting against the public interest, decide by a two-thirds majority to appeal through the provincial headquarters of the Austrian Trade Union Federation against the management's actions. This provision applies to the kind of undertakings listed in Art. 12, para. 1, provided that the total number of employees exceeds 500.

'A national economic commission to be established under the Federal Ministry [for Incomes and Economic Planning][1] shall be competent to decide upon such appeals. The commission shall be presided over by the Federal Minister [for Incomes and Economic Planning] or by a representative appointed by him. The other members shall be appointed in equal numbers by the Federal Industrial Association and the Chamber of Labour Conference.

'In the event of closure of undertakings, the appeal by the works' council must obligatorily go forward for decision by the national economic commission which must be notified within four weeks, counting from the day on which the company owner informed the works' council.'

A particularly important provision in the law relates to time off for educational purposes. This is most significant from the standpoint of education and training and by providing the opportunity to large numbers of works' council members to obtain instruction regarding the scope of the law and its application, lays the foundation for the exercise of the right to co-determination at the company level. The text reads as follows:

'Each member of the works' council shall be entitled to time off from his work without loss of pay up to a total of two weeks during his term of office, for participation in education and training activities. In exceptional cases, and on proof that special

---

[1] The Federal Ministry for Incomes and Economic Planning was replaced by the Federal Ministry for Trade and Industry which is now responsible for implementation of the Law.

training is required, the period of time off may be extended to four weeks. If a substitute member permanently replaces a titular member on the works' council, during the latter's term of office, he shall be entitled to time off for educational purposes to the extent that the member who has resigned did not exercise his entitlement.

'Time off is to be granted for participation in educational and training activities organized by employers' or workers' bodies able to conclude collective agreements, or recognized as suitable by both parties, and having as their purpose the communication of knowledge that serves in the exercise of the functions of a member of a works' council.'

JOB SECURITY

One of the most important questions for workers' representatives that arise in connection with co-determination at the company level is that of job security. A dynamic economy is always subject to all kinds of changes. Structural weaknesses from the past must be eliminated in order to remain competitive. But such structural changes often give rise to reductions in the labour force. The same is true of the nationalization measures that often become necessary and the application of new technological processes. Of course, the employment structure in a company cannot be expected to become fossilized while all other structures in the same company are undergoing various necessary modifications. Under a practical system of co-determination inside the company, the aim will therefore be to avoid social hardship to the extent this is possible, and on the other hand to ensure that any displaced workers will find other employment either in the same company or in another nearby. From the standpoint of effective reductions in production, plant reorganization, co-determination or closures should never result in any considerable number of workers losing their means of subsistence and having to rely on inadequate unemployment insurance benefits.

In Austria recently we have seen examples of plants being closed down as a result of structural changes, the burden of which was borne exclusively by the workers. This happened with the closure of unprofitable paper and cellulose plants. The recklessness that was shown on this occasion convinced wide sectors of the Austrian people that the trade unions' demand for co-determination was justified from the standpoint of job security.

Another recent example occurred with a large petroleum company. In the process of adjustment to the needs of a future European market, changes had to be made that rendered a reduction in the labour force necessary. However, agreement with the works' council and the responsible trade union ensured that none of the workers concerned had to suffer any reduction in his means of existence.

As may be seen, there are cases in which consultation in connection with maintenance of jobs or avoidance of social hardships brings positive results. In other cases, however, economic conditions mean that there is only the possibility of equalizing the burdens – by avoiding other jobs in the event of plant closures and ensuring that the transition to new employment takes place with as little friction as possible.

Recently, an Austrian corporation was proposing to close down one of its paper mills, and at the urging of the responsible trade union the central works' council of the corporation called for the convocation of the national economic commission in accordance with the law quoted above. It was contended that the management of this corporation was harming the economy as a whole. The workers' representatives concerned saw an opportunity here not only to obtain a favourable settlement for the specific plant, but also to establish principles for the solution of the problems of the entire paper industry which is facing economic difficulties at the present time. In this connection, mention should be made of the efforts of the competent trade unions to conclude a contract with employer representatives covering the entire industry and involving the creation of a social fund to be financed by the employers which would contribute to reducing the existing difficulties in the event of future plant closures.

In a number of countries, the workers' demand for an active labour market policy has led to the adoption of legal provisions and government measures that benefit employers as well as workers. A well-known, outstanding example of this is to be found in Sweden.

Following long years of effort in this field, the Austrian labour movement has finally succeeded – though relatively late in the day – in obtaining the adoption of a law that corresponds to the needs of our time, as may be seen from the following outline.

The law corresponds to the recommendations made by OECD

and takes account of the new demands that are being made, and will be increasingly made, of labour market administration as a result of international developments. It was adopted in parliament in December 1968, and came into force on 1 January 1969 as the Labour Market Development Law, having as its purpose an extension of the responsibilities of the labour market administration. In addition to the provision of vocational guidance, placement in employment and unemployment insurance, the administration will in future make a considerably greater contribution to the maintenance of full employment and the prevention of unemployment. Special significance attaches to measures for promoting geographical and occupational mobility of workers as well as re-adaptation. This feature is of great importance in relation to the structural changes which are already taking place and which may be expected in the future. The new law provides a legal basis for the necessary measures.

The law provides for financial aid to preserve jobs or training, for job security, adjustment of short-term disequilibria in employment and prevention of structural unemployment. In 1971 about 350 million Schillings were allocated for this purpose.

DECISIONS OF THE AUSTRIAN TRADE UNION FEDERATION

The whole complex question of co-determination inside and outside the undertaking was the subject of discussion at the Seventh Congress of the Austrian Trade Union Federation (ÖGB) in autumn 1971. A working group had previously drafted a statement on co-determination, and this was then unanimously approved by the congress delegates. The social policy spokesman of the Federation, Dr Gerhard Weissenberg, has presented and explained this statement in detail in *Arbeit und Wirtschaft*, the joint publication of the Austrian Chamber of Labour Conference and the Trade Union Federation. Dr Weissenberg makes the following observations:

'At the national and provincial level, we demand that the workers' right to co-determination should be laid down in the basic labour laws, and that the laws establishing co-determination should be guaranteed in the Constitution.

'At the company level, extension of the works' council's law is the centre of our demands. This means appropriate organizational structures, simplification of election procedures and improvement in the functioning of works' councils. Communications between workers and the works' council must be improved by all suitable measures, including in particular legal authorization for the creation of sub-committees or department spokesmen which would provide the opportunity of achieving such an improvement.

'However, the essential feature of a reform of the Works' Council Law must be a revision of their responsibilities and functions. Existing rights of co-operation on personnel questions, particularly with regard to new hirings, transfers, promotions, dismissals and lay-offs, must be greatly expanded. Agreements at the plant level must be based on sound principles so as to serve as an instrument for the legal application of co-determination.

'In future, therefore, a distinction should be made between measures relating to organization of work in the plant, which cannot be taken in the absence of such an agreement; measures that require the co-operation of the works' council but can be decided upon by an outside body (conciliation office) even in the absence of such an agreement; agreements about matters that can be settled on the basis of legal provisions or collective agreements; and finally plant agreements that do not lay down any standards for action.'[1]

Since 1948, the Austrian trade unions have campaigned for co-determination. This is true as regards both the Federation and the sixteen industrial unions that comprise it. The Seventh ÖGB Federal Congress brought a positive result that found expression in the revision of the Works' Council Law. The power of one-and-a-half million organized workers had brought further important progress. Thus the Seventh ÖGB Congress was a turning point, and the decisions taken by the delegates will be of vital importance in future developments in Austria.

ON THE WAY TOWARDS CO-DETERMINATION

Generally speaking, the principles embodied in the Works' Council Law, together with specific provisions concerning personnel representatives and certain special legal texts and ordinances, can be considered as forming the legal basis for co-determination. This is also the case with the Law on Collective

[1] *Arbeit und Wirtschaft*, September 1971, no. 9/1971.

Agreements which in practice gives the unions the opportunity, when concluding agreements, to obtain co-determination for the works' council at the company level and for the union at the industry level with regard to matters that are important to them.

Closer examination of the responsibilities and functions laid down for works' councils in the law shows that in most cases the active co-operation of the unions guarantees observance of the collective agreement, conclusion of internal agreements at the plant level, protection against dismissal and supervision of provisions for the protection of workers.

The Law on Collective Agreements guarantees the unions the right to co-determination with regard to working conditions and renumeration of employed persons. In Austria this occurs at the industry level, the agreement being concluded between an employers' association and one of the sixteen industrial unions composing the ÖGB.

The above-mentioned co-determination at the provincial and national levels through the Chambers for Workers and Employees also favours the unions, because there is close co-operation between the Chambers and the Trade Union Federation and in many cases the same persons occupy leading positions in both bodies. Our major preoccupations are the maintenance of full employment, economic growth and the competitiveness of Austrian industry. Another of the most important demands of workers' representatives is for improvements in social security.

Austrian social legislation is very progressive in many respects. This is the result of decades of intensive efforts by the unions and the Chambers of Labour.

At the present time, it is not possible for the trade unions to restrict themselves to making their voice heard with regard to wages and working conditions. Special attention must be paid to the evolution of prices in order to maintain and improve workers' real incomes. Immediately after the Second World War, the Trade Union Federation concluded an agreement on wages and prices with the top employer association – the Federal Chamber of Industry. This removed the danger of inflation, and also made it possible gradually to raise real wages in step with the successful reconstruction of the Austrian economy. This wage-and-price agreement is also an important element in co-determination at the national level and hence an example of industrial democracy in Austria.

For many years this problem has been under the control of

the Joint Commission for Wages and Prices. This is composed of representatives of the Federal government, the Federal Chamber of Industry, the Chambers of Labour and the Trade Union Federation. Any proposed price increases must be submitted to this Commission for approval. Similarly, agreement must be obtained from the Joint Commission before entering into wage negotiations. It has been possible by this means to stem price increases to some extent. However, a fully-fledged wages and prices freeze was not intended, nor was it feasible because the Joint Commission for Wages and Prices operates on the basis of voluntary agreements between employer and unions.

Since the Seventh ÖGB Congress in September 1971, the weight of the unions' campaign for co-determination has been at the company level. The decisions taken there lay down a combination of factors determining a company's size and economic importance and hence subjecting it to co-determination. These factors are the number of employees, the amount of capital and turnover as an expression of the company's performance. On this basis the participation of union representatives in the supervisory boards is determined on the following scale:

In all medium-sized undertakings employing more than 200 persons, or with an annual turnover of at least 100 million Schillings and a balance sheet of at least 50 million Schillings, one-third of the members of the supervisory board shall be appointed by the works' council. In all undertakings employing more than 500 persons, with a balance-sheet of 100 million Schillings and a turnover of 200 million Schillings, in which two of these conditions are fulfilled, the following arrangement shall be made. The supervisory board must be composed of an odd number of members. One member shall be appointed by agreement between the shareholders and the workers; the others shall be appointed in equal numbers by the shareholders and the workers' sides, two-fifths of those from the workers' side being nominated by the trade union concerned.

It will be seen from this structure that decision making will take account of the interests of all concerned and not merely the employers' profit interest.

We in the trade unions are conscious that such a system of co-determination can only work successfully if the workers' representatives are intellectually equipped for their task and have access to the necessary basic training.

Both in the Chambers of Labour and the Trade Union Federation, and also in many cases the individual unions, have already taken on this responsibility. The Trade Union Federation is giving consideration to using correspondence courses to transmit information to the greatest possible numbers. There is already a correspondence school that successfully provides instruction in trade unionism and union activities. The Chamber for Workers and Employees in Vienna will also provide special courses, probably for graduates from the Social Academy and other officials interested in these questions. The Vienna Chamber of Labour has for many years been providing training in accountancy on behalf of the Chamber of Labour Conference, and this has proved most successful.

Together with the unions and the works' councils, the Chambers of Labour are part of the organizational structure of the labour movement. The close relationship between the Chambers and the unions is also seen in the composition of the Chambers.

INDUSTRIAL DEMOCRACY INITIATIVE OF THE KREISKY GOVERNMENT

A new amendment to the law on plant committees proposes a one-third participation of the workers' representatives on the board of directors of the holding companies as of 1 January 1973. This participation will give the employees' representatives in the supervision bodies of the holding companies the chance of exercising a veto through Preference holdings.

'TRADE UNION STRATEGY'

The project will differ in one major point from the German model: it will not be possible to appoint outside persons to the board of directors, including trade union officials not belonging to the enterprise. However, delegates from other enterprises which have a close economic relationship to the 'democratized' enterprise (i.e. enterprises with direct or indirect joint ventures) will be permitted membership. The trade union representatives shall be responsible only to the assembly of employees: their tenure of offices will be independent of the limits fixed in the corporation law or in the statutes of the enterprise. The trade union representatives shall not receive director's fees, but shall be compensated for their expenses. Amendments to the legislation on incorporated companies and private limited companies will not be necessitated by this innovation. Only the board of directors of the Austrian Industrie-Verwaltungs–AG (ÖIAG) for the nationalized enterprises will not be effected by this new form of industrial democracy as they are already under special law.

The Social Ministry refers in its reasons in favour of the initiative to demands of the Austrian national trade union centre, to the draft proposal of the EEC Commission in Brussels on the Status of European Registered Companies, and to the German practice.

Further, the Ministry underlines that trends towards concentration within the Austrian economy necessitate an increase in workers' participation. Trade union commentators have made particular reference to the increased influence exercised by foreign capital, over which control is urgently sought. However, further extension of the industrial democracy scheme is to be dealt with by the redrafting of the labour legislation which promises among other things to consolidate industrial democracy in a real constitutional plant law. A committee of the Social Ministry has been working on this for a long time.

As we all know, progress cannot be made without meeting obstacles, and industrial democracy will only be achieved step by step, by overcoming such obstacles. However, it would be quite false to state, as is widely said on the employers' side, that the introduction of co-determination at the company level would place the whole system of private enterprise in peril. It is obvious that co-determination also implies co-responsibility. It is not just management that takes risks, and in the long run nobody is going to accept risks while being subject to decisions taken by others. Co-determination will bring a change in social policy and social psychology that will give the assurance that people are participating in shaping their own destinies. Mistakes will certainly be made, but experience has shown that mistakes are already made as a result of unilateral management decisions. This is not an agreement against co-determination, since everyone knows that all human effort is subject to error.

In conclusion, experience in Austria has demonstrated that it is only through close co-operation between works' councils and unions that it is possible to bridge the gap between company interests and national interests. It is the unions' responsibility to give intensive training to works' council members so that they understand the implications of what they do for the economy as a whole, and it is the works' councils' responsibility to pass on this knowledge to the workers and also to bring their own concrete problems to the unions. Co-determination at the company level should never be in contradiction with co-determination at the provincial and national levels.

We can say without exaggeration that Austria is a socially progressive, democratic country. There are already the beginnings of workers' co-determination in industry and the economy. However, as far as industrial democracy as understood by the trade unions is concerned, a great deal of effort is still required to attain our objectives in this important sector of public life.

Chapter 13

Canada

HENRY LORRAIN
*First Vice-President, United Paper Workers' International Union
Vice-President, Canadian Labour Congress*

The most striking aspect of industrial democracy in Canada is its elusiveness. It's a bit like the case of the striker walking the picket line back in the thirties who was questioned by a woman about his activity.

'I'm picketing this plant because I'm on a strike', said the worker.

'Why are you on strike?' asked the woman.

'Madam', said the worker, righting his picket sign and marching proudly past her, 'I'm on strike for the right to collective bargaining . . . whatever the hell that is.'

The point is that it is unlikely that a significant number of Canadian workers would say 'Yes', they favoured industrial democracy, because until very recently the subject has not been seriously examined in Canada; and the results of the limited discussions that have taken place have demonstrated that Canadians have a rather remarkable ability for saying what industrial democracy is not.

Generally, the concept is not regarded as something separate and apart from the traditional North American collective bargaining process. Hence Canadian reaction to industrial democracy may appear to be negative. The mainstream of thought on the subject among Canadian labour leaders does not endorse 'worker control'. Nor are works councils looked on with favour, although there is growing support for continuous consultation between the local union and local management.

If Canadian workers were asked whether they favoured industrial democracy they probably would reply cautiously and ask for an explanation of the term. But if they were asked whether they favoured job protection through some mechanism which would give them the right to negotiate technological change, there is little doubt that they would say 'Yes'. However, this would be viewed as an extension of the collective bargaining system.

The following views on 'industrial democracy' in Canada do not represent a concensus in the Canadian labour movement. They are ideas which we have talked about in our own union and have presented to management and government from time to time in recent years. It would be false to suggest that they have wide currency or are close to being accepted. On the other hand the concepts are not simply ethereal. We look on them as logical and necessary adjustments in the Canadian collective bargaining system, or if you prefer, the development of a Canadian 'industrial democracy'.

EXPANSION OF COLLECTIVE BARGAINING

Early collective agreements in Canada were relatively limited in scope. Through the years they have expanded in a number of directions. Labour has been successful in establishing rules governing the behaviour of management in such matters as promotions, demotions, lay-offs and rehires, but regrettably only as they relate to the question of seniority. Collective agreements now include grievance procedures and the office of the shop steward has been recognized. Management's absolute right to impose disciplinary measures has been curtailed. In addition, unions have put some new twists into the wage package, so that it now includes various forms of indirect and deferred economic benefits such as pensions, group insurance, prepaid medical care, sickness and accident insurance, supplemental unemployment benefits, severance pay, and so on. Year by year, collective agreements have become more extensive and increasingly we have established bilateral control over more conditions of employment.

Unions have never conceded that there could be any absolute boundary surrounding the subject matter of the collective bargaining process. Fundamentally, the purpose of a trade union has been to convert the government of an enterprise from autocracy into a semblance of industrial democracy. Or put in other terms, there has been an attempt to replace the unilateral decision-making powers of management by a bilateral arrangement involving both union and management.

The reasons for extending the collective bargaining process are threefold. There is the immediate need to reinforce the countervailing power of the union on behalf of the employees, in what is basically an unequal relationship between the two parties.

Secondly, there must be a vehicle which will enable workers, directly, and through their union, to express their intelligence, creativity, knowledge and interest in their work. And the basis for this type of activity means workers will have to have more control over certain areas directly related to their own work. This agrees with the social scientist's concept of 'self-control' over the performance of their own work.

Finally, management must come to accept *in practice* greater responsibility towards employees and the community for decisions which affect both. This acceptance implies much more than the institution of mechanisms which ensure accountability to constituencies other than the enterprise. It implies also the re-examination and redefinition of the 'criteria of performance' by the enterprise. A government minister responsible for the environment has said that economic development can no longer be measured or defined simply in terms of economic growth if we are really concerned about improving and preserving our environment. If by 'environment' we mean not only the physical and ecological impact of management decision, but also *its* social effect on people, then the labour movement must strike the theme of World War I French Premier Clêmenceau when he told his generals: 'War is much too serious a matter to be left to the generals.'

How then do we go about developing these extensions to the collective bargaining system? There are two dimensions to the solution.

DUAL ASPECTS OF INVOLVEMENT

Consider first a vertical dimension which involves two processes, both of them aimed at the unilateral decision-making powers of management, but which are at different levels. At the top level of decision making, both from the point of view of impact and the responsibility of those making the decisions, management must accept a new 'criteria of performance' concept. Decisions which, by their very nature, affect the lives of employees and the entire community cannot be based on the traditional yardstick of the profitability of the firm. This is especially true when profits are measured by the firm itself in accordance with internally developed policies. Therefore, decisions to close or to reduce operations, to locate or to relocate, to modernize or to build new facilities, are all matters of tremendous importance to employees and to the community. Similarly, policies of pricing, marketing, product mix, productive capacity and production levels are *privately* made, but are *public* in their impact. To state simply that all such matters are regulated by the mechanisms of the marketplace in a market-type economy is all right for economic textbooks, but it is just not good enough as the foundation for a modern industrialized economy. To rely upon the marketplace under modern conditions as a self-regulating mechanism is to rely on a bent and distorted framework.

Now we have to face up to the question whether these matters can be brought into collective bargaining as we know it, given our present economic and social system. The answer seems to be probably not, if we think in terms of precise clauses in a collective agreement covering a single plant. However, by extending the *concept* of collective bargaining, we can envisage mechanisms for reducing the *privacy* (in the sense of both secrecy and interest) from these major decision areas. Such mechanisms would involve a three-way *consultation* and *information* process aimed at least at *influencing* crucial management decisions. And in this connection it must be stressed that the full and complete provision of information by management to the union, the employees and the community *before the decision is made* is crucial. Without specific and complete information any subsequent 'consultation' becomes at best symbolic, at worst pure manipulation.

Recent legislation in Quebec and Ontario dealing with mass lay-offs and dismissals shows a belated and extremely timid recognition of the principle advanced here that privacy cannot be tolerated in decisions which have major public impact. Both acts require employers who plan mass lay-offs or dismissals to give advance notice to the affected employees and the government. The length of notice required is based on the number of employees affected and it should be noted in passing that the time provided in the regulations is far from adequate. The philosophy behind the law is fairly simple and sound. Since the cost of the decision is to be borne largely by the employees and the community, there is a need for something in the manner of an 'early warning system'. So far so good. But there are at least two key elements missing here. Firstly, the advance notice does not have to be given to the union. Secondly, and more importantly, the only requirement is for a simple notice of the pending lay-off. There is no requirement for the company to say why it is taking the action. The company is not called on in any way to *justify* its action. It can say, in effect, 'We'll tell you what we intend to do since you insist on knowing, but we're damned if we'll tell you why we're doing it. After all it's *our* business. And anyway, you wouldn't understand even if we did try to explain it. And finally, we're accountable, in the last analysis, only to the stockholders.'

This kind of attitude just doesn't stand up to inspection.

Recent developments which have resulted in massive lay-offs in the pulp and paper industry in Quebec serve to throw into bold relief the stark realities of 'private' decision-making and its effects. They also reveal the limitations of plant unit bargaining, as a legal framework, in the face of company-wide and even industry-wide policies and decisions. Some type of consultative or 'watchdog' agency is called for which will represent an industry, its employees through their unions and the community at large through government. Instead of fighting a rearguard action, and instead of waiting until crisis is on the doorstep, such an agency should be taking initiatives to make sure it is constantly and fully informed about the plans, projects, problems and general situation of the industry. Functioning on a continuing basis it should be able to analyse this information and make proposals to the decision-making areas of responsibility based on the results. Nor can it be said that such a system of information, consultation and recommendation would be ineffectual.

In the case of the pulp and paper industry, there are plenty of 'teeth', perhaps 'incentives' might be a more polite word, in the form of timber rights and a host of other concessions and subsidy arrangements which could be withdrawn, modified or otherwise used to 'influence' even the most powerful corporations. Strong measures are now being considered to force corporations to stop polluting the air and water. The pollution issue is new. It's the newest and hottest thing since the motherhood syndrome. This is not to deprecate the environmental crisis, but surely it is more than time that basic questions of employment, the standard and quality of life in a host of industrial environments, receive similar attention and treatment.

The second area where we should enter the decision-making process is at the opposite end of the power structure – at the level where work is executed day-to-day. Here, a different type of collective bargaining could be imagined, whose basic objective would be to obtain a much greater degree of autonomy at work for employees. This might help us to eliminate some of the ham-fisted attitudes of some employers who still insist on tyrannizing the workplace. The aim would be to reduce substantially the amount and severity of direct and immediate supervision by management over such things as work schedules, crew or shift organization, the methods and the pace of work.

This is far from being the 'pie in the sky' or pipe dream that some detractors would suggest. It is not even very original. The British Tavistock Institute of Human Relations has published several authoritative studies on successful experiments with 'self-directed' work groups which operated under very general directives from top management. This type of development is closely tied in with, and operates as a complement to, the other information–consultation–recommendation process. That is to say, the autonomous, 'self-directed' work organization at, say, the department or process level, would operate on the basis of general objectives and targets set fairly well in advance which had been arrived at through the information–consultation–recommendation process.

The second dimension of the extension of the bargaining process is a horizontal one. It would involve extending, within the limits of the conventional plant unit type of agreement, the bilateral decision-making process to cover issues which remain at present the unilateral preserve of management. In other words, we would extend the bargaining system to those items within the jurisdiction of *local* management. This extension would cover such matters as plant rules and regulations and the selection of front line supervisors, for example.

Of course, none of these developments will come easily. In fact the concepts posited here fly in the face of the autocratic and highly structured organizations which tie people to machines instead of to each other. But if we are really concerned about resolving conflicts in the workplace then we ought to re-examine some of the current methods and look to more humanizing alternatives. It is clear that where these changes have been made, the rewards have been substantial, both in terms of resolution of conflict and in more efficient production. These surely are powerful incentives to overcome prejudices about management rights and prerogatives.

If man is to have real social power he must have the right to make decisions about those things which affect his life. He must be able to participate effectively, that is to say, to build, alter or reserve the way in which things shape his life. In our system of participation by representation, trade unions are the only practical vehicle for such participation in working life. Such participation must be real, effective and complete, based on full access to information. It must not be merely symbolic, with unions confined to consultative functions.

Just as there are matters now subject to collective bargaining which were heresy two or three decades ago, so there are prerogatives of management today which must yield to bilateral decision-making. Organized labour will not be satisfied to concentrate only on negotiating technological change. Our position will be to oppose firmly any arbitrary limitations on collective bargaining and the obvious implications which limit the ability of the union to protect its members in their work life. It's our job to do so. It's what labour unions are all about.

Chapter 14

Switzerland

EWALD KAESER

National Secretary, Federation of Textile, Chemical and Paper Workers

GENERAL BACKGROUND

In Switzerland, the workers' right to co-determination has very seldom been given real legal or institutional form. Of course, the trade unions have always striven to extend workers' rights and have achieved some successes, but this extension of workers' rights has always been in the field of *consultation*.

The establishment of representative workers' bodies inside the undertaking (works' committees) goes far back into the past. The first works' committee was set up in 1872 in the firm Rothfärberei Neftenback in the Canton of Zürich. With the growth of the trade union movement, the Swiss Engineering Industry Association recommended its members in 1897 to establish works' committees and negotiate with them rather than with the trade unions. The same thing happened in the 1905 labour conflicts and in a similar fashion in 1942 in the chemical industry at Basle. Efforts to give these works' committees a legal institutional basis remained unsuccessful. Over the years, the trade unions have adopted a positive attitude towards these works' committees and have tried to see that they are composed as far as possible of trade union members.

This has been achieved in many instances, and with the assistance of the trade unions, the works' committees have today become very widespread in private industry and have developed into important workers' organs within the undertaking. The existence and functions of works' committees are also generally laid down more or less precisely in collective agreements and general labour contracts between companies and trade unions. There are considerable differences as between companies and economic sectors in the extent to which these works' committees have won recognition of their right to represent workers within the undertaking. They have achieved their greatest success where they have based themselves on the trade unions.

The works' committees' right to consultation relates to the workers covered by collective and general labour agreements, namely those employed in manufacturing (industrial workers). It is true that works' committees collaborate in the social sector: pension funds, sickness funds, housing schemes financed by undertakings, etc. In certain cases they are active with regard to wage determination – incentive wages, piece-rates, job rates. The works' committees have an important role in human relations.

With very few exceptions, there is no right to consultation with regard to certain management decisions: for example, appointments, dismissals, promotions, transfers, finance, personnel administration, etc. (We shall come back to the exceptions.)

The *legal framework*, as it exists today (beginning of 1972), is often characterized by opponents of co-determination as *entirely* satisfactory. However, it provides no institutional form of co-determination.

The Swiss constitution contains an article 34 ter, relating to employer–worker relations, as follows:

'1. The Federation is authorized to promulgate regulations:
   (a) about protection of workers;
   (b) about relations between employers and workers; particularly with regard to the joint settlement of questions relating to the undertaking and the occupation;
   (c) about declaration of universal applicability of general labour agreements and other general arrangements by employers' and workers' organizations for the promotion of labour peace;
   (d) about appropriate compensation for loss of wages and earnings owing to military service;
   (e) about employment placement;
   (f) about unemployment insurance and unemployment assistance;
   (g) about occupational training in industry, manual occupations, commerce, agriculture and domestic service.'

Thus, the Federation has the power to issue directives concerning protection of workers and employer–worker relations. Articles 31 to 44 also give powers that could be used in favour of increased rights for workers: 'The Federation shall take appropriate measures within the framework of its constitutional authority to increase the welfare of the people and the economic security of citizens.' The same is true of article 31 quinques, which states: 'The Federation shall take measures in co-operation with the Cantons and with private enterprise for protection against economic crises and where necessary to combat unemployment when it occurs.'

In Switzerland there also exists the so-called 'advisory opinion' procedure. Under this, the Federation and the cantons can submit important draft laws, particularly of an economic or social character, to the competent bodies (trade unions, employers' associations, etc.) for an advisory opinion. Representatives of the workers also participate in various technical and expert committees.

There is a Federal law on employment in industry and commerce (labour law). This contains important provisions for the protection of workers, including the maximum weekly working hours, special protection for women and young workers, and directives on safety and health. This law also contains a single reference to freely elected workers' representatives (art. 37, para. 4): 'Work rules in the undertaking shall be agreed in writing between employers and freely elected workers' representatives, or issued by the employer after consulting the workers.' There are provisions under which the individual worker has to be consulted (e.g. acceptance of night work) or to be given the opportunity to express his opinion (e.g. art. 48, exceptions from ordinary working hours).

All these provisions are thus restricted to consultation, *the final decision remaining with the employer alone.*

Another law which contains provisions for the regulation of employment relations between employers and workers is the 'Federal Law on revision of Parts 10 and 10 bis of the Code of Obligations' (Contract of Employment). This law contains both absolutely binding and relatively binding directives to be observed in establishing an individual employment contract, a collective agreement or a general labour agreement. This law gives no right to co-determination by workers or their organizations.

Finally, mention may be made of company law. Here, too, there are no binding provisions benefiting the workers: for example, the obligation to inform the workers of an undertaking belonging to a limited company, or the right to representation on the board of directors. Under existing law, no one who is not a shareholder may be elected to the board of directors of a limited company (art. 707 of the Code of Obligations).

This brief and incomplete survey appeared necessary for the understanding of the campaign being carried on by the Swiss trade unions for co-determination and industrial democracy.

TRADE UNION CAMPAIGN FOR CO-DETERMINATION
AND INDUSTRIAL DEMOCRACY

Although the achievement of industrial democracy is embodied as one of their objectives in the statutes or programme of individual trade unions, their activity in this field was limited until 1967–8 to extending the workers' right to consultation. At the level of the undertaking, this occurred through the workers' education provided by the trade unions for members of works' committees and emphasis on problems of worker representation. Efforts were usually also made to anchor the progress achieved in collective agreements or plant rules.

Industrial development, increased concentration in industry and the consequent concentration of power, with all the visible effects of an economy operating solely to maximize profits – all this, as well as the world-wide campaign for industrial democracy, awakened Swiss workers and their trade unions to the need to fight for a real right to co-determination.

At the beginning of 1969 the Textile, Chemical and Paper Workers' Union set up a special commission. This had the task of examining co-determination problems, taking into account the conditions existing within this union's jurisdiction. The commission's report and recommendations were adopted by the union congress in September 1970 under the heading 'co-determination as a principle of collective bargaining policy'.

After setting out the basic principles and objectives of workers' co-determination and industrial democracy, this statement puts forward concrete proposals for the realization of co-determination. These proposals take as their starting point the idea that co-determination can be achieved both through collective bargaining and through legislative action.

The basic principle of co-determination is set out briefly as follows:

'Co-determination by workers on an equal footing will bring about democratization of the economy. This also constitutes the solution of the problem of equitable distribution between the workers and the community as a whole of the surplus value produced by the economy.'

Co-determination is to be realized at all levels: 'in labour and personnel matters; technical organization, wage determination, social insurance, accident prevention and hygiene, appointments, dismissals, transfers, promotions, etc.'

Plant management: joint participation in in-plant management, the board of directors, administration, supervisory bodies, right to take part in elections, right to supervise, right of recall or termination.

At supra-plant level: participation of workers in national economic affairs and legislation (company law, labour law), possible establishment of an economic and social council, works' constitution law.

'Those responsible for co-determination within the plant in respect of the whole field of operations of the undertaking are the bodies representing those employed there – namely, committees of workers and salaried employees united in a single body depending on the scope of the problem.' Co-determination in specific cases will operate through joint committees. Co-determination will be guaranteed and supported by the unions and their shop stewards in the plant.

The trade union programme aims at winning rights and guarantees (freedom of movement within the plant, protection against dismissals, right to information, right of assembly, right to carry on educational activities, etc.). A programme in stages is proposed to this end, and under this co-determination would be achieved step by step, accompanied by the necessary education activities.

In Stage I, co-determination would be achieved with respect to: wage determination, social insurance, personnel welfare, workers' housing provided by the company, disciplinary matters, suggestion schemes, accident prevention and hygiene, appointments, transfers, dismissals, training.

In Stage II, promotions, investments relating to equipment for each individual job, social and hygiene installations, organization of production schedules (job planning, etc.).

In Stage III, production policy, sales policy, finance policy, personnel matters.

The statement on co-determination by the Textile, Chemical and Paper Workers' Union also sets out the conditions that must exist or be created to assure co-determination within the plant: for example, effective works' committees and union stewards. Election rights of employees, works' committees and union stewards are defined. The right of workers and their organizations to supervise and recall management is also laid down.

This is a co-determination programme that keeps close to the plant and is firmly based on the plant's employees and their organizations, but at the same time it is made clear that this cannot be put into effect without the co-operation and support of the trade unions.

Great emphasis is placed on the need for solid technical training of worker members of co-determination bodies. The union intends to achieve co-determination in stages as set out in the statement, on renewal of collective and general labour agreements. At its congress in October, 1969, the Swiss Trade Union Federation (SGB) also set up a special commission for the study of the co-determination problem.

This commission presented its report in January 1971. After being discussed and revised at various levels, it was published in September 1971 under the title 'The SGB's Co-determination Programme'. Its conclusions and proposals are similar to those in the statement on co-determination by the Textile, Chemical and Paper Workers' Union. After a brief survey of the present situation, the report notes that 'despite the most favourable evaluation it cannot be denied that in general plants and companies are still run in an authoritarian manner. Co-determination within the plant still has to be achieved.'

The SGB's co-determination programme states: 'Democracy is indivisible.' It must be equally valid in all fields – hence also in the economy. Under the SGB's co-determination programme, co-determination must be on an equal footing and operate in all fields and at all levels. It must be worked towards in matters relating to organization of the plant, social affairs, personnel matters and in the economic and financial field. 'Co-determination must also extend to company boards of directors and similar bodies in other institutions.'

Co-determination is demanded in trusts, parent companies and holding companies. Joint participation in boards of directors is aimed at, with representatives of the public interest also being on the boards, particularly in major companies. The most important campaign so far for co-determination by workers and their organizations relates to the so-called 'co-determination initiative'.

The widely favourable reception given to the publication of the statement by the Textile, Chemical and Paper Workers' Union in autumn 1970 led the Christian National Trade Union Federation to make a declaration saying that it was considering launching an initiative for a constitutional amendment on co-determination.

It made the same proposal to the Swiss Trade Union Federation. The initiative started early in 1971 and within a few months more than 160,000 signatures were collected – as against the 50,000 signatures that are necessary. Very rarely in Switzerland has an initiative obtained such a large number of signatures. This shows that there is strong popular support for workers' co-determination. For the first time, the three trade union organizations came together in this action.

The initiative presented by the Swiss Trade Union Federation (SGB), the Christian National Trade Union Federation (CNG), and the Swiss Evangelical Workers' Union (SVEA) aimed at adding the following text to the above-mentioned article 34 of the Federal Constitution: 'The Federation is authorized to promulgate regulations: ... about co-determination by workers and their organizations in plants, companies and the administration.'

The Federation is now obliged to submit this initiative to a popular referendum. The trade union and the labour movement as a whole have the task of carrying on a campaign to ensure that the initiative is adopted by the people. This will not be an easy task and will require complete commitment.

This brings us to a further fact worth mentioning: in 1968 or 1969, almost nobody in Switzerland, either in trade union circles or still less among the employers, believed that a demand for co-determination would ever be put on the table. In January 1969 the following text could be read in the Swiss employers' journal:

'It is no accident that the example of co-determination as it has developed in the Federal Republic of Germany, has found very little echo among the workers in our country. The Swiss trade unions place great importance on the right of consultation on everything that affects the worker in his job and his company and there is no doubt that this consultation will be extended still further. But the Swiss workers' organizations leave the responsibility for management to those who also take the risks of management. This division of responsibilities has proved itself in our country and it is a sign of maturity and wisdom that our workers recognize and accept this.'

Since 1970, however, three factors can be set against that statement:

1. The statement on co-determination as part of collective bargaining policy by the Textile, Chemical and Paper Workers' Union.
2. The co-determination programme of the Swiss Trade Union Federation.
3. The constitutional initiative presented by the SGB, CNG and SVEA.

How little the employers welcome this development can be seen in their violent defensive campaign. We cannot resist quoting some of the pearls from their arguments: workers' co-determination as demanded by the unions is said to mean 'cold-blooded socialization, destruction of the free market economy, crippling of freedom of decision, blocking of rapid decisions that are necessary in management, power to the trade unions, and the workers cannot exercise co-determination since they don't understand anything'.

Of course, widespread intensive discussions and talks are now taking place in all kinds of organizations and bodies. The press, radio and television have taken up the problem of co-determination. Publications are being issued, and the Swiss Federation of Employers' Associations has announced that it will set forth its position in detail. The conflict of opinion is going into matters of principle and in the author's view this can bring nothing but good.

FIRST STEPS AND SUCCESSES

Even before there were any general discussions or concrete proposals about co-determination in Switzerland, the works' committee in the Firestone Produkte A. G. plant in Pratteln, belonging to the Dättwiler Holding Company, had obtained co-determination on certain points. The Textile, Chemical and Paper Workers' Union had concluded a collective agreement with this firm. On renewal of this agreement in 1967, the works' committee of this 100 per cent organized plant was able to insert practical co-determination in the agreement. The relevant clause of the contract reads as follows:

'Art. 15: *Works' Committee*. The composition and activities of the works' committees are governed by the existing statutes and election rules. The purpose of the works' committees, in addition to defending the workers' interests, is to promote mutual discussion, co-operation, confidence and good understanding between management and workers.

'The works' committee has a right to co-determination with regard to job evaluation, evaluation of performance, transfer, piece-rates and bonuses, suggestion schemes, disciplinary matters (except dismissal without notice), sickness insurance and termination because of employment shortages or rationalization measures.

'With regard to other problems directly affecting the workers covered by the collective agreement, the right to consultation is maintained.'

The corresponding clause in the previous contract read:

'Art. 15: The composition and activities of the works' committee are governed by the existing statutes and election rules. The purpose of the works' committee, in addition to defending the workers' interests, is to promote mutual discussion, co-operation, confidence and good understanding between management and workers.'

Thus, since 1967 co-determination with regard to certain matters has for the first time been given institutional form in Switzerland. Co-determination is exercised by representatives of the works' committee in the joint committees set up for specific questions. These joint committees (e.g. on transfers, suggestions, etc.) deal independently with their problems and their decisions are final. This joint system functions very well and has greatly improved the workers' attitude towards their company. Their self-confidence has grown.

In the beginning, management representatives also spoke in praise of co-determination. They even went so far as to say that 'co-determination had brought to life psychological reserves among the workers and this was to the company's advantage'.

Today one has the impression that as a result of the employers' attempt to construct a defensive front against co-determination, the Firestone management in Pratteln is also trying to fix narrower limits or even to push backwards. The workers and the union are watchful and will not surrender the rights they have won.

This example shows that workers' co-determination in the plant will have to be fought for against the will of the employers. Company managements put in place by capitalists have no desire to give up any of their unilateral decision-making powers.

This first co-determination model in the Firestone plant in Pratteln which, as we have seen, was established in the 1967 collective agreement, has helped a great deal to give inspiration to the co-determination demands of the Textile, Chemical and Paper Workers' Union. Again, this union was the first in Switzerland to propose a trade union model and inspired the trade union federation.

Another case in which co-determination has been institutionalized according to the model laid down in the statement on co-determination as part of collective bargaining policy was a renewal of the collective agreement with the firm Model A. G. Kartonund Kartonagerfabrik in Weinfelden. Co-determination established under the contract relates to job evaluation, suggestion scheme, and accident prevention and industrial hygiene.

However, even more important are the first steps towards co-determination in the chemical industry. This is also important because it relates to the Swiss plants of such major corporations as Ciba-Geigy A. G., Hoffman-La Roche A. G. and Sandoz A. G. Altogether about 15,000 workers are covered by collective agreements.

For more than twenty-five years works' committees freely elected by the workers have been operating in these companies. Efforts to extend the works' committees' competence as laid down in their statutes (more operational rights, right to information, right to take part in decisions, etc.) made little progress. However, the practical activities and responsibilities that result from the collective agreements have enormously increased in the course of time.

The works' committees' activities were strongly supported by their trade union through co-ordination, training, teaching and so on. In the general collective agreements concluded between the companies and the union, the institution and functions of the works' committees are defined in article 41, as follows:

'(1) The composition and activities of the works' committee are governed by the existing statutes and election rules in each company.

(2) The responsibility of the works' committee is to defend the workers' interests and promote co-operation, mutual consultation, confidence and good understanding between workers and management.

(3) Members of the works' committee are free to carry out their mandate as laid down in the statutes and shall not be penalized for so doing.'

The general collective agreement for the chemical industry in Basle was due for renewal on 1 January 1972. In accordance with the programme for co-determination as part of collective bargaining policy, the strongest union in the chemical industry – the Textile, Chemical and Paper Workers' Union – put forward demands for extending trade union rights within the undertakings (field of activities of works' committees, consultation and co-determination).

In lengthy and arduous negotiations some concessions were gained from the employers. The new clause defining the activities of the work's committees reads as follows:

'Art. 41: *Works' Committee*

(1) The works' committee is the legitimate representation vis-à-vis the company of all workers covered by this collective agreement. Co-operation between the works' committees and the company is based on readiness to exchange information and on the principle of trust and good faith.

(2) The works' committee supervises observance of provisions of this collective agreement inside the company. It co-operates in all fields in which co-operation is laid down in law, collective agreement, works' committee rules and any other in-plant regulations or agreements. Such co-operation takes place in the following fields:
 – Extension of probation
 – Warning
 – Dismissal on economic grounds
 – Termination in the event of damage to health due to work in the company
 – Shift work
 – Washing facilities
 – Work compensation regulations
 – Longer holidays
 – Working conditions

- Incentive wages
- Transfer of large groups of workers.

(3) Co-determination by representatives of the works' committee shall be provided for with regard to establishment and application of wage systems, accident prevention and industrial hygiene, suggestion schemes, rewards and bonuses, vocational education and training of workers covered by this collective agreement.

(4) Subject to the agreement of the competent management representative, the works' committee may in particular cases invite inside or outside experts to take part in its sittings.

(5) The works' committee has the right, subject to the agreement of the competent management representative and as appropriate, to inform the workers covered by this collective agreement by means of posters or circulars. Detailed procedures shall be laid down in works' rules.

(6) The chairman of the works' committee shall be relieved from his work in the plant in proportion to his responsibilities, in order to carry out his leadership of the works' committee as a whole, to expedite current business and participate in the committee set up by the firm.

In firms or plants with more than 1,000 workers covered by this collective agreement, the chairman of the works' committee shall be relieved for at least half his ordinary working time. In firms or plants with more than 2,000 workers covered by this collective agreement an additional member of the works' committee shall also be relieved for half his ordinary working time.

In particular cases as necessary, and with the agreement of the competent management representative, the other members of the works' committee shall be allowed appropriate time off for urgent matters, account being taken of the needs of the company.

(7) Members and substitute members of works' committees in the individual companies have the right during their three-year term of office to as many multiples of 10 working days' paid leave as there are members (excluding substitutes) of the works' committee, for the purpose of courses and arrangements for training and further training in the activities of a member of the works' committee.

Distribution of the available paid leave among the members and substitute members is the responsibility of the works' committee. Any leave lasting more than 10 working days for an individual member of the works' committee shall also require the agreement of the competent management representative.

(8) The composition of the works' committee is laid down in election rules. The works' committee's rules and the election rules shall be issued by the firm, after agreement with the works' committee.

(9) The firm shall inform the works' committee at least once a year about the evolution of the personnel situation.'

If we compare this article with that in the previous contracts, the progress is clearly seen. Progress has also been made in the new agreement in other respects. For example, there is possibility of consultation of the works' committee and the union with regard to lay-offs on economic grounds. The relevant text reads as follows:

'Lay-offs on economic grounds
'Art. 8 (1) Lay-offs due to work shortages or for other causes unrelated to the worker himself, such as mergers, reductions in production, nationalization measures, closure of plants, shall be thoroughly discussed with the works' committee. As far as possible, hardship cases shall be avoided and opportunities given for re-training.

'(2) If the discussions between the company and the works' committee do not lead to a result satisfactory to both sides, the employers' association and the trade union can be brought in.'

In the light of current economic developments in Switzerland (automation, mergers, closure of plants, etc.) this clause is of great importance. To be sure, in other countries there are more far-reaching measures for protection against dismissals in law or collective agreements, but in the Swiss situation this provision is unique in a collective agreement.

The chemical industry contract also includes 'directives concerning incentive wages'. Here too, the works' committee has some right of co-determination. Three clauses may be quoted in this connection:

'Incentive wage supplements shall be established as a proportion of the individual wage in the form of a supplement, which shall be taken into account in determining holiday and sick pay as well as supplements for working time subject to supplementary payments.

'Companies shall establish a central joint evaluation committee for carrying out job evaluation, and also work and evaluation groups as required. The works' committee shall be represented in such groups by at least two persons nominated by it.

'Evaluation of performance shall be carried out by the supervisor. At the request of the person concerned, an explanation of the evaluation shall be given and reasons stated. After receiving this explanation, he shall be free to have recourse within three working days to an appeals committee, composed of a majority of management delegates together with representatives of the works' committee. No further appeal can be made against decisions of this body.'

The provisions of the general collective agreement for the Basle chemical industry have been taken over into the contracts with five other firms, the text being identical. These are Rohner A. G., Henkel & Co., Schweizerische Teerindustrie A. G., Pratteln Säurefabrik Schweizerhalle A. G. and Lanza A. G. (Schweizerhalle).

The above-mentioned provisions in collective agreements are the first steps towards co-determination on a contractual basis in Swiss industry. There is no doubt that we shall move forward from this beginning.

CONCLUDING REMARKS

Detailed examination of the co-determination provisions in these collective agreements reveals that their scope is restricted to specific sectors of the workforce. Foremen, supervisors and technical and commercial personnel are not covered. Moreover, in the Basle chemical industry laboratory staff are not covered by the same collective agreement. The workers not covered by the contract represent the majority in the bigger companies.

This shows that there are still difficulties as regards the realization and implementation of co-determination and that great efforts are still needed to overcome them. It must also be remembered that agreements between companies and unions are contracts under civil law.

A civil law contract is a voluntary agreement: it can be cancelled at any time either on expiry or subject to the agreed

L

period of notice. Thus, if for any reason (for example, too weak union organization) the contract no longer exists, the right to co-determination is also lost. This is the reason for establishing co-determination *legally*.

Attention must also be paid to the attitude of other employers' organizations towards co-determination. In this connection, we may mention the Swiss Commercial Union (72,000 members). This body was asked to sign the initiative launched by the trade unions. It refused but stated that it was in favour of extension of consultation and co-determination. So-called 'house unions' (internal employee associations), mostly of workers not covered by collective agreements, are either opposed to such schemes or interpret co-determination as meaning complete integration into the existing economic systems. Some managements also have the intention of introducing 'co-determination' of the latter kind within their companies as part of their management policy.

Then there is the public sector: Federal government, cantons, local authorities. Here too there are staff committees which are the elected representatives of the employees but they are entitled only to consultation. On the railways and in the postal services the unions have the right to participate and co-operate in certain matters. The civil service law also provides for a joint committee at the Federal level. In banks and commerce there is consultation but no co-determination. All these factors must be taken into account when talking about comprehensive co-determination.

Switzerland is a small country, but it too has economic giants with power and influence far surpassing that of the state. It must not be forgotten that Switzerland is a centre of international finance and a major power in capitalist terms.

Production geared to profit maximization has the same effects in Switzerland as everywhere else: capital accumulation in a few hands, unsolved infrastructure problems, rent problems, environmental destruction, shutting down of plants, mountains of trash, exploitation, etc. It is the responsibility of trade unions to fight for progress, for more rational production to benefit the consumer, mankind and the world.

As far as the Swiss trade unions are concerned, co-determination for workers and their organizations inside the plant and in the administration does not just mean integration of workers into the existing system. It is their responsibility to work out a form of co-determination that can be put into practice at all levels – on the job, at the plant level, in the board of directors, in management, at the national level and in co-operation with trade unions in all countries at the international level.

Let us conclude by underlining one satisfactory point: within a relatively short time the Swiss trade unions have managed to break through with their demands for co-determination and for 'Equality between Labour and Capital'. The march towards the goal of industrial democracy has started: it will be a Long March.

Chapter 15

France

EDMOND MAIRE

Secretary General, Confédération Française Démocratique du Travail assisted by Pierre Rosanvallon and Marcel Gonin

When talking of industrial democracy or workers' control, there is always a danger of getting lost among definitions of the new institutions and losing sight of the real, everyday aspects of workers' conditions. Yet these are the aspects that leave the deepest mark on every individual's personality and provoke in him his first aspiration to break out of his status as a wage earner.

We therefore believe it is first necessary to set out the present situation of workers before outlining a strategy that will result in each individual becoming responsible for the development of his own personality and of society as a whole.

THE WORKER IN CAPITALIST SOCIETY

EXPLOITATION AT WORK

As the birthplace of capitalist society, and as the temple of industrial society, the factory determines and conditions the worker's life. A wage earner in a factory is subjected to two main pressures: exploitation and dependence.

For a long time the sense of exploitation was what the worker felt most directly. As part of the labour force, as a machine used to produce or conceive, the worker is nothing but a piece of equipment in the factory. In the early stages of capitalism, wages were just enough to keep the worker and his family at a miserable level of subsistence. Worker opposition to the employer thus mainly expressed itself in a struggle for higher wages. This situation has evolved, due to two factors: trade union action and the consumer society. The powerful weapon of trade union organization has enabled the worker to arrive at a certain power relationship that forces the employer to negotiate and pay higher wages. But this evolution in wages has gradually become an essential economic element in capitalism: as industry develops and the number of wage earners increases, what is produced has to be sold. The worker as wage earner can therefore no longer be distinguished from the worker as consumer, and this double personality has inevitably brought a new behaviour pattern on the part of employer. It is in an employer's interest to pay the lowest wages possible, but development of capitalist society requires an adequate distribution of purchasing power, particularly among wage earners (in France wages represent about two-thirds of national income for three-quarters of the active population). Consumption by the upper and middle classes was enough to absorb what was produced in the early stages of capitalism, but would no longer provide a large enough market for industrial production today.

DEPENDENCE

Notwithstanding these economic developments, we know that wages continue to be one of the essential factors in workers' demands. This is often explained as being due to pressure of consumer needs, these needs being either basic or artificially created by the dominant system of development. This explanation is correct, but only as far as it goes. The real reason is that wages are not just money, but also an expression of the social relationship of dependence and domination to which the worker is subjected.

The worker has no independence and no responsibility, but is merely a pawn in the hierarchical system of the undertaking, which is fundamentally alien to him. The undertaking is centred on the exploitation of capital and on the profit motive, and uses those who work there as a means of increasing its production potential.

The worker's personality is deeply affected by this situation to which he is subjected eight or ten hours a day, day after day, particularly in the case of monotonous, repetitive work on the assembly line, where above all he must not think but be a human cog that costs less than the machine that might replace him.

For many years, the optimistic view of technical change has

preached that human beings would be progressively replaced by machines, or that uninteresting work would find its compensation in leisure outside work. Today, this is recognized as a mistake. Leisure is no cure for lack of interest in one's work. At the present time, leisure is escape, a search for oblivion, a means of re-constituting one's working capacity. It is pointless to try to construct a democratic society – still less a socialist society – on such a basis. It is the situation of men and women in the factory that has to be changed.

Some capitalists understand this. They see why large numbers of young people rebel against the alienation and depersonalization due to repetitive assembly line work. They understand the threat to the system under which they profit that is contained in this rebellion, which is at the same time a demand for another way of life. They realize that scientific and technical progress depends on making it possible for as many people as possible to be creative, to make innovations. For this reason, they try to introduce new ways of interesting workers in their jobs, of getting them to participate. Hence the attempts that are being made to re-design production, because the time has come when productivity diminishes as a result of splitting up the work into too many uninteresting jobs. However, these attempts can have only limited results because the employers' aim is to maintain their domination, and therefore what they are really doing is trying to manipulate the workers. This is one of the major contradictions of the present time.

In this context, wage claims retain their priority, but their significance has changed. They no longer represent a demand for a 'decent' or a 'fair' wage, but are the expression of a widespread feeling of revolt opposing labour against capital. Many of the conflicts and disputes that arise on wage issues really reflect a rebellion against the employer's authority, against the aged hierarchy and working conditions on the job. So-called 'quantitative' demands have a tendency to become part of a struggle for 'qualitative' objectives.

This change in the type of conflict also reflects the fact that workers have a clearer and more global view of their own predicament. The fight for higher wages, the fight against the hierarchical system, the fight for better working conditions – all these represent a revolt against the system as such. It is a conflict between labour and capital and is not limited to the single aspect of redistribution of wealth.

OUTSIDE THE FACTORY

Extension of conflict within the undertaking leads inevitably to conflict outside the factory and to demands that take into account the whole development of industrial society.

In the nineteenth century, capitalism had to change traditional social structures in order to develop. Since then society has gradually been organized in response to the needs of industrial growth and capital accumulation, so as to ensure that human beings accept a hierarchical social system.

As society develops and becomes more complex, life becomes more and more compartmentalized: life at work, life at home, life in travel between the two . . . and so on. As people become aware of this they want to re-create unity among these distinct segments of their life, to raise living conditions and working conditions.

In the consumer society the worker's money is all that counts. Any means will do to take it away from him – including lying advertisements. Planned obsolescence is an essential factor in the operation of the economy. The consumer society as idealized in publicity reinforces social distinctions which already exist in the hierarchical system of the factory.

In present-day society, collective social equipment is increasingly necessary to satisfy individual wants by socialist means (housing, transport, communications, health, education, household services, services for small children). Yet the logic of the market economy, in France perhaps more than elsewhere, is opposed to the collective satisfaction of individual wants. Insistence that these services must show a profit means that social distinctions are reinforced by wage differentiations, which are very wide in France.

This differentiation is clearly seen in the way in which urbanization proceeds in France, with the sole aim of concentrating the manpower needed to keep the capitalist system going. Profit is the only motive and so workers are housed in large-scale projects further and further away from city centres. They are factories for eating and sleeping, and hence for re-creating their working capacities.

Men and women resent these poor conditions as regards housing and transport just as much as they resent the brutal conditions in which they work.

Capitalism is no longer restricted to industrial production but has taken over the whole of human society, and everywhere seeks to impose the same kind of social relationships based on subordination and authority.

The logic of the development of industrial capitalism has as its consequence an extension of trade union action from inside the undertaking to the world outside.

For a long time, emphasis was placed on increases in nominal wages only; then came claims based on the cost of living, following the reduction in real wages due to price increases. Now we see claims for improvements in living standards which involve indirect or deferred wages as well as the total amount of services and opportunities provided by society as a whole. Workers today base their objectives and their activities on what they judge to be the evolution in the value of this total amount.

Inside the plant, workers have seen how wage increases are accompanied by job speed-up. On the one hand, there is an increase in purchasing power and hence theoretically in opportunities to enjoy leisure and culture, but on the other hand, pressure of work increases physical and nervous fatigue.

Similarly, relatively rapid increases in purchasing power may be gained by union action while housing, transport and health conditions may deteriorate as a result of defective urbanization and too slow development of collective social equipment.

The workers are therefore conscious that trade union action cannot be limited to the factory since this would dangerously restrict the possibilities of improving their lot. Workers are subject to exploitation and alienation outside the factory as well as inside it.

Industrial capitalism has become a totalitarian society encompassing all economic and social relationships buttressed by an ideology of efficiency and growth, and based on individual enterprise and the pursuit of profit. This system is being increasingly imposed on all the mechanisms of our society.

In these circumstances, the CFDT's struggle against the authoritarian hierarchy in the factories is an integral part of a revolt against hierarchical social relationships in society. If workers refuse to be treated as instruments of production like machines inside the plant, they demand to be treated outside the plant as human beings, having their own dignity and responsibility and not just as consumers who can be manipulated – poorly housed, badly transported, poorly informed.

In May 1968 the CFDT was close to the student movement

because different aspects of the same authoritarian society were being attacked. The students wanted to shake up the traditional university and express their own personalities just as the workers were fighting for the right to take responsibility, and the people as a whole wanted freedom of speech in a society that was trying to gag them. Revolt inside the factories, which are the heart of industrial society, and revolt in the schools supported each other and led to a global revolt against our entire society.

Thus, at the present time, trade union action based on the real living conditions of workers means action within society as a whole, and not just within the factory. The whole of daily life (urbanization, environment, health and transport) and information media (culture and education) are the battlefields where trade unionism must fight for real industrial democracy.

THE CFDT'S SOCIALIST PROGRAMME

The dominant classes in today's capitalist society are making various attempts at adjustment – new management techniques and consultation are two recent examples. The labour movement has also developed certain ideas, either of a reformist character or proposing a global alternative: some are interesting and all contain some useful elements, but none of them provide the answer to the real problem.

(a) ROADS TO NOWHERE

Management Techniques
Certain firms are aware that there is a real problem of 'participation' and try to solve it by a new management method called 'management by objectives'. This method is half-way between decentralization and delegation of authority and is interesting for only two reasons:

- it is limited to having executives 'participate' and not the majority of workers;
- decentralized responsibility is still left within the restrictions imposed by top management.

There is absolutely no change in the workers' situation: all it means is an extension of the technocratic structure.

The 'Autonomous' Workshop

Another extension of new management techniques can be seen in the attempts made in certain leading firms to bring decision making about work organization down to the level of the individual workshop. Such experiments are too recent for a judgement to be made on their real psychological value. Will workers develop aspirations towards responsibility to the extent that they undermine the decision-making system at higher levels? Or if there is a real danger of this happening, will these experiments remain marginal and without real significance? Whatever happens, the fundamental problem remains: there cannot be any real democratization at one level without corresponding democratization at all other levels. If the firm's objectives do not correspond to those of the community as a whole, if production and investment functions remain in private hands, if essential decisions are taken by the ruling class and imposed on those who have to carry them out, then workers' participation in certain minor decisions will only serve to disguise their powerlessness on essential decisions. Developing initiative and creativity among workers or creating a better social climate is not industrial democracy, but employer self-interest. The best that can result is some improvement in working conditions.

Consultation

Gaullist theories about association between labour and capital, French planning based on 'consultation' among social groups, the various incomes policies advocated by Western governments or institutions such as OECD and EEC – all these are attempts to evade reality, which is the class struggle. All are attempts to integrate workers into the aims of the ruling classes by gaining their agreement for the preservation of 'basic principles' and the continuation of the existing system – that is, the existing disorder.

Institutional Solutions

A number of reforms have been proposed in France in recent years with a view to spreading responsibility and reducing the power of owners of companies.

While these reform proposals recognize the need for change in the way companies now operate, they are unsatisfactory because they assume that workers' conditions can be changed by setting up institutions but without questioning the principles underlying the capitalist system. There is a need to increase the power of works' councils to achieve better balance and reduce employers' power, but it would be illusory to think that this is the way to transform social relationships and thus modify the status of subordination to which workers are subjected. What all these 'institutional' proposals have in common is that they are based on theoretical models and abstract concepts of the problem of responsibility, and not on an analysis of workers' conditions as they really are.

Socialism in Eastern Europe

The most important point about what has happened in Eastern Europe is that no distinction is made between changing society and changing workers' conditions. However, the means by which power was seized and the exercise of that power by a single party transformed into a totalitarian bureaucracy have created a new form of subjection for the workers. To be sure, workers are no longer exploited in the sense that private ownership of the means of production no longer exists, but they remain in a state of dependence at all levels. They have no power of decision over the purpose or organization or use of the product of their labour. The dominant capitalist class has been replaced by a technocratic, bureaucratic apparatus with different aims from those of capitalism but using mechanisms to keep power and consolidate itself as the dominant social group. While their material conditions may improve faster (in spite of 'mistakes' by the bureaucracy), workers remain imprisoned in a system of hierarchical and authoritarian social relations.

(b) THE CFDT CONTRIBUTION

For various reasons, deriving from their very nature, these proposed solutions cannot be accepted by the CFDT as providing a valid way of changing French society.

Our criticism is not of abstract nature, or because they go too far or not far enough, but realistic, based on whether or not they really change workers' conditions.

In this field, the labour movement's experience is limited, and the conclusions and theories that are derived from that experience vary from one person to another; we still have to achieve a synthesis that takes all factors into account and expresses the common aspirations of all workers. This is a great responsibility for the international labour movement, in particular the trade unions, and requires discussions, exchange of experiences, an open and progressive mind. It is beyond the capacity of a single national organization, however well-meaning it may be.

Nevertheless, the CFDT believes it should make its own contribution to this effort, and integrate its activities in this field with those of others. This is why the CFDT, recognizing the changes that have taken place in capitalist society, and the lessons to be drawn from the international experience of the socialist movement, has declared itself in favour of a democratic socialist, self-governing society.

The 35th Congress of the CFDT defined this democratic socialist programme as a society which assures to every man and woman the opportunity to develop his or her personality in the context of social relationships, structures, types of production and consumption, and to be in control of the development process: in other words, a self-governing society.

Only such a society can create new kinds of relationships between persons and groups at all levels, ensure equality of opportunity and give mankind equality of opportunity and free mankind from the alienation that hinders the development of the human personality.

This society will eliminate all traces of inequality or segregation on a social, cultural, sexual or racial basis, and will therefore be able to work in solidarity with the peoples of the Third World, without imperialism or exploitation, with full respect for the type of civilization these peoples aspire to.

This is the outline of a society to be created by the workers and the majority of the population.

The CFDT Congress set forth three features of this future democratic socialist society:

– workers' control;
– social ownership of the means of production;
– democratic planning.

The distinguishing feature of the CFDT concept is its idea that socialism is not just a change in the economic system (ownership or income distribution).

The three aspects of the socialist society we are proposing do not have the same importance or the same weight.

The fundamental issue for the CFDT is the programme of workers' control, because it is at this level that the workers' situation has to be profoundly changed. Obviously, this does not mean just a change in the exercise of power and responsibility within the undertaking – every sector of society must be subject to workers' control. A change in workers' responsibilities within the firm must also mean a change in power relationships in public life, and vice versa.

By becoming freely and responsibly integrated into the community, the workers will regain that mastery over the nature, purpose and organization of work of which capitalism has deprived them.

Social ownership of the means of production is a feature of democratic socialism because it is a basic, indispensable condition for transforming society. It is one of the principal methods to be adopted from the outset to suppress the powers and functions attributed to the legal right to property. But it is obviously not enough in itself to construct a democratic, socialist society. Experience in the Eastern countries has unfortunately shown that property relations can change without basically changing the workers' subordinate position.

Democratic planning aims at making major decisions for the community on the basis of priorities. This does not mean that undertakings under workers' control would have to be subject to all its aims and operations, otherwise workers' control would have no real meaning. A balance must be achieved between workers' control and democratic planning so as to achieve the closest possible identity between the interests of the community as a whole and those of lesser decentralized communities (undertakings, regions, cities, etc.). If it is to express the basic decisions of the entire people, democratic planning must overcome the distortions to which it has been subjected under capitalism. Planned decisions will correspond more closely to the aspirations of decentralized community and will not be imposed from above on condition that the workers develop their social awareness, understanding and education. In other words, there is a close and direct link between workers' control, the primary factor in eliminating alienation, and the development of democratic planning.

Both democratic planning and workers' control should aim at ensuring that the nation as a whole has an advanced social awareness resulting from exchange of ideas. In this connection, workers' control will play a basic role because, by enabling workers to exercise responsibility, to free themselves from alienation, it will help to eliminate bureaucratic control over society.

In a democratic socialist society, democratic planning has the essential task of preparing a social programme for every social group. Any society – even the society we want – may be threatened by the appearance of a privileged caste, as well as by groups left on the margin of social progress. Thus, if the plan is widely debated and if authority is widely diffused, the plan's objectives will take account of the need to redress any distortions that may have appeared.

The socialist society we want to build is not a model whose mechanisms can already be exactly described. The CFDT's primary aim is to lay down the major guidelines for the construction of the new society. The kind of socialism we shall achieve will depend on external factors and on the people's growing social awareness. The essential point is for us to integrate the workers' aspirations in a global programme to make a fundamental change in the workers' present mode of existence.

There are those who will call us utopian: we ask them to open their eyes. Conflict in Italy, renewal of interest in workers' control in Britain and Belgium, the recent strike at Renault at Le Mans, the programme to change working life in the Federal Republic of Germany – all these show that the workers in Western Europe are rebelling against their lot, even if their rebellion is sometimes confused and incomplete. In the United States, blacks, women and students are in revolt. In the countries of the Third World, the people's demand for independence is another manifestation of the same kind: the irrepressible aspiration of each individual to be recognized as someone different and special. Even in France there are the first beginnings of collective action about public transport, parks, access to private beaches, against pollution, for town planning in the Paris market area to take account of people's social and cultural needs. There is growing revolt about the scandalous situation with regard to health protection, the people are slowly becoming aware of the exclusion from society of old people and immigrants, the subjection of women, the isolation of young people – all these show the possibilities of revolt against inhuman conditions and are a yardstick for measuring the chances of socialism with a human dimension.

CFDT STRATEGY

Our strategy may be defined at four levels:

(a) OUR IDEA OF SOCIAL TRANSFORMATION

Our analysis of workers' conditions inside and outside the factory, their aspirations, demands and the struggles now taking place reveal that the CFDT's proposals correspond to a profound need. Our strategy is based on the same appreciation. It also brings in the experience of international socialism which demonstrates the deadly peril for democracy – and therefore for socialism, because it cannot be effective without democracy – in the conquest of power by a minority elite, however well-meaning it may be. The masses are not yet prepared for the responsibilities and difficulties involved in total transformation of a whole society with its economic and social structures, and this inevitably means that the minority will become totalitarian if it wishes to retain power at all costs. For this reason, the CFDT refuses to look upon history as a dichotomy – 'before' and 'after' the revolution; it refuses to envisage progress by fixed stages, because this idea requires a party or an elite group with power over others to decide when the move should be made from one stage to the next.

Trade union action should aim at making irreversible progress towards responsibility. The struggle to change power relationships and to break up capitalist structures must be based on development of democracy in all phases of social transformation. There is no better guarantee of continuous expansion of rights, liberties and power for all those who have decided to develop their own personality and the new society.

The CFDT's strategy is conceived of as a continuous process, some periods being more intense and rapid, others less so, but without predetermination, changes in rhythm coming from the developing awareness and combativity of the workers themselves. It is the role of the trade unions to act in the different fronts so as to develop the workers' social consciousness and bring them to see how they can emancipate themselves. We have no wish to impose a theoretically perfect programme but merely to show the workers the direction their struggle should take.

(b) PREPARATION OF DEMANDS

Our strategy does not make a distinction between preparation of demands and the content of those demands. The CFDT has no interest in sticking a socialist label on every trade union claim. However, this does not mean that any solution can be accepted on the pretext that it is easier to achieve: for example, paying a bonus when there is a problem of working conditions. What we want is to prepare claims that move in the direction of a global solution of all the problems involved and bring all the workers into action in the struggle to modify power relationships.

The workers themselves should prepare their demands on the basis of their own experience and problems. Our ambition is to bring the workers to the point where they can solve their own problems. In other words, on the basis of their experience and the knowledge at their disposal, they must participate in decision making. They must sift information, decide, make experiments, criticize results – all this is part of the movement from confusion to awareness. The trade union's role is to help them analyse and understand their situation, and prepare demands corresponding to their aspirations, by providing them with information and making suggestions.

The value of such demands lies in the fact that they are collective class actions with a specific content. They are expressing the independent reaction by workers against the passivity and depersonalization that capitalism requires. Their contents reflect the degree of consciousness attained by workers with the help of trade union organization.

There is no doubt that this kind of trade union action is difficult and we do not claim to have reached a satisfactory standard. But a trade union that is striving to help the workers to become more responsible cannot allow them to depend on it all the time for assistance, and must keep moving forward in the right direction. The point about the struggle against capitalism is that it develops the workers' capacity to take decisions for themselves.

If our struggle against capitalism is to be really effective, our demands must move towards socialism: in other words, they must lay the foundations for a new social order. Opposition to hierarchical structures is a move towards socialism because it implies a more egalitarian society both as regards distribution of incomes and as regards power.

The same is true of claims in respect of women workers, except those relating to maternity, because such claims imply a move towards a society in which roles are not predetermined by sex and in which there is a new relationship between men and women. It is most important to achieve effective participation by marginal groups (women, immigrants, young people, etc.) in the preparation of demands, so that each demand reflects the total situation of all the workers involved, and thus reflects the new society we are fighting for. The union's role in preparing the workers' demands is thus very important, and we cannot see how this situation can be modified because we cannot expect a reaction to an inhuman situation always to arise spontaneously. Every worker has his own individual contribution to make, based on his own experience and knowledge, but his can be only a partial contribution. It is not intellectual capacity that is lacking but the opportunity to compare, communicate and present. Without a global, collective vision of the historical process, without a capacity to analyse and synthesize past experience and new struggles – in other words, without a trade union organization – spontaneous reactions will often be smothered by the alienating pressures of the capitalist system. In such circumstances, there will be a tendency for workers' demands to reflect the needs inspired by the ideology of the ruling classes. The quality of the information supplied by the union, the indications it provides about the path to be followed, the extent to which it can engage in a dialogue with the workers – all these will contribute to the workers' understanding of their own demands. In this way, intermediate aims can be put forward as solutions for workers' problems within a socialist context in which long-term objectives harmonize with short-term goals.

(c) PRINCIPLES OF ACTION

The CFDT sees each trade union action as an opportunity to develop the social consciousness of the masses subjected to the capitalist system, and that consciousness will see that it is the whole system that is at fault and must be replaced by the workers' own socialism. Each action is therefore aimed at constructing the future. To achieve this, it must be based on an analysis of the situation and the prospects of success; it can only be carried out on the basis of what exists and what is aimed at. We have explained how this can be achieved in preparing workers' demands.

This takes place at all phases in the development of union action. A first step is to win the right to hold meetings in the plant, and thus make democratic discussion and exchange of information possible so as to put into practice the principles of spreading responsibility which will change our society. Trade union education and training will develop members' capacity to take decisions to deal with the specific problems of all kinds of workers in a single context, to be a vital link between workers and leaders – all these are actions that enable a trade union to arrive at a fusion of workers' control and planning within over-all collective action.

It is essential that this process should function correctly, because upon it depends:

– whether the workers realize the true nature of the global capitalist system and understand that it is possible to replace it;
– whether the struggle for a socialist society becomes intense and effective.

More generally, social change can only occur in a democratic system if it is supported by the conscious mobilization of the majority of the social groups concerned in establishing demo-cratic socialism, and these groups are not all wage earners. We are not against the ballot box, but we do not count on it ex-clusively, though we do believe that the ballot should confirm any change in the social system achieved through struggles.

The transition to socialism must be a dynamic process, involving increasing appropriation of power by the workers – a process of permanent enlargement of liberty and progressive mastery by mankind over his own environment.

Two Examples

In the present trade union situation in France we have to come as close as possible to the strategy we have just outlined, which in our view, based on historical experience, is the only way to achieve democratic socialism.

We present two examples of our tactics in using intermediate aims: limitation of the employers' authority in personnel management, and compression of wage differentials.

Both arose in response to aspirations that were given new life in May 1968, though in a confused form. Subsequently, the unions tried to put them into clearer form so as to constitute a basis for action. In their turn, the demands put forward by union members and workers at the factory, regional, local or sectional level have enriched them and made them more concrete – thus synthesizing them at a new level. Our strategy moves forward in this complex fashion. The following passage sets out how the CFDT sees these two intermediate aims.

1. Limitation of the Employers' Arbitrary Authority in Personnel Management

In May 1968 the workers rebelled against the everyday concrete effects of the employers' arbitrary authority. On this understanding, it has been said that the 1968 strikes and sit-downs were the expression of a revolt against management actions rather than against the capitalist system as such. Indeed, many of the demands put forward to limit employers' authority are not incompatible with the system itself.

Some people are afraid that if union power is exerted in the first instance against management decisions, this will lead to integration of the workers in the system, to acceptance by the workers of the capitalist undertaking and the existing organization of society.

It is true that democratization of a power structure must take place within a given framework. It is therefore necessary to avoid this danger of integration and make clear to the workers the contradictions that exist at all levels of society. Full democratization at one level is impossible without democratic transformation at other levels. The information and training provided by the unions must help the workers to understand how they can emancipate themselves, by explaining the causes of the situation in which they live.

Furthermore, while Gaullist-type 'participation' is put forward as an end in itself and responds to workers' aspirations by distributing what is left of profits, paid for by the state, our aim to limit employers' authority is only one stage in a series of transformations. Our aims are incompatible with the concentration of power and absolute authority that is widespread among French employers. In present circumstances, our demands contain an explosive force for social transformation, and are the best basis for improving consciousness, democratization and progress towards workers' control.

The struggle against the employers' authority is an essential part of all union activity, but in the field of personnel management it is particularly important and that is why we have put forward two priority claims: agreements at the plant level, and control over employment contracts.

(a) *Generalization of negotiation, particularly at the plant level:* Collective bargaining is an essential aspect of the democratization process. When negotiation is the result of action by workers with regard to objectives on which they fully agree, it is a manifestation of a power relationship and expresses that relationship in the contacts between the workers and the company.

It is at that crucial moment that fresh liberties are won and trade union power stands up against that of the capitalist company.

It is also important from the standpoint of workers taking up union membership.

There must be co-ordination between the various levels at which bargaining takes place, for two reasons:

– negotiations at the national, regional or local level must be accompanied by negotiation at the plant level, and must contribute to it and not eliminate it;

– negotiations at the national, regional or local levels must not allow problems at the plant level to be negotiated by bodies other than the union: for example, the works' council.

Co-ordination of negotiations should therefore be designed to emphasize the importance of bargaining at the plant level and not try to eliminate it.

Plant agreements supplementing the collective agreement should become the general practice and should settle those aspects of the employment contract that cannot be validly dealt with outside the plant.

To achieve this, the contents of these agreements should deal not only with the structure and rates of real wages, hours of work, collective guarantees, but also with the general application of the contract; criteria for hiring and firing, principles applying to vocational training, etc.

(b) *Trade unions should deal with all aspects of employment:* At present, the union's role is too limited to certain aspects of the employment contract and should be extended to cover all aspects of working conditions.

This means that trade union action should deal with those

problems that have the greatest immediate impact on workers, and make them the centre of its day-to-day activities.

To be sure, this is already the case and is particularly seen in the role of shop stewards. But collective action has not yet been successful in really influencing the authoritarian decisions affecting the workers' daily life in the factory. For example, when he is hired, the worker is alone face to face with the personnel manager who lays down the conditions.

Similarly, with regard to a transfer that he does not want or that he has asked for and been refused, a worker does not always inform his shop steward, or if he does so it is after the decision has been taken by management. Then there is the system of promotions at the discretion of management which can overcome a workers' will to oppose his boss. Or there is the case of the worker who is called in by management and 'advised' to leave 'honourably' with a small sum of money, unless he would prefer to see his shop steward and be sacked without warning and without indemnity. One could go on for ever. . . .

Union effectiveness depends on union control over every individual aspect of working conditions. A union branch can win the right to be obligatorily informed in every individual case, before any decision is taken, about all measures being considered by management with regard to specific aspects of working conditions: hiring, promotion, transfers, penalties, downgrading, premature retirement, firing, etc. The trade union representatives will give their views, argue, make counter-proposals.

When management is obliged to inform the union branch directly or through its elected representatives before it takes any decision affecting an individual worker, this gives the union the opportunity to bring pressure to bear on the employer to remedy abuses or prevent flagrant injustice.

The mere fact that an employer has to make known and justify his decisions means that he has to reason with the trade union. If he tries to evade this obligation, he will be faced with the collective opposition of the workers.

Conquest of the right to be informed does not mean becoming a party to management decisions, because major decisions remain the management's prerogative. For example, how could a union agree to choose fifty workers to be fired when there is a reduction for economic reasons for which the union is in no way responsible?

We have given one example, but that is not enough. On the contrary, we must look for others. We must invent new forms of organization and make new demands that will enable us to extend trade union control over all aspects of the individual employment contract. For example, we must fight to reverse the onus of proof in case of dismissal or make the works' council a forum for collective discussions of working hours or work organization. This is how we can develop our activities in the right direction.

2. Compression of Wage Differentials

Differentials in wages and job classifications are wider in France than in other countries at the same stage of development. We can base our action on this fact, and also move towards our goal of establishing greater equality among workers by fighting for compression of wage differentials.

But it is not enough just to limit ourselves to this aspiration towards equality. In the first place, we have to admit that, at the present stage of human consciousness, different levels of competence are accepted as justifying different levels of remuneration. Furthermore, if we bring to light the fundamental causes of the excessive differentials in wages, we also attack the entire authoritarian organization of society under the capitalist system.

Present wage and job classifications are not based on so-called objective criteria or on the value of the work performed. The very logic of the system prevents objective evaluation.

If a capitalist undertaking is to function properly, the best qualified workers, particularly supervisors, must devote themselves exclusively to the company's interests; they must not question its objectives and must place all their energy at its disposal. Management's wage policy is in accordance with this principle.

In private enterprise, decisions are by definition arbitrary since the workers in general may not participate. Profit and power command, and authority 'cannot be divided'. Arbitrary decisions must therefore be transmitted from the top downwards to those who have to carry them out. This would seem to require compensation for all employees having a command function: higher salaries and a clearly distinct social status to facilitate the exercise of authority.

Our educational and cultural system selects the children of

well-off families and co-opts them into the ruling classes, thus maintaining the social system of which scales of remuneration are an integral part, with barriers and artificial differences between categories.

The dynamism of economic development based on individual consumption, which is the motive-force of capitalism, requires certain goods to be reserved primarily for the 'upper classes' and thus become an object of envy for the mass of people and then an object of mass production. Afterwards new luxury products are launched to keep the pump primed. A system like this links economic development with wide wage differentials.

It can be seen how compresson of wage differentials provides an opportunity for social criticism and a spur to class consciousness and democratization.

The use that is made of an issue such as this depends on each particular situation in a given sector. But in every case everything should be done to ensure that all categories of worker are united in the struggle. In particular, we believe that large numbers of supervisory staff are capable of joining in the fight for access to responsibility, for job and wage classifications based on competence and for recognition by each person of a different role for everyone in the execution of collective decisions.

Other intermediate aims could be defined: for example, with regard to health, we could demand a health protection system that relates problems within the factory (working conditions, safety and health) to those outside (general problems of hospitalization, prevention, etc.). What matters is to define the objectives in such a way as to throw a spotlight on the realities of the capitalist system and at the same time put forward our conception of socialism.

(d) AT THE INTERNATIONAL LEVEL

As capitalism develops on a world-wide scale, the SCDT is involved in developing an international struggle, since the growing interdependence of capitalist states raises the question of construction of socialism in an industrialized country surrounded by capitalist states.

International trade union activity is urgently necessary because we have already fallen behind the strategy of the multinational corporations. However, we must not fall into the trap of thinking of the international scene as something that is permanent. It is noteworthy that May 1968 in France was preceded by movements in Italy and followed by the 'warm autumn' in that country. The relationship between the struggles in France and Italy is very clear: it derives from the same kind of aspirations, the same rebellion against the present organization of society and of work, with its excessive fragmentation of labour and rigid hierarchical structure in companies (for example, strikes at Renault in France, Pirelli and Fiat in Italy). Similar aspirations for a new social order were expressed at the last congress of the Belgian FGTB which discussed workers' control and social ownership of the means of production. In Germany, too, we see the trend to bring 'co-determination' down to the workshop level. In Sweden, the wildcat strikes at Kircina reflect a revolt against existing social relations. Similar movements are evident in Britain.

Obviously these experiences are not identical but in their different ways, depending on local conditions, they reflect the same kind of aspirations for a new form of social order and exercise of power. This spontaneous movement is still hesitant in its protests but it is a factor to be taken into account in the international struggle. Businessmen's Europe is being consolidated. The workers' Europe will be constructed slowly but surely and will be durable on condition that it is based on the workers' fundamental needs. Trade unions must consolidate and develop this movement which is essential to achieve the social transformation of each country, and in particular must prevent the ruling class in one country from defeating the workers' movement in another.

The CFDT believes that the social structure of France cannot be transformed without the support of workers in other countries, and also that French workers must demonstrate effective solidarity with the workers' struggle in other countries.

We may seem to have gone a long way away from 'industrial democracy'. This is true if we restrict this term to meaning an institutional reform within the framework of capitalism. But if we share the CFDT's view that it means workers' action and an increase in workers' power, that its real meaning relates to democratic socialism, that it requires a close link between analysis, planning and strategy, then it is the starting point for the emancipation of all workers, and we have tried to make our contribution to this cause.

Index